Editor:
Paul Gardner

Editorial Project Manager:
Evan D. Forbes, M.S. Ed.

Editor in Chief:
Sharon Coan, M.S. Ed.

Art Director:
Elayne Roberts

Associate Designer:
Denise Bauer

Production Manager:
Phil Garcia

Imaging:
James Edward Grace

Acknowledgments:
HyperStudio® is a registered trademark
of Roger Wagner Publishing, Inc.

Trademarks:
Trademarked names and graphics
appear throughout this book. Instead of
listing every firm and entity which
owns the trademarks or inserting a
trademark symbol with each mention of
a trademarked name, the publisher
avers that it is using the names and
graphics only for editorial purposes and
to the benefit of the trademarked owner
with no intention of infringing upon
that trademark.

Publishers:
Rachelle Cracchiolo, M.S. Ed.
Mary Dupuy Smith, M.S. Ed.

SCHOOL
CURRICULUM LABORATORY
UM-DEARBORN

S0-BHW-023

HyperStudio®
for
Terrified Teachers

Authors:

Tim Fleck, Syble C. Isbister,
Chris Carey, Ann Brundige,
Mike Westerfield

Teacher Created Materials, Inc.
P.O. Box 1040
Huntington Beach, CA 92647
ISBN-1-55690-180-7

©1997 Teacher Created Materials, Inc.
Made in U.S.A.

Table of Contents

Hyper...what?

"What is HyperStudio, and why use it in the classroom?"

Okay, you have bought this wonderful book because you are a teacher who has begun to use *HyperStudio* in your classroom. Or maybe you bought it because you are a teacher who would *like* to begin using *HyperStudio* in your classroom. Maybe you even bought it because your administration has decided to make *HyperStudio* a part of the curriculum, or you are just curious about this "*HyperStudio*" program colleagues, parents, or students keep telling you about. Whatever description best describes your particular situation, one thing is clear—the thought of teaching and using *HyperStudio* in your classroom terrifies you!

It is natural to experience some fear or hesitation when trying something new, especially when it involves the use of computers. For many of us who are teachers, experience with computers was not a part of our college education degree program. Yet we are trying to educate young people who are growing up unaware that there was ever a time *without* computers. Ten years ago, few students had a computer at home. Now when you ask students how many of them have computers at home, practically every hand is raised, and many children report having *two or more* computers. They are far more computer-savvy than students used to be, and their expectations for using computers in the classroom are far greater.

Computers impact our lives daily. They are in many of the appliances we use and the automobiles we drive. They provide the special effects we have become used to seeing in commercials, television shows, and movies. They run our ATM machines, and price the products we buy at stores. They are used in everything from medicine to weather forecasting, stock market analysis to standardized test scoring. Why? Well, one reason is that computers can help us do things more quickly and efficiently, barring the periodic bug or glitch that is inherent in any type of technology. Let's face it, even a pencil lead breaks once in a while, and ballpoint pens run out of ink at the most inopportune moments. But the value of computers goes far beyond just their speed and efficiency. Computers are also interactive. We can communicate with them, and they can communicate back. They can display colorful images that engage our attentions, and provide us with on-screen areas which react when we click on them. They can enable us to access vast amounts of up-to-date information—information which can speak to us, play an animation, or a video.

Not only is it possible to communicate with a computer, but, like the pencil and the pen, the computer is a tool that can enhance the ways in which we communicate with *one another*. That is where *HyperStudio* can play a key role.

So, what is *HyperStudio*? *HyperStudio* is computer software that enables us to create our own interactive projects and presentations. These projects and presentations can communicate thoughts, ideas, and information through multiple types of media—sound, graphics, text, animation, video, and Internet access—just to name a few. As educators, you know that our students learn most effectively when more of their senses are stimulated, and when they are actively involved in the creation of their own learning. With its multimedia capabilities at our fingertips, we and our students can teach and learn from one another in ways that we never before thought possible.

HyperStudio is not a fancy multimedia encyclopedia or some flashy video game. It is not an interactive testing program or an animated history simulation. Not that there's anything wrong with these types of programs; they are effective learning tools in their own right. However, these kinds of programs are designed primarily to be *used* or *referenced*. Not so with *HyperStudio*. It is a resource of simple, yet powerful, tools that await our creative inspiration. If we can imagine it, *HyperStudio* can help us create it. We become the *creators* of our own interactive, multimedia programs. *HyperStudio* empowers us to be effective communicators through technology. If we want to, we can design our own multimedia encyclopedias or video games. We can author our own interactive tests or animate our own historical simulations. They may not be as polished or professional-looking as commercial products, but they are *ours*. And that is rewarding.

Students actually don't mind doing work when it involves *HyperStudio*. In fact, they feel a great deal of pride and satisfaction in the process. They love showing off their projects to their parents, or to friends they drag in from other classrooms. They can hardly control their enthusiasm. They feel a true sense of ownership in their work, and as a result, are more likely to put forth their best efforts.

You will enjoy serving as a facilitator to your students as they work on their multimedia projects. Try to coach and encourage them through each stage of a project's development. *HyperStudio* is a vehicle through which you can collaborate with your students.

Still terrified of *HyperStudio*? Then that is an attitude we have got to change in the course of this tutorial. Students sense fear. They know which subjects their teachers enjoy teaching, and they know which subjects make their teachers anxious. They know that if their teacher never uses the computer(s) in his/her classroom, then he/she is either afraid of computers, lacks the knowledge to use computers, or does not place a great deal of importance on the use of maybe all three. We need to be confident and knowledgeable when using *HyperStudio* with our students, so that they, in turn, will be excited about and comfortable with using it.

Unlike some other tutorials, ***HyperStudio for Terrified Teachers*** is not a "quick fix" or "quick start" manual. This tutorial is structured into a series of Beginner, Intermediate, and Advanced lessons to help you and your students acquire a strong working knowledge of and appreciation for *HyperStudio* authoring. The successful completion of each lesson will require commitment on the part of both teacher and students. Whether we teach in a one-computer classroom, or have access to several computers, the learning of *HyperStudio* will happen best if we set aside time on a regular basis to teach the material to our students, and time for them to use it. Learning this should culminate in the development of student projects that...

(a) demonstrate the student's knowledge of the software, and

(b) fulfill a requirement(s) for one or more of the subjects you teach.

By requiring our students to create multimedia projects that will be evaluated in some manner, we will be emphasizing both in words *and* actions that *HyperStudio* authoring is a legitimate means of learning, and is as valid a product to be "graded" as work done with paper and pencil.

Each lesson throughout this tutorial is broken down into the following sections:

HyperOverview

At the start of each lesson a summary of what the lesson is all about will be presented. You will also use this section to share any reflections or anecdotes gained from using *HyperStudio*.

HyperHardware

It is assumed that you already have a computer and *HyperStudio*. This section will listing of *additional* materials needed (if any) in order to complete a given lesson. And yes, *HyperStudio* is *software,* not hardware. But hey, "HyperHardware" is kind of catchy.

HyperPrerequisites

This is a listing of the skills, tools, and other capabilities both teacher and students should already have some knowledge of and experience with in order to accomplish the objectives of each lesson.

HyperClinic

This is the "nuts and bolts" of each lesson. We will present detailed and specific steps and information concerning the use of *HyperStudio*. This section is written for you, the teacher. Please take the time to practice and learn the skills involved, which can then be used as the basis for a whole-class presentation *before* permitting students to go to the computer.

HyperStudio for Terrified Teachers is based specifically on the Macintosh 3.0 version of HyperStudio. Certain commands and functions may be different in earlier Macintosh versions, as well as the Apple IIGS and Windows versions, but the overall techniques should be applicable regardless of the platform.

Included in this section will be occasional *HyperHints*. HyperHints are additional bits of information on particular skills, or extra tips on using certain tools or features of *HyperStudio*. And sometimes they are simply pieces of advice based on other's experiences using *HyperStudio* in the classroom.

There are also *HyperHorizons* here and there. These are sneak peeks into the next Macintosh upgrade (3.1) for *HyperStudio*, which is currently undergoing extensive beta testing. It is very likely, in fact, that this version will be "officially" released prior to the printing of this tutorial. It promises to be quite an exciting upgrade!

HyperHands-On!

This section is written for the students. It is a simplified, step-by-step application of the material covered in the HyperClinic—presented in the form of student task cards. Copying these cards for students to take with them to the computer is encouraged, as this will help them keep track of each task as it is completed.

A word of caution: Don't depend on the tasks cards to teach *HyperStudio to* your students. Please work through the HyperClinic first, and then present a whole-class lesson(s) to your students. The task cards do not cover everything found in the HyperClinic, and don't go into nearly as much depth. They are intended to help your students practice some of what you have preached. Your students will no doubt have questions along the way, and they will be depending on you to help provide answers.

Beginner Level

Goal/Objectives/Final Project

Level Goal: While completing the lessons in the Beginner Level portion of this tutorial, students will learn basic *HyperStudio* skills in art, text, sound, and card links necessary for the creation of a small two to four card stack.

Level Objectives: Throughout the Beginner Level, the student will acquire the ability to…

- evaluate and discuss school-produced sample stacks. (Lesson 1)
- create original artwork using the various *HyperStudio* paint tools, selection tools, and color palette. (Lessons 2 and 3)
- add clip art and import background files. (Lessons 3 and 4)
- create painted and object-based text. (Lesson 5)
- create visible and invisible buttons (with and without icons) to play/record sounds and link cards. (Lesson 6)
- perform basic stack operations—create a new stack, add new cards, manually move from card to card, and save a stack. (Lessons 1–6)

End-of-Level Project: Upon completion of the Beginner Level lessons, the student will create a two to four card stack that…

- features original artwork.
- includes prepackaged clip art and background files.
- uses examples of painted and object-based text.
- uses visible and invisible buttons (with and without icons)…
    - to establish links between cards
    - to play student-recorded sounds
    - to play prepackaged sound files.

Suggested topics include an "All About Me" stack, an illustrated short story or poetry stack, a small research report stack, or an art portfolio stack.

Lesson 1: Get With the Program!

"Taking a look at student and teacher-created sample projects"

HyperOverview:

HyperStudio practically teaches itself. It's one of the most user-friendly pieces of software available, and requires no previous computer programming knowledge on the part of its user. However, while learning to use its basic features is easy to do, learning *how* and *when* to use each feature to its fullest requires time and practice. Even after using this program for many years, you will continually learn and discover new techniques and ways of creating with *HyperStudio*.

HyperStudio was originally designed for use on the Apple IIGS computer. Within a few years, it became available for Macintosh computers. And a few years after that, a Windows version was introduced. You will not find too many companies that are supporting these three computer environments the way that Roger Wagner Publishing (the producer of *HyperStudio*) is.

HyperStudio ships with a very nice resource CD, along with a well-written reference/tutorial manual. It is strongly recommend that you utilize these as you use and learn the program. This tutorial is not intended to take the place of the information addressed on the CD and in the manual. What it is intended to do is complement this material by providing insights, tips, and information based on classroom experience—which should help you and your students avoid common mistakes and hours of frustration. So, let's *get with the program.*

HyperHardware:
- *HyperStudio* Program Resource CD (essential for Macintosh 3.0 and Windows versions—no CD needed for Mac 2.0 or Apple IIGS versions)

HyperPrerequisites:
- A basic understanding of and experience with using your particular model of computer and its system software (essential)

HyperClinic:

Start up *HyperStudio*. After a few moments, you will notice a screen looking like the one in Figure 1 (page 9). This is, in fact, not *HyperStudio*. (It is the Home Stack, which will be discussed in a moment.) There should be a menu bar with words across it at the top of your screen. The items contained in this menu bar and in its branching sub-menus make up *HyperStudio*. The program is basically behind-the-scenes. It will occasionally display messages and dialog boxes on the screen as you are creating, but most of the time it is off-stage—like a stagehand working the necessary props and effects to spotlight your performance.

HyperHint ➔ *There's nothing more annoying than digging through folders on your hard drive every time you want to run a program. Making an alias of your HyperStudio startup icon and placing it in your Apple Menu Items folder is one way to save time starting up the program. If you are using System 7.5 or later on your Macintosh, this process is a snap. First, click **once** on the HyperStudio startup icon to select it. Then, click on the multi-colored apple in the Finder Menu, hold the mouse down, and move to Automated Tasks. Then, with the mouse button still down, select "Add Alias to Apple Menu" from the submenu. Your computer will display the message "The Alias(es) have been added to the Apple menu" when it is finished. That is it. Now whenever you want to run HyperStudio, just click on the Apple in the Finder menu, move the mouse to HyperStudio, and then let up on the mouse button. You'll be using the program in no time.*

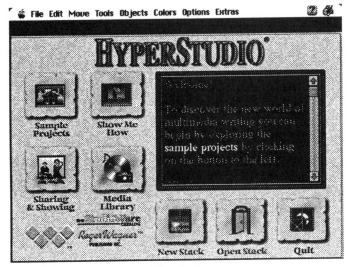

Figure 1

You have launched *HyperStudio* and are now in the Home Stack. This is the default (or preset) manner in which the program starts up. We will discuss other ways to have *HyperStudio* start up in a later lesson. The Home Stack is designed to take you on a tour of the many features of *HyperStudio*. It also includes links to the Program Resource CD which contains a number of art and sound files that are available for your use, along with sample stacks for you to take a look at.

The word "stack" is used a number of times and its meaning should probably be explained. *HyperStudio* "projects" and "presentations" were referred to earlier in the introduction. Well, the multimedia world often refers to these creations as stacks. Why? The projects and presentations you make with *HyperStudio* consist of a series of interactive screens (or cards) that are linked together. These cards can be organized in any number of ways, just like a deck of playing cards. Makes you wonder why they are not called "decks" doesn't it?!

Sometimes the best way to get ideas before making something of your own is to see what others have done. For this lesson, try exploring some of the sample school stacks that have been included with *HyperStudio*. Some of the favorites are "Brown is Brown, Bobcats," and "A Tour of Rwanda, Africa." These stacks were created by teachers and students at Peakview Elementary. Some of the most amazing things are being done with *HyperStudio* at this school. "Brown is Brown" is a sample of an interactive class poetry book. It uses a very simple design, original student artwork, and recorded readings of a couple of poems by the actual students who wrote them. Even the school principal joined in to add some original theme music. "Bobcats" is a student report with original artwork and an easy-to-use main menu. And "A Tour of Rwanda, Africa" demonstrates how a teacher and student can team up to create a project together. It features very nice digital photos, an easy-to-use main menu, and informative authors card. You can bet the students involved in making these stacks learned a great deal, and had a lot of fun doing so.

From the above-mentioned samples, you might get the idea that *HyperStudio* is being used only to create primary and elementary stacks. However, a whole host of well-done educational stacks are featured on the resource CD, covering the entire range of grade levels, and on topics ranging from "The Apollo Program to Ionic and Covalent Bonding" to "The Pythagorean Theorem." There are even a few stacks included for use with special needs children. Further, while showing and having your students explore the many educational stacks is recommended, the CD also contains many family, community, and work-based stacks. These range from family albums to interactive resumes to geologic structural analysis. There is really no limit to the type and complexity of stacks that can be created with *HyperStudio*.

Since your students will be touring various sample stacks, it is recommend that you hold a post-*HyperHands-On* class discussion. You might also consider having each student fill out a short questionnaire about the stack(s) he/she has viewed. Suggested questions for a class discussion and/or questionnaire could include the following:

- What stack(s) did you look at during your *HyperHands-On* session?

- What did you like most/least about this stack(s)?

- What things were included in this stack(s) that could not be included in a written report on paper?

- Do you think you would like to create your own stacks like the one(s) you looked at, even if it meant having to do more work and research than for reports on paper? Why or why not?

HyperHands-On!

Student Task Card—Lesson 1
"Take a Look at Some Sample Stacks"

Step 1. Start up *HyperStudio*.

HyperStudio will automatically open the **Home Stack** for you. If you are using the Macintosh 3.0 or Windows versions, make sure your teacher has provided you with the Program Resource CD, and that it is in your CD-ROM drive. If you are using the Macintosh 2.0 or Apple IIGS versions of *HyperStudio*, you won't need a CD.

Step 2. When you get to the Home Stack, use the on-screen "hand" (it is called the browse tool) to click on the **Sample Projects** button.

Step 3. When you get to the Sample Projects card, click on the **At School** button.

Step 4. When you get to the At School card, you will find a series of buttons at the bottom.

You can click on the **Back** and **Next** arrows to move back and forth through the list of stacks available for you to see. Clicking on the **Sample Projects** button will take you back to the Sample Projects card. You can click on the **?** button to learn more about a sample stack before you open it. When you come to a stack that you'd like to take a look at, just click on its picture. When you finish looking at a stack, just click on its **home** button to return to the At School card.

Step 5. Remember: you are just *looking* at stacks right now.

You'll only need to use the browse tool at this point.

Step 6. When your time is up, be sure to return to the At School card so that the computer is set for the next student.

If you are the last student to use the computer, your teacher may want you to quit *HyperStudio*. To do this, click on the word **File** in the menu bar at the top of the card, and continue to hold the mouse button down. While still holding the mouse button down, select **Quit *HyperStudio*** from the pop-up menu, and then let up on the mouse button. Your computer will exit *HyperStudio*.

Lesson 2: A True Work of Art

"Learning to use the Paint Tools and Color Palette/Exporting Screens"

HyperOverview:

Using *HyperStudio* is like using many programs in one. Because it has paint tools and colors of paint, it can function as a graphics program. With its text capabilities, it can function as a word-processor. Since it can combine text and graphics, it can function as a desktop publishing program. It can also play and record sounds, music, and speech, or be used to create and run animations and video sequences. In so doing, *HyperStudio* is a fully-equipped audiovisual production tool. Add to all of this *HyperStudio*'s interactive capabilities, and it is of little wonder why it is becoming the most popular multimedia software in education today.

HyperStudio is aptly named. "Hyper" means over, above, beyond, and exceeding. And the *American Heritage Dictionary* defines a "studio" as…

- an artist's workroom
- a photographer's establishment
- an establishment where an art is taught or studied
- a room or building for movie, television, or radio productions
- a room or building where tapes and records are produced

As its name implies, *HyperStudio* is the ultimate creative environment in which media can be used and combined in all of its many forms!

It is the first definition of "studio" that we will be exploring in this lesson— *HyperStudio* as the artist's workroom. Just imagine what Michelangelo or Leonardo could have done with *HyperStudio*. That would truly be something to see. But what is more important is that *HyperStudio*'s complete set of paint tools, colors, and patterns can bring out the artist in each of us. You and your students will be creating your own masterpieces in no time.

HyperPrerequisites:

- A basic understanding of and experience with using your particular model of computer and its system software
- Familiarity with using a mouse, trackball, or other input device

HyperClinic:

This lesson is based specifically on the Macintosh 3.0 version of *HyperStudio*.

Start up *HyperStudio*. You have probably noticed by now that whenever you do this, the familiar computer pointer arrow becomes a "hand" with a pointing finger. This is *HyperStudio*'s **browse tool** or **cursor.** As its name implies, this tool lets you "browse" through a stack. It's what you use to click on things like buttons and text object scrollbars. You can even use it to move "draggable" objects. We will learn more about using this handy little tool later on—including how to use alternative cursor designs.

To use *HyperStudio*'s paint tools, first create a new stack. Move the browse tool up to the menu bar at the top of your screen. (The browse tool will temporarily revert back to the computer pointer.) Click on the word **File**, continue to hold the mouse button down, move the pointer to the first submenu choice **New Stack**,

and then let up on the mouse button. A message box will appear. Addy (the program mascot, and the beloved family pet of Roger and Pam Wagner) will appear from time to time to inform and assist you

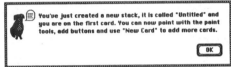

You've just created a new stack, it is called "Untitled" and you are on the first card. You can now paint with the paint tools, add buttons and use "New Card" to add more cards.

[OK]

as you work with *HyperStudio*. What a hyper little helper she is—pardon the pun. Click on the **OK** button, and your new stack will be displayed. What appears to be a blank card is really a digital "canvas" waiting to give life to your artistic energy.

There are two items in the menu you will be using: **Tools** and **Colors.** Clicking on **Tools** will display all of the tools you see here. We will not be using all of these tools in this lesson, just those that are specifically for drawing and painting—which we will take look at in just a few minutes. Clicking on Colors will display the palette of 64 colors and 16 patterns that you see on the right.

HyperHint→If you are using an earlier Macintosh version or the Apple IIGS version, your color palette will contain 16 colors and 16 patterns, like the one on the next page.

The 3.0 version of *HyperStudio* for Macintosh, as well as version 1.0 for Windows, both default (or are preset) to display stacks in 256-color mode. Earlier Macintosh versions defaulted to 16-color mode. The Apple IIGS version is **limited to** 16-color mode. (Well, that is not entirely true. There are ways around this, but they are a little complicated and time-consuming, and cannot be achieved directly from within *HyperStudio*.)

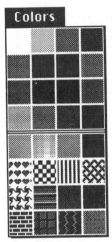

As just stated, the latest Macintosh and Windows versions of *HyperStudio* default to 256-color mode. This is currently the color limit of these versions as well. A number of people would like to see *HyperStudio* support thousands or millions of colors, and that capability may become a reality some day, considering how hard the programming team at Roger Wagner Publishing is working to continually improve *HyperStudio*. But for now, 256 colors is the limit. However, that just means that *HyperStudio* can only display up to 256 colors on a card at one time. But each card can have its own set of 256 colors from the millions that are available!

Okay, so if *HyperStudio* can support up to 256 colors, why does the color palette only display 64? For convenience, primarily. In a later lesson, we will explore how to gain access to the full palette of 256 colors, but you will have to be patient for now. Not only is the 64-color palette designed to be easier to use than displaying all 256 colors at once, but it also features 16 patterns. If all 256 colors were displayed at the same time in the pull-down palette, there would be no room left for any patterns.

All artists need to hold the tools of their craft. They need to see the colors of their medium laid out on a palette. For this reason, the **Tools** and **Colors** not only function as pull-down menus, but can be "torn off" and placed right out on the card if desired. Doing this is very easy. Just click on the word in the menu bar, continue to hold the mouse button down, move the pointer down into the tool set or color palette itself, and then any direction except up. The moment the

pointer gets to one of the edges of the tool set or color palette, the set or palette itself will separate from the menu bar. While still holding the mouse button down, you can then place the palette anywhere on the screen you like. If you are successful in placing the Tools and Colors out on the screen, each one will take on a slightly different look, as you can see here. The color palette gets longer. Most important is that both the tool set and color palette now sport little bars across the top. If you click on this bar and hold the mouse button down, you can drag each one to another location. If one gets in your way, or if you just don't need to use it any longer, just click in the little white square on the far left of the bar. This puts it back away. Try it. Cool, huh?!

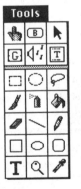

For convenience, make sure both the tool set and color palette are out on the screen, and let's take a brief look at each of the drawing and painting tools.

The **paintbrush,** as its name implies, allows you to apply "digital" paint onto your card. To use it, just click on it once in the tool set, and then click on the color or pattern in the color palette that you would like to paint with. To apply a dab of paint, just click on the card itself. Or click on the card, hold down the mouse button, and move the mouse around to apply lots of paint. The default shape of the brush is a medium-sized circular tip. There are two ways you can change this shape. One method is to click on **Options** in the menu bar and select **Brush Shape.** This will bring up a dialog box featuring 24 different shapes to choose from. Select your new shape and click on the **OK** button. The other way to change brush shapes is to rapidly click twice in succession (called "double-clicking") on the paintbrush tool itself in the tool set. This will also bring up the Brush Shape dialog box.

HyperHint→You can only double-click on a tool if the tool set has been torn off and is on the screen.

The **spraypaint tool** sprays a somewhat circular array of paint dots onto the card. You can click on the card once to put down one set of dots, or draw with it by clicking and holding down the mouse button. You might note as you practice with this tool that the faster you move the mouse around, the more "dotty" your drawing will be. The slower you move the mouse, the more filled-in the dots will be. As with the paintbrush, you can change the color or pattern of paint by selecting it from the pull-down **Colors** menu. Having the color palette already out on your card (as suggested above) makes this even more convenient.

The **fill tool** (or paint bucket) looks like a bucket tipped over with paint spilling out of it. It "pours" a color or pattern of paint onto the background. *The active area of this tool is the tip of the spilling paint.* This bucket of paint does not just pour paint everywhere, though. The paint only goes into connected areas that are the same color as the color where the paint was "spilled." If the whole background of your card is one solid color, then the paint will fill the entire card. If you already have some paint on the background, then this tool will only fill areas that are *connected to* and *the same color as* the area into which you first clicked or "spilled" the paint.

HyperHint→This tool is best suited for use when you want to fill in solid blocks of color on a card. Patterns can be very difficult to alter with the fill tool, due to their small, disconnected areas of color.

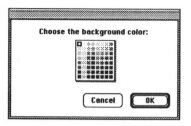

Where would any artist be without an eraser? So, *HyperStudio*'s tool set has an **eraser tool.** Erasing can be done using any color or pattern in the color palette. You can erase areas manually by holding down the mouse button and moving the eraser around on the card. Or, you can have *HyperStudio* erase the entire background of a card for you by either double-clicking on the eraser tool, or by selecting **Erase Background** from the **Edit** portion of the menu bar. Either method will bring up a dialog box that asks you to select the color you wish to erase with. Notice, though, that this dialog box only allows you to select colors—not patterns. If you want to erase the entire card with a pattern, you will have to do so by hand.

HyperHint→ You might think that erasing is really no different than painting in HyperStudio. However, that is not entirely true. While erasing with a color or pattern may look the same as painting, erasing actually removes *paint from the card. For example, there is a difference between a "white" canvas and a canvas with white paint on it. Whenever you use a tool like the paintbrush or fill tool, you are* adding *paint to the card. Not that important, right? Maybe not, but there* is *a difference. Also, whenever you create a new card in a stack, the entire background of that card is set in whatever color or pattern the eraser is currently set on. If you ever create a new card and it doesn't come in looking the way you were expecting, check to see what the eraser is set to. If necessary, you can always re-erase the background using the steps mentioned above.*

While on the subject of erasing, it is not always necessary to erase mistakes you make while drawing or painting. *HyperStudio* always allows you to undo any change you make to the background. To take advantage of this capability, click on **Edit**, hold the mouse button down, move the pointer to **Undo Painting**, and then let up on the mouse button. Keep in mind, though, that *HyperStudio* lets you undo only the last change you made.

Drawing straight lines can be very difficult without using a straight edge. That is where *HyperStudio*'s **line tool** comes in handy. It creates straight lines in whatever color or pattern you select. To set its color or pattern, just click once on the tool and once on the color or pattern you wish it to be. To use it, just click on the card where you want the line to start, hold the mouse button down, and drag the line out however long and in whatever direction you want it to be. Double-clicking the line tool (or selecting **Line Size...** from the **Options** menu) will enable you to set your line to one of five different thickness settings.

HyperHint→ *Want to draw perfectly horizontal, vertical, or 45° lines? It's easy. Just hold down the shift key on your keyboard while making your line. This will constrain, or restrict, the direction of your line to 45° angle multiples. So, you can draw lines that are straight up and down, left to right, or halfway in between. In fact, you can use the shift key to force any of* HyperStudio's *paint tools to create perfectly horizontal or vertical lines, but only the line tool has the added ability to be shifted 45° as well.*

The **pencil** draws with a small, one-pixel-wide point in the currently selected color or pattern—and never needs sharpening. It's great for doing detailed work, since its tip is much finer than the smallest shape available for the paintbrush. Double-clicking on the pencil will allow you to magnify the card's background twice as big (or 200%). You can double-click on the pencil again to go to 400%, and a third time to 800%. When you magnify, a small window appears to show the portion of the card you are working on in normal size (100%). You can also magnify the card by selecting **Magnify** from the **Options** menu, and then selecting the percent magnification. However, the easiest way to magnify the background is to use the **magnifying glass**, which we will learn about in a few minutes. Wait until then to play around with HyperStudio's magnification features.

Holding down the command key (the key with a ⌘ and an open apple on it on your keyboard) while clicking the pencil on the card enables you to quickly change the "lead" of the pencil to whatever color you clicked on. The same thing can be accomplished using the **eye dropper**, which we will cover later.

Want a handy way to draw geometric shapes? Then you will appreciate HyperStudio's **rectangle, oval,** and **rounded rectangle tools**. These tools can create outline or filled versions of their respective shapes, in whatever size you would like. Normally, each tool is featured in the tool set with a white center and a black outline. Double-clicking on any them will cause them to become filled. Double-clicking again will cause them to become their original outlined versions. (You can also "toggle" back and forth between these capabilities by selecting or deselecting **Draw Filled** in the **Options** menu.)

Check out the examples on the right. The first one was created by using the rectangle tool in "filled" mode with the rock pattern. The second example was created in "outline" mode with the same pattern. To get a thick outline, set the

Line Size to the fourth thickness. (Yes, you can set the thickness of the outlines of these tools by selecting **Line Size…** from the **Options** menu, or by double-clicking on the line tool itself.)

If you want to draw shapes from the inside out, instead of from edge to edge, you can select **Draw Centered** from the **Options** menu.

HyperHint→Want to draw perfect shapes, such as a square or a circle? Just hold down the shift key while making your shape. You will notice that you can still size the shape however you'd like, but that its horizontal and vertical dimensions are restricted proportionally.

Remember *Spirograph®*—that really cool kit that helps you draw awesome geometric patterns? Well, you can do this with *HyperStudio* too—and with a lot less effort. Set your line size small, the shape tools to outline mode, and select **Draw Multiple** from the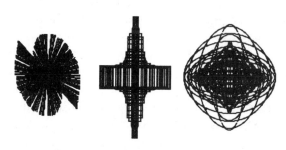

Options menu. The designs shown here were created in just seconds with the **line, rectangle**, and **circle** tools respectively (smallest line size, with draw multiple and draw centered features selected).

T Although the **text tool** is one of the paint tools, a separate lesson is devoted to it later on. You are free to experiment with it, but do not encourage your students to use it at this time. While its features are many, its limitations can make it quite frustrating to use. Have your students wait to use it, especially if they plan to make text of any great length.

The **magnifying glass** lets you get "up close and personal" with your art. Using this tool instead of double-clicking the pencil, allows you to select the particular portion of the card you would like to see magnified.

Draw some kind of pattern or image on your card. Then, select the **magnifying glass** and click on the card in a location where you'd like to do some detailed work. In the example below, a portion of the designs above were magnified. (Notice the magnifying glass takes on the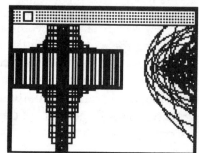

shape of a **transparent rectangle tool** when you move it over the card.) Included with your magnified view (also known as working in "fat bits") will be a small window displaying the magnified area in its normal size. This window gets smaller and smaller as you increase the amount of magnification. Increasing the magnification can be done by either clicking the magnifying glass on the card again, or by selecting **Magnify** in the **Options** menu. Clicking inside the tiny window will take the entire card back to normal size again. Clicking on the bar at the top of the window and holding down the mouse button will enable you to place it elsewhere on the screen. This is handy if the window gets in your way. You can get rid of the window entirely by clicking inside the little white square on the left side of the bar. Of course, that will prevent you from being able to click inside the window itself to return the card to normal size. But not to worry. Remember, you can always use **Magnify** in the **Options** menu and set your magnification to 100%—or easier yet, just press the escape key on your keyboard, or select the **browse tool**.

*HyperHint→Suppose you are working in fat bits and you would like to move to an area of the card that you currently cannot see. Well, believe it or not, you can use the browse tool to do this. There is a way to get the **browse tool** and still work in fat bits. While using the **magnifying glass** (or one of the other paint tools), press the option key on your keyboard. Presto. That tool temporarily becomes the **browse tool**, and the card stays magnified. Now, just click and hold down the mouse to "drag" to a new location on the card. The moment you let up on the option key, the **browse tool** will return to whatever tool you were using.*

The **eye dropper** "soaks up" color from the background. It is used to change the paint color of the tool you are using. Sometimes it is easy to forget a particular color you have used in a picture you are working on. In that case, just get the **eye dropper** and click it on an area of your card containing the color you would like to get. Voila. The **eye dropper** will soak it up and make it available for your **paint tool**.

Remember how the color palette got longer when you placed it out on the screen? What made it longer was the addition of the section pictured here. With the color palette out on the screen, *HyperStudio* allows you to see the current colors or patterns you are using for the **text tool**, **eraser**, and **painting tool** (in this case, the **pencil**). If another tool was being used, such as the **paintbrush**, its icon (or picture) would appear where the **pencil** is located. Basically, this section of the color palette serves as a handy "tool color indicator" to show you the current foreground color (top), background color (middle), and text color (bottom) that you are using. Clicking the **eye dropper** on the background changes the foreground color (the color being used by whatever paint tool you are using). Clicking the **eye dropper** on the background while pressing the option key changes the background color (the color being used by the eraser).

HyperHint→The color of the tool you are using will also be selected with an outline in the palette of 64 colors itself. However, since it is possible to use all 256 colors on a card (which we will learn to do later), there is a chance that the selected color may not be among the actual 64 colors displayed in the color palette. In that case, the color will not be selected with an outline in the 64-color palette. However, it will appear in the tool color indicator portion at the bottom of the palette.

Well, that is quite a bit of information on, but a rather brief overview of, *HyperStudio*'s many paint tools. You will be amazed out how quickly you and your students become adept at using these tools.

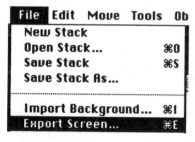

One last piece of information. You and your students may want to save some of your masterpieces as art files. These can then be printed later, or, better yet, included as part of your first stack. *HyperStudio* provides an easy way to save what you have painted or drawn on a card. Simply select **Export Screen...** from the **File** menu.

Don't be too hasty to click on Save however. *HyperStudio* automatically defaults to a folder called "HS Art" which is inside the "HyperStudio for HD" folder on your hard drive. The "HS Art" folder is a collection of art files that are included with *HyperStudio*. (we will learn more about using these files in a later lesson.) By exporting the screen, you have indicated to *HyperStudio* that you wish to create another art file, and so it takes you to its default art folder. It is recommend that you do *not* save your artwork here. Rather, make a custom folder, either on your hard drive, an external drive, or floppy disk, for saving the

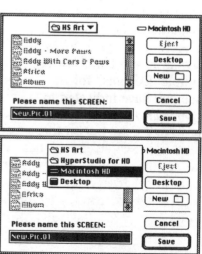

art you and your students create. To do this, first click where the dialog box says "HS Art" and pull down the list of levels.

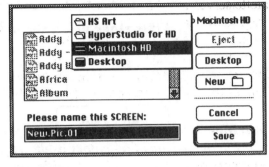

If you will be saving to another drive or to a floppy disk, you will want to select Desktop and then select the drive or disk. In the example to the right, a folder was created on the built-in hard drive.

To create the actual folder, click on the button that says "New" with a folder icon beside it. Another dialog box will pop up, allowing you to give your new folder a name. In this example, the folder is saved as "Student Art Files." After typing the folder's name, click on the Create button.

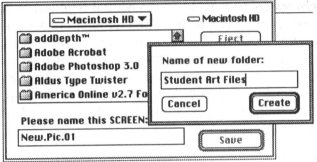

Your new folder now becomes the location where your screen will be saved. Be sure to give your screen file a name. *HyperStudio* offers "New.Pic.01" as the default name. Do *not* use this name.

Create a specific name that identifies what the picture is. In this example, the designs included earlier in this lesson, were saved in "Tim's 'Draw Multiple' Designs" folder. Once you have indicated to *HyperStudio* where you want to save your file and what you want to name it, click on the Save button. That is all there is to it.

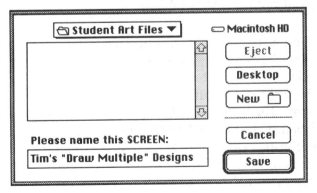

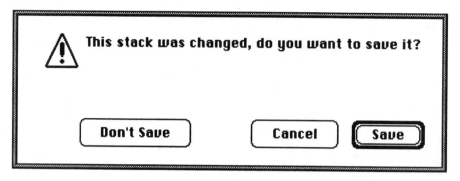

After creating your art (and saving it if you like), it is time to Quit *HyperStudio*. In Lesson 1, you only browsed through sample stacks. In this lesson, you created a new stack and actually made changes to it. When you quit this time, *HyperStudio* will display the message shown here. Since the emphasis of this lesson has been on experimenting with the paint tools and creating original works of art, click on Don't Save. You and your students have a few more lessons to run through before acquiring enough of the basics to create your first fully interactive stack.

HyperHands-On!

Student Task Cards—Lesson 2

"Practice Using the Paint Tools and Color Palette"

Step 1. Start up *HyperStudio*.

Step 2. When you get to the Home Stack, click on **File** in the menu bar at the top of the screen and continue to hold the mouse button down. Move the arrow to **New Stack**, and then let up on the mouse button to select it.

You can also create a New Stack by clicking on the **New Stack** button at the bottom of the Home Stack card.

Step 3. When the little dog, Addy, (the *HyperStudio* mascot) appears telling you that you have just created a new stack, use the **browse tool** (the "hand") and click on the **OK** button.

Step 4. In your new stack, click on the word **Tools** in the menu bar. A set of tools will pop up. Let up on the mouse, and the tools put themselves back away. To use any tool, click on **Tools**, hold the mouse button down, move the arrow onto the tool you wish to use, and then let up on the mouse button.

To place the whole tool set out on your card, click on **Tools**, hold the mouse button down, move the arrow down into the tool set, and then move it off in any direction except up. You can then place the tool set wherever you'd like on the card. In fact, you can move it around at any time by clicking in the little bar at the top of the tool set and holding the mouse button down. If you click on the little white box inside the bar, the tool set will put itself back away.

Step 5. Place *HyperStudio*'s color palette out on your card by clicking on the word **Colors** in the menu bar, and then follow the information covered in Step 4.

Step 6. Practice using the **paintbrush**.

To use it, just click on it once in the tool set, and then click on the color or pattern in the color palette that you would like to paint with. Want to change the shape of the brush? One way is to click on **Options** in the menu bar and select **Brush Shape....** This will bring up a dialog box featuring 24 different shapes to choose from. Select your new shape and click on the **OK** button. The other way to change brush shapes is to rapidly click twice (called "double-clicking") on the paintbrush tool itself in the tool set. This will also bring up the Brush Shape dialog box. (You can only double-click on a tool if the tool set is out on the screen.)

Step 7. Practice using the **spraypaint tool**.

The faster you move the mouse around, the more "dotty" your drawing will be.

Step 8. Practice using the **fill tool**.

This tool looks like a bucket tipped over with paint spilling out of it. It "pours" a color or pattern of paint onto the background. The active area of this tool is the tip of the spilling paint. This bucket of paint does not just pour paint everywhere, though. The paint only goes into connected areas that are the same color as the color where the paint was "spilled." If the whole background of your card is one solid color, then the paint will fill the entire card. If you already have some paint on the background, then this tool will only fill areas that are *connected to* and *the same color as* the area into which you first clicked or "spilled" the paint. *Patterns can be very difficult to fill because they are made up of so many different colors.*

Step 9. Practice using the **eraser tool**.

You can erase areas by hand, or you can have *HyperStudio* erase the entire background of a card for you by either double-clicking on the eraser tool, or by selecting **Erase Background** from the **Edit** portion of the menu bar. Either method will bring up a dialog box that asks you to select the color you wish to erase with. The dialog box only allows you to select colors—not patterns. If you want to erase the entire card with a pattern, you will have to do that by hand.

HyperHint→It is not always necessary to erase mistakes you make while drawing or painting. HyperStudio *always allows you to undo any change you make to the background. Just click on Edit, hold the mouse button down, move the pointer to Undo Painting, and then let up on the mouse button. Keep in mind, though, that* HyperStudio *only lets you undo the last change you made.*

Step 10. Practice using the **line tool**.

To set its color or pattern, just click once on the tool and once on the color or pattern you wish it to be. To use it, just click on the card where you want the line to start, hold the mouse button down, and drag the line out however long and in whatever direction you want it to be. Double-clicking the **line tool** (or selecting **Line Size...** from the **Options** menu) will allow you to choose from five different line thicknesses.

HyperHint→Want to draw perfectly horizontal, vertical, or 45° lines? It is easy. Just hold down the shift key on your keyboard while making your line. This will constrain, or restrict, the direction of your line to 45° angle multiples. So, you can draw lines that are straight up and down, left to right, or halfway in between. In fact, you can use the shift key to force any of HyperStudio's *paint tools to create perfectly horizontal or vertical lines, but only the line tool has the added ability to be "shifted" 45° as well.*

Step 11. Practice using the **pencil**.

It's great for doing detailed work, since its tip is much finer than the smallest shape available for the **paintbrush**. Double-clicking on the **pencil** will allow you to magnify the card's background twice as big (or 200%). You can double-click on the **pencil** again to go to four times as big (400%), and a third time to go eight times bigger (800%). When you magnify, a small window appears to show the portion of the card you are working on in normal size (100%). You can also magnify the card by selecting **Magnify** from the **Options** menu, and then selecting the percent magnification. However, the easiest way to magnify the background is to use the **magnifying glass.** Wait until then to play around with *HyperStudio*'s magnification features. Holding down the "command" key (the ⌘ key with a and an open apple on it on your keyboard) while clicking the pencil on the card is a quick way to change the color of the pencil to whatever color you clicked on.

Step 12. Practice making shapes with the **rectangle, oval,** and **rounded rectangle tools**.

These tools can create outline or filled geometric shapes in whatever size you would like. Normally, each tool is featured in the tool set with a white center and a black outline. Double-clicking on any them will cause them to become filled. Double-clicking again will cause them to become their original outlined versions. (You can also use Draw **Filled** in the **Options** menu to do this.)

HyperHint→*Want to draw perfect shapes, such as a square or a circle? Just hold down the **shift** key while making your shape.*

Step 13. Practice using the **magnifying glass**.

This tool lets you get "up close and personal" with your art. You might prefer using this tool rather than double-clicking the pencil, because it allows you to select the particular portion of the card you'd like to see magnified.

Step 14. Practice using the **eye dropper**.

This tool "soaks up" color from the background. It's used to change the paint color of the tool you are using. Sometimes it is easy to forget a particular color you have used in a picture you are working on. In that case, just get the eye dropper and click it on an area of your card containing the color you'd like to get. The eye dropper will soak it up and make it available for your paint tool. If you press the **option** key while clicking the **eye dropper**, you can change the color of the **eraser tool**.

Step 15. Create and save an original piece of art.

If your teacher wants you to, use the paint tools to create your own picture. Ask your teacher to help you save the picture (also called exporting the screen).

Lesson 3: Making the Right Selection

"Learning to use the Rectangle Selector, Circle Selector, and Lasso"

HyperOverview:

What do rodeo cowboys and theater marquees have in common? More than you might first realize. Each one uses "selection" as an important means to an end. The cowboy must accurately throw his lasso while on horseback to stop and capture a running calf. The faster and more accurate he is, the more points he earns in the competition. A theater marquee must draw people's attentions to the production title around which the lights flash. A bit of a stretch? Maybe, but sometimes you have got to stretch things in order to make a point.

In this lesson, you and your students will gain experience in using *HyperStudio*'s "selection" tools. These tools, while not so useful at a rodeo or theater production, *will* help you "capture" portions of your art and "produce" effects that are not possible with the paint tools alone (covered in Lesson 2). You will also learn each tool's strengths and limitations. Teach how to use these amazing tools and you will "score big points" with your students.

HyperPrerequisites:

- Experience using a mouse, trackball, or other input device

- Experience creating new stacks and new cards (Lesson 2)

- Experience using *HyperStudio*'s paint tools and color palette (Lesson 2)

HyperClinic:

Included in the *HyperStudio* tool set are three tools used for selecting, moving, and manipulating artwork—the rectangle selector, circle selector, and lasso. These tools enhance your ability to make alterations to your artwork. With them, you can scale, rotate, flip, cut, copy, and paste areas of the background—actions that are just not possible with the paint tools alone.

Start with the **rectangle selector** (sometimes referred to as the **marquee tool** in other paint and drawing programs, such as Adobe's *Photoshop*®). First, create a new stack and paint some kind of an image or design onto the background. (Nothing fancy, just something you can try out each of the selection tools on.) After painting your image/design, get the **rectangle selector** from the tool set. (It's just above the **paintbrush**.) Notice that while this tool is a rectangle with dashed lines in the tool set, it takes on the shape of a "cross" when placed over the card itself. Position the cross anywhere on the card. To select an area, click and hold down on the mouse button while dragging the cross.

As you drag it, you will notice that a dashed rectangle will be created. When you have selected an area the size you want, let up on the mouse button. The dashes will turn red and begin to move. (Just like the lights on a theater marquee—get it? Because of the size and color of the moving dashes, some people affectionately call this action "marching ants." But it is your selection, and you can call it anything you like.)

HyperHint→The easiest way to use the rectangle selector is to position the cross just above and to the left, and then drag just below and to the right of the area you wish to select. You will soon find a way that is easiest and most comfortable for you.

With the area *still* selected (with the ants still marching), place the tool anywhere inside the selected area. The tool's cross design will become a cross with four arrow points. This new design indicates that you can now move the selected area. Try it. With the tool as a four-pointed cross, click and hold down the mouse button while dragging the selected area to a new location on the card.

If you ever want to deselect the area, just place the tool anywhere outside the selected area and click the mouse button one time. But don't do this just yet. KEEP THE AREA SELECTED.

Now place the **rectangle selector tool** along one of the four sides of the selected area. The tool itself will now become a line with an arrow point on each end. If you place it on a top or bottom side, the line is vertically oriented. If you place it on the left or right side, the line is horizontally oriented. This design indicates that you can increase or decrease the height or width of the selected area. With the tool as a two-pointed line, click and hold down the mouse button while dragging the side (up or down or left or right, depending on which side you are moving). As you increase or decrease the height or width, your original artwork will become distorted.

HyperHint→Don't panic if you accidentally click off the selected area when trying to click on one of its sides, causing it to deselect.

*You can easily reselect the area by choosing **Undo Deselection** in the **Edit** menu. Just make sure that you do this as your very next card action. Remember, HyperStudio can only undo the very latest action you have taken. In a case where you may inadvertently carry out another action after deselecting the area, you would just have to use the rectangle selector and reselect the area yourself.*

While the area is selected, you can adjust both its height and width at the same time by moving the rectangle selector to one of the area's four corners. In this case, the tool will become a diagonal, two-pointed line. You can scale both dimensions by clicking and holding down the mouse button while dragging the corner. If you want to scale both dimensions proportionally, just press the **shift** key while dragging a corner.

So far, you have been *manually* moving or resizing a selected area of your card. Using the same selected area (or select a new area if you'd like), it is time to get

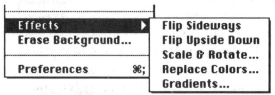

HyperStudio to do some of the work for you *automatically*. With an area selected, you can click on **Edit** in the menu bar, hold the mouse button down, and move the pointer to **Effects.** This will cause a submenu to appear with choices ranging from **Flip Sideways** to **Gradients.** Try each one of these effects.

Get the **Effects** submenu and choose **Flip Sideways.** Your selection will become a mirror image of itself as it is "flipped" along an imaginary vertical axis running through the middle of the selection area. To undo this effect, choose **Undo Flip Sideways** in the **Edit** menu.

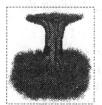

Now choose **Flip Upside Down** from the **Effects** submenu. Your selection is flipped over along an imaginary horizontal axis running through the middle of the selection area. It becomes a mere reflection of its former self. To undo this effect, choose **Undo Flip Upside Down** in the **Edit** menu.

Choose **Scale & Rotate,** and *HyperStudio* will bring up a little dialog box in which you can set the **scale factor** and **rotation angle.** The scale factor is set in %, with 100% being the default.

For example, if you wish to double the size of your selected area, you would enter "200%" as the scale factor. To rotate your selected area, just enter the number of degrees you wish to rotate it, and specify whether you want it rotated clockwise or counter-clockwise. Obviously, if you set the rotation angle to 360°, the selection would not appear to be affected, since this results in placing the selection back in its original position. The selection is always rotated along an imaginary point at the very center of the selection area. To undo this effect, choose **Undo Stretching** in the **Edit** menu.

If you choose **Replace Colors**, *HyperStudio* will bring up a dialog box in which you can replace or exchange colors in the selected area. Two identical 64-color palettes are displayed in this dialog box. These palettes can be used either to replace one color with another in your selected area, or to exchange two colors. If you **Replace colors**, the color you click on in the left-side palette is replaced with the color that you click

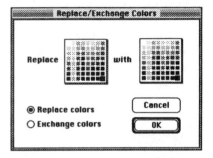

on in the right-side palette. For example, if you select white in the first palette and black in the second palette, any white pixels of color in your selected area will become black pixels. Exchanging colors is a little different. When you **Exchange Colors**, the two selected palette colors are swapped for each other. Using the example mentioned above, any previously white pixels in your selected area would be transformed into black, and vice-versa. Exchanging colors can be used to produce some interesting "negative" photo effects. To undo this effect, choose **Undo Painting** in the **Edit** menu.

HyperHint→You only need to click once on each color to select it. If you double-click, the entire 256-color palette will appear. It is recommended that you refrain from using this palette in this lesson, since the artwork you have created up to this point has been based on the 64-color palette. We will talk about the 256-color palette in a later lesson.

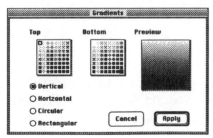

The last item in the **Effects** submenu is **Gradients**. Choosing this will bring up a dialog box in which enables you to create simple shades and color blends. Just select your starting and ending colors from the two color palettes, and *HyperStudio* will provide the necessary in-between colors to create a smooth gradient. You can create a **vertical, horizontal, circular,** or **rectangular** gradient. Unlike the other **Effects, Gradients...** completely fills in the selected area, replacing the original image. By combining different selected areas and gradients, you can create some amazing three-dimensional effects. To undo this effect, choose **Undo Painting** in the **Edit** menu.

*HyperHint➔By now you have probably noticed that the **Undo** command has a slightly different wording depending on the last action you have taken. If you last created a painting effect, it reads as "Undo Painting." If you scale and/or rotate a selection, it reads as "Undo Stretching." If you undo a selection, it reads as "Undo Selection." Regardless of the wording, though, this command will always undo the last action you have taken. Without a doubt, this is a command you will be using over and over again as you work with* HyperStudio. *So, why not make its use even easier. By now maybe you have noticed the keystroke combination at the far right of the command itself? That means that as an alternative to always clicking on **Edit** and selecting **Undo,** you can just press and hold down the command key (⌘) while pressing the letter **Z** on your keyboard. Try it. It is easy, and a whole lot faster. In fact, quite a number of* HyperStudio *commands have keystroke combination alternatives. As you continue to use* HyperStudio, *try to memorize these "keyboard shortcuts." Using them will increase your speed and efficiency while using* HyperStudio.

The circle selector behaves in a similar manner to its rectangular sibling. With this tool, you can make circular and oval selections of areas on the card. If you want these selections to be perfect circles, just press the **shift** key as you hold down the mouse and drag the tool.

As with the rectangle selector, this tool looks like a cross when placed over the card itself. Select an area of your card with the circle selector, move the tool inside the selected area, and notice that it becomes a four-pointed cross. This indicates that you can move the area, just as you did with the rectangle selector. But unlike the rectangle selector, you cannot manually resize the area. Moving the tool to the edge of the selection does not change the tool's design to a two-pointed line.

With the area still selected, get the **Effects** submenu. Notice that **Flip Sideways** and **Flip Upside Down** are printed in gray, not black. This indicates that these effects are not available to areas selected with the circle selector. Notice, too, that the **Scale & Rotate...** command only reads as **Scale....**. Choose this command and a dialog box will appear allowing you only to scale your selection. You cannot rotate areas selected with the circle selector. The **Replace Colors...** and **Gradients...** effects are fully functional, however, just as they were for areas selected with the rectangle selector. That about sums it up. The circle selector is basically a circular version of the rectangle selector, with a few limitations thrown in. What it lacks in capability, though, it makes up for in utility. For example, it is a great tool for creating cameo effects. And it creates fantastic three-dimensional spheres when used with circular gradients.

HyperHint→Replace Colors... and Gradients... are fully functional whether you have an area selected or not. HOWEVER, if you use either of these effects without first selecting an area, the effect will be applied to the entire card. Not that this is bad. If you want to replace/exchange two colors wherever they are on the entire card, then choose this effect without making a selection. If you want a nice gradient effect for the entire background, just choose this effect without making a selection. BUT, if you only want the effect to occur in a given area, you must first select the area.

The **lasso** is a very unique tool. Its selection capabilities are more discriminating. While the rectangle and circle selector tools select everything within their borders, the **lasso** selects only certain parts, while ignoring others. To really understand what this does, you need to try it out. Use the following example or experiment on your own.

If you are following this example, you will need a clean card. Either erase the card you are on (use black as the erase color), or create a new card with a black background. Using the **paintbrush**, paint an area of the card with the repeating cloud pattern from the bottom row of the color palette. The **lasso** can be a little difficult to use at first, so it is recommended to use the magnifying glass to magnify the background 200%

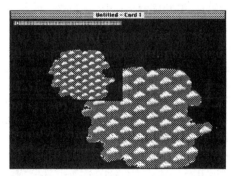

(twice its normal size). Get the **lasso tool**. Notice the tool keeps its design when placed against the card itself. To use it, click and hold down the mouse button in the blue color of the cloud pattern while "drawing" around a group of clouds. A freehand selection "line" will be "drawn" as you do so to indicate the area you are selecting. Make sure you close this "line"—that is, connect the selection back to the point at which you began. Otherwise, *HyperStudio* will close the selection automatically by drawing a straight line from the point at which you finished back to the point where you first began. This "line" is only a temporary indication of your selected area.

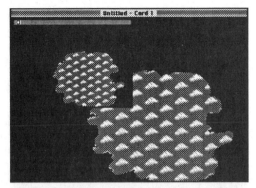

When you have selected your area, let up on the mouse button. The "line" will disappear, and something interesting will occur. If you began and finished your selection in the blue portion of the cloud pattern, the **lasso** will enclose each of the clouds in your original selection area. Cool, huh. This is what is meant by the tool being very discriminating. The **lasso** works by ignoring the color in which you first clicked and began your selection. So, since you first clicked on a blue pixel, the lasso ignored anything that was this same color of blue. Another way of looking at it is that the color in which you start to lasso an area becomes transparent or invisible to it. The **lasso** "shrinks" to capture any other colors but the one you first clicked on, which, in this case, are the little clouds.

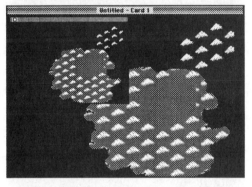

While the clouds have little marching ants around them, move the **lasso** over one of them. Notice that it becomes the familiar four-pointed cross. Now you can move the clouds. When the lasso becomes a four-pointed cross, click and hold down the mouse button while dragging the

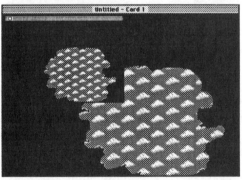

clouds outside the pattern you painted. The clouds move while the blue remains behind. And it does not matter which cloud you click on, as long as it is one with marching ants around it. Although the selected clouds are disconnected from each other, they act as one unit when moved. Definitely a much more unconventional tool effect than the rectangle selector.

While the clouds are still selected, undo this last action. The clouds will return to their original positions. Click once anywhere off the clouds to deselect them. Now try something a little different. Click the **lasso** first in a black portion of the

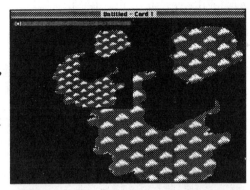

card, hold the mouse button down, and select an area of your cloud pattern. This time, the entire area of the pattern you lassoed is selected. Why? In this instance, since your selection began on a black-colored pixel, black became the transparent color, so the lasso shrank to fit your selected portion of the cloud pattern. With this portion still selected, you can move it away from the rest of the pattern.

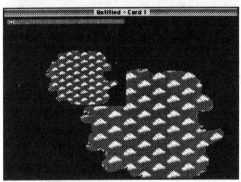

Like its real-world counterpart, the lasso surrounds and shrinks to capture its target area—whether it is a rodeo animal or a pattern of clouds. But *HyperStudio*'s lasso has another trick up its sleeve. It can expand outward as well. Press the **option** key while clicking the lasso once inside the blue portion of the cloud pattern. You don't need to continue holding the mouse button down. Just click the lasso *once*. The lasso will expand to select all of the blue portion of the cloud pattern. While the ants are marching, select **Replace Colors.** When the dialog box appears, replace the fourth blue down in the blue color column of the first color palette with black in the second color palette. If you are successful, all the blue in your cloud pattern will disappear, leaving just the clouds themselves.

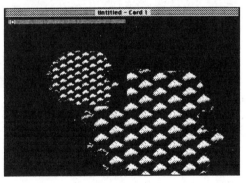

The lasso—what an amazing tool. It does, however, have its limitations. Like the circle selector, you cannot manually resize selected areas, and the only menu effects available when using it are **Scale, Replace Colors,** and **Gradients.** The fact that the lasso works by ignoring one color and selecting others, while extremely useful, can also make it quite challenging to work with. You will understand this better when you learn about clip art and backgrounds in the next lesson.

More can be done with selected areas than just moving, resizing, and other effects. You can also **Cut, Copy, Paste,** or **Clear** them. Whenever you select an area (regardless of which selection tool you use), you can choose one of these four actions from the **Edit** menu (all but **Clear** have keyboard shortcuts as well). When you **Cut** a selection, it is like taking a pair of scissors and removing the selected area. This area is then temporarily stored in the computer's memory on the clipboard. It can then be pasted onto any card in your stack. When you **Copy** a selection, it is like taking a snapshot of the area. The original selection remains, while an exact copy is temporarily stored on the clipboard. This copy can be pasted onto any card in the stack. When you **Clear** a selection, it is as if the area has been erased. The area is removed, but unlike cutting it, nothing is stored on the clipboard. (You can get this same effect by selecting an area and then pressing the **delete** key.) **Paste** is used to get a copy of the last selection stored on the clipboard. This copy is placed on the current card while remaining selected, allowing you to move it to where you would like to, or to perform additional effects to it.

*HyperHint→there is a shortcut to cutting/copying a selected area and pasting it back onto the same card. Just select the area, move the tool into the selection area so that it becomes a four-pointed cross, and then press the **option** key while moving it. Instead of actually being moved, a copy of the original selection will appear. As if this were not enough, try doing this after selecting **Draw Multiple** in the **Options** menu. This allows multiple copies to be created in a path as you continue to move the mouse. This capability was used to produce the name below from one small area of the cloud pattern selected with the circle selector tool.*

And here is something else that is really cool... Make sure you have a card with something drawn or painted on it. Pull off the toolset and set it out on the card. Then, double-click each one of the selection tools in the toolset and see what happens. You will be pretty amazed.

Believe it or not, even more possibilities await you in upcoming lessons for making use of *HyperStudio's* selection tools.

HyperHands-On!

Student Task Cards—Lesson 3

"Learning to use the Rectangle Selector, Circle Selector, & Lasso"

Step 1. Start up *HyperStudio*.

Step 2. Make a new stack.

Step 3. Create a small design or picture on the background using any of the paint tools.

Step 4. Get the **rectangle selector** from the tool set.

Notice that while this tool is a rectangle with dashed lines in the tool set, it takes on the shape of a "cross" when placed over the card itself.

Step 5. Select an area of your design/pattern with the rectangle selector.

To select an area, click and hold down on the mouse button while dragging the cross. As you drag it, you will notice that a dashed rectangle will be created. When you have selected an area the size you want, let up on the mouse button. The dashes will turn red and begin to move—they look kind of like "marching ants."

HyperHint→*Don't panic if you accidentally click off the selected area when trying to do the following steps—or if you do something you didn't mean to do or don't like. Every* HyperStudio *user has done this, and it is no big deal. You can easily "undo" your last action by choosing* **Undo...** *in the* **Edit** *menu. Just make sure that you do this as your very next card action.* HyperStudio *can only undo the very latest action you have taken.*

If you accidentally do another action after deselecting the area, just use the rectangle selector and reselect the area yourself.

Step 6. Move your selection to another part of the card.

With the area *still* selected (while the ants are still marching), place the rectangle selector anywhere *inside* the selected area so that it will now look like a cross with four arrow points.

This new design indicates that you can now move the selected area. Try it. With the tool as a four-pointed cross, click and hold down the mouse button while dragging the selected area to a new location on the card.

If you ever want to deselect the area (get rid of the marching ants), just place the tool anywhere outside the selected area and click the mouse button one time. But don't do this just yet. KEEP THE ANTS MARCHING!

Step 7. Change the size of your selection.

Now place the **rectangle selector** along one of the four sides of your selected area so that it looks like a line with an arrow point on each end. (If you place it on a top or bottom side, the line points up and down. If you place it on the left or right side, the line points left and right.)

Try making your selection wider or thinner or taller or shorter. With the tool as a two-pointed line, click and hold down the mouse button while dragging the side (up or down or left or right, depending on which side you are moving). As you change the size of your selection, your original artwork in this area may become distorted (chunky or grainy).

Step 8. Scale your selection.

When you "scale" something, you change both its height and width at the same time.

Move the **rectangle selector** to one of the area's four corners until it becomes a diagonal, two-pointed line. You can now scale the area by clicking and holding down the mouse button while dragging the corner.

If you want to scale the area proportionally (exactly like the original, only bigger or smaller), just press the **shift** key while dragging a corner.

Step 9. Flip your selection sideways.

With an area of your design or picture selected, click on **Edit** in the menu bar, hold the mouse button down, and move the pointer to **Effects.** This will cause a branching menu to appear. Choose **Flip Sideways.**

Your selection will become a mirror image of its original form. Either leave it this way, or undo it to flip it back to its original position.

Step 10. Flip your selection upside down.

Now choose **Flip Upside Down** from the **Effects** menu (remember you first have to click on **Edit** in the menu bar).

Your selection will become a reflection of its original form. Either leave it this way, or undo it to flip it back to its original position.

Step 11. Scale and rotate your selection.

Choose **Scale & Rotate...** from the **Effects** menu (remember, you first have to click on **Edit** in the menu bar).

HyperStudio will bring up a little dialog box in which you can set the **scale factor** and **rotation angle.** The scale factor is set in % (percent), with 100% being the default (or preset) size. If you wish to double the size of your selected area, you would enter "200%" as the scale factor, since 200% means the same as "twice as big."

To rotate your selected area, just enter the number of degrees you wish to rotate it, and click on whether you want it rotated clockwise or counter-clockwise.

HyperHint→There are 360° in a circle, so type in a number from 1 to 359. If you type 360, you won't notice any change in your selection. Since 360° is a full circle, the selection will be rotated all the way around to its original position. If you type a number larger than 360, it won't hurt anything, but there is really no reason to, since there are only 360° in a circle. So, typing 361° is the same as typing 1°.

Either leave your selection this way, or undo it to scale and rotate it back to its original form.

Step 12. Replace colors in your selection.

Choose **Replace Colors . . .** from the **Effects** menu.

HyperStudio will bring up a dialog box in which you can replace or exchange colors in the selected area. Two identical 64-color palettes are displayed in this dialog box. These palettes can be used either to replace one color with another in your selected area, or to exchange two colors.

If you **Replace colors,** the color you click on in the left-side palette is replaced with the color that you click on in the right-side palette.

When you **Exchange colors,** the two selected palette colors are swapped for each other.

Either leave your selection this way, or undo it to scale and rotate it back to its original form.

Step 13. Create a gradient in your selection.

Choose **Gradients...** from the **Effects** menu.

A dialog box will appear which allows you to create simple shades and color blends. Just select your starting and ending colors from the two color palettes, and *HyperStudio* will provide the necessary in-between colors to create a smooth gradient.

You can create a **vertical, horizontal, circular,** or **rectangular** gradient. Unlike the other effects you have used, **Gradients...** completely fills in the selected area, replacing the original image.

Step 14. Get the **circle selector** from the tool set, and select a new area of your picture.

The **circle selector** works a lot like the **rectangle selector**. With this tool, you can make circular and oval selections of areas on the card. If you press the **shift** key as you select an area, the "ants will march" in a perfect circle.

This tool looks like a cross when placed over the card itself (just like the rectangle selector did). Select an area of your card with the circle selector, move the tool inside the selected area, and notice that it becomes a four-pointed cross. Now you can move the area, just as you did with the rectangle selector.

Unlike the **rectangle selector**, you cannot manually resize the area. Moving the tool to the edge of the selection does *not* change the tool's design to a two-pointed line.

Step 15. Flip your selection sideways and upside down.

With the area still selected, click on **Edit** and get the **Effects** branching menu. Notice that **Flip Sideways** and **Flip Upside Down** are printed in gray, not black. This means that these effects are not available when you select areas with the **circle selector**.

Step 16. Scale your selection.

Click on **Edit** and get the **Effects** branching menu. The **Scale & Rotate...** command only reads as **Scale.** You cannot rotate areas selected with the circle selector.

Choose this command and a dialog box will appear allowing you only to scale your selection.

Either leave it this way, or undo it to scale it back to its original size.

Step 17. Replace colors in your selection.

This works just the same as when you were using the **rectangle selector**. Using the circle selector, repeat Step 12.

Either leave it this way, or undo it to scale it back to its original size.

Step 18. Create a gradient in your selection.

This works just the same as when you were using the **rectangle selector**. Using the circle selector, repeat Step 13.

Either leave it this way, or undo it to scale it back to its original size.

*HyperHint→You can **Replace Colors...** and create **Gradients...** whether you select an area first or not. HOWEVER, if you use either of these effects without first selecting an area, the effect will be applied to the entire card. If you want to replace/exchange two colors wherever they are on the entire card, then choose this effect without making a selection. If you want a nice gradient effect for the entire background, just choose this effect without making a selection. BUT, if you want the effect to occur only in a given area, you must first select the area.*

Step 19. Get the lasso from the tool set.

The rectangle and **circle selector** tools select everything within their borders. But the **lasso** is special. It only selects certain parts, while ignoring others.

Lesson 4: A Tour of the Art Galleries

"Importing Backgrounds/Adding Clip Art"

HyperOverview:

Up to this point, you and your students have been creating and modifying your own original artwork masterpieces. In terms of creativity, this is far more important than the skills you are about to learn. An outspoken *HyperStudio* user, Gordon Russell, said, upon hearing this book was being written, that from his firsthand experience, "Clip art can kill creativity, in kids and adults. The best student stacks are hand-drawn. Clip art narrows their thinking to what is **available,** not what is **possible.**" there is a lot of truth in Gordon's admonition. Prepackaged artwork (or "clip art" as it is often called), while able to give projects a professional look, can also become a crutch for teachers and students as they create stacks. Adding clip art is easier and takes less time than creating original artwork from scratch. And because clip art is often of very high "technical" artistic quality, it is very tempting for teachers and students to use it to the exclusion of original artwork.

This is not to say clip art should never be used. Far from it. But avoid the indiscriminate use of prepackaged art. Clip art should not be used in a stack simply because it looks nice—it should be used because it enhances the information the stack is trying to communicate in ways that the user can't achieve as well through original artwork. To this end, you must become art critics. You need to "tour the art galleries" for just the right pieces to accent your own multimedia works of art. Accordingly, you should give credit in your stacks for any sources you access, and make sure that your use of clip art does not violate its copyright.

In this lesson, you will learn how to bring prepackaged artwork into a stack. Knowing which pieces of art to add to your stacks is something you and your students will have to learn on your own.

HyperHardware:

- HS Art folder (should be installed on hard drive)
- *HyperStudio* Program Resource CD (optional)

HyperPrerequisites:

- Experience creating new stacks and new cards (Lesson 2)

- Experience using the paint and selection tools, and a basic understanding of how each tool functions (Lessons 2 & 3)

HyperClinic:

Bringing artwork into a stack is quite easy once you have spent time learning to use *HyperStudio*'s selection tools. Although prepackaged art is often generically referred to simply as "clip art," a distinction needs to be made before proceeding with this lesson. *HyperStudio* offers two basic alternatives for placing artwork on a card: as a "background" and as "clip art." Art can either be added to a card so that it fills the entire "background," or it can be added to the card in small "clips."

Whenever you import a "background" in *HyperStudio*, the entire art file is placed on the card, completely replacing whatever art was previously on the card. The chosen art file becomes the entire background of the card.

Whenever you add "clip art," *HyperStudio* allows you to select a portion of a piece of art. This selected portion is then added to the already-existing background, becoming a part of it.

Here is a simple exercise to help clarify the difference. Start up *HyperStudio* and create a new stack. For this stack we will need two cards, so create a new card.

HyperHint→There are a number of ways to manually move back and forth between cards in a stack. If you click on **Move** *in the menu bar you will be presented with the many options you see here. (Of course, it is even better if you memorize their keyboard shortcuts.)* **Back** *retraces your steps, basically moving you to whatever card you were on prior to the current one. It can also move you through the entire sequence of cards (even from stack to stack) that you have been to if you continue to select* **Back.** **First Card** *always takes you to the very first card in your stack.* **Previous Card** *takes you one card back (numerically) in your stack.* **Next Card** *advances you one card.* **Last Card** *takes you to whatever card is last (no matter what its actual number is).* *Choosing* **Jump To Card...**

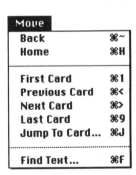

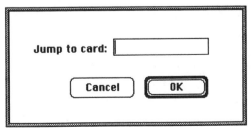

causes HyperStudio *to display a dialog box in which you can enter the exact number of the card you wish to move to.*

On Card 1 of your new stack, load an art file as a background. To do this, simply click on **File** and select **Import Background...** from the menu. This will bring up a dialog box from which you can choose the source for the art file. To locate the file you need, you first have to tell *HyperStudio* the method you want to use to get the art. Selecting **Disk file** indicates that the art you want is already stored on a disk (floppy disk, hard drive, cartridge drive, CD-ROM, etc.). Selecting **Video** indicates that you want to capture and digitize an image from a video source (VCR, camcorder, laserdisc player, TV, etc.). Selecting *QuickTake camera* indicates that you want to obtain a digital image stored on an *Apple QuickTake* camera. For this lesson, select **Disk file** as your source. (you will learn about incorporating video/digital images into your stacks in a later lesson in this tutorial.)

Selecting **Disk file** brings up another dialog box in which you can specify the file you wish to import. *HyperStudio* automatically defaults to a folder called "HS Art." This folder is located in the main *HyperStudio* folder that was placed on your hard drive when you first installed the software. "HS Art" is provided as a basic starter kit of art files. You aren't limited to the files in this folder, however. For example, you could click on the **Desktop** button, and then select a file from a floppy disk or CD-ROM. *HyperStudio* can load art files from a wide range of file sources, and in a variety of standard file formats (PICT, TIFF, GIF, JPEG, EPS, *MacPaint*, and others).

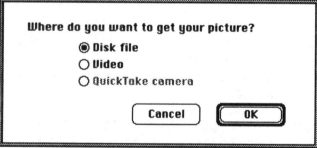

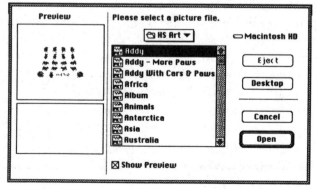

For now, let's stick with the "HS Art" folder since it is already handy. Open the very first file in the list—"Addy."

*HyperHint→To select a file, you can either highlight it and then click the **Open** button, or you can double-click on the file name. Further, any buttons that appear with a double outline (like the **Open** button, for example) can also be activated by pressing the **return** or **enter** keys. You can locate a file by scrolling through the list, but a quicker way to locate a particular file is to press the letter key on your keyboard corresponding to the first letter in the file's name. And, if several files begin with the same letter, you can type the first couple of letters to locate one in particular. (These letters have to be typed fairly quickly in succession for this to work, however.)*

Almost immediately your first card will resemble the sample shown here. The entire "Addy" file has been imported as the card's background. At this point you could then use any of the paint and selection tools to make changes to this background. Or, you could always import another file to replace this one. Just remember that importing a background means that the current background is completely replaced by the chosen art file.

Some files are really not well-suited for use as backgrounds. "Addy" is one such file. It features several small versions of Addy, along with some objects for Addy to use. Chances are that someone accessing this file would not want all of it, just selected pieces of it. "Addy" is designed for use as clip art —not a background. The files below, also from the "HS Art" folder, have been created specifically for use as backgrounds.

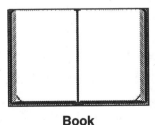

Book **Gazette** **USA**

Not that these files cannot be used as clip art, too. In fact, if they are scaled down in size, they make wonderful clip art accessories for a card. But backgrounds, on the whole, are files created and intended for use primarily for whole-card coverage.

HyperHint→At some point, especially if you start importing backgrounds from other file sources, Addy may appear with the following message. This is HyperStudio*'s way of indicating to you that the screen size of the file you intend to import as a background is either larger or smaller than the size of your card.*

If you click on the "Yes" button, HyperStudio *will scale the file so that it fits on the entire card. This can bring about mixed results, depending on the dimensions of the original file. If you click on "No,"* HyperStudio *will bring the file in and center it on the card. However, since the file is not*

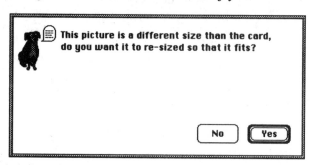

resized as it is imported, any parts of it that are beyond the dimensions of your card will not be included. You will just have to experiment to get the results you are looking for. You should know that at this point your stacks are limited to a card size of 512 pixels x 342 pixels (about 7" x 4.75"). This is HyperStudio*'s standard card size, as it fits nicely on just about any size monitor. In a later lesson, we will learn how to make adjustments to* HyperStudio*'s default settings—including how to create stacks with card sizes larger or smaller than standard size.*

Erase the background of Card 1 in black. Then, click on **File** and choose **Add Clip Art...** from the menu. *HyperStudio* will display the same dialogs you saw when you imported a background. As before, select "Addy" from the "HS Art" folder. This time, however, *HyperStudio* will not immediately place the file on your card. That is because you indicated that you wanted it for use as clip art—not a background. Instead, a "Clip Art" dialog box is displayed. This dialog shows the top portion of the "Addy" file, a "scroll bar" along the right and bottom sides, a "rectangle selector" and "lasso," a "Get another picture..." button, a "Cancel" button, and an "OK" button.

File	
New Stack	
Open Stack...	⌘O
Save Stack	⌘S
Save Stack As...	
Import Background...	⌘I
Export Screen...	⌘E
Add Clip Art...	⌘A

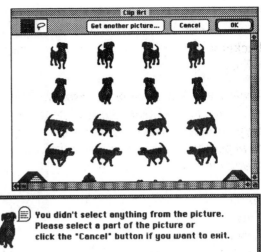

HyperStudio has provided you with several options. The **scroll bars** allow you to move up, down, or across the picture to locate the portion you are interested in. If you accidentally choose the wrong file, or if you decide that this is just not the file you want, you can get another picture file. You can even cancel your decision entirely. If the file is the one you want, you need to select a portion of it before clicking on the **OK** button. (Don't worry if you forget to do this. Addy will appear to remind you. What a faithful companion she is.)

In Lesson 3, you gained experience using the rectangle selector and lasso tools. As you may recall, the rectangle selector "selects" a piece of art by placing a rectangular frame around it. Make sure this tool is highlighted in the clip art dialog box, and then select a portion of the "Addy" picture file. You should see the familiar "marching ants." Once you have selected it, click on the **OK** button (or, as mentioned earlier, you could press **return** or **enter** on your keyboard).

For the example shown here, one of the little doghouses was selected. After you click on the **OK** button, *HyperStudio* will place the selected clip art in the center of your card (in this case, Card 1). Notice that it has a rectangular area of white around it, and the ants are still marching. You can now place the clip art wherever you would like on the card, resize it, flip it, etc. Since you used the rectangle selector to obtain this piece of art, you can apply any of the effects you used with this tool in Lesson 3. Remember, you need to leave the clip art selected to apply any changes to it, and you need to click off it to place it down on the background. No matter what effects you use, the white area surrounding your clip art will still remain.

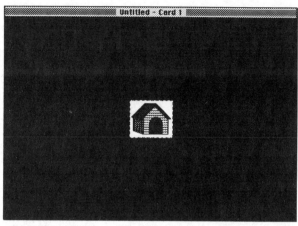

(Well, that is not entirely true. In this example, white could be replaced with black to eliminate the white area, but some of the detail would be lost in the doghouse. White could be exchanged with black, but this would create an undesired "negative" effect to the doghouse.)

This is one of the drawbacks to selecting clip art with the **rectangle selector**. Nothing in the "Addy" file is perfectly rectangular, so, when using the **rectangle selector**, you end up selecting a part of the white area around any clip art you select. If the background of Card 1 were white, this extra white area would not be noticeable. But on a dark background this is very noticeable. An easy remedy for this is to get the **fill tool**, select black from the color palette, and then fill the white area in with black. This works fine as long as your background is one solid color, or has large areas of solid color on it. But if the background you place the clip art on is detailed, then this solution does not work. In a few moments you will learn how to work around this potential problem, as well as problems arising with lassoed clip art.

While still on Card 1, use the **Add Clip Art...** command again, and get another object from the "Addy" file. This time, however, use the lasso. To get the lasso, make sure you highlight it first at the top of the clip art dialog box. Take a moment first to recall the lasso's unique feature—it ignores any color in the selection area that is the same as the color on which it is first clicked. For the sake of comparison, the same doghouse as before is selected. To get the entire doghouse, start the **lasso** in the white area surrounding it. However, by doing so, the lasso ignored all the white pixels in the doghouse itself.

If the doghouse were added to a white background, this would not cause any problem. However, it was added to a black background, which caused an undesired loss of detail (much the same as if white had been replaced with black). If the background you place lassoed clip art on is detailed, then this becomes an even more of a problem to deal with, UNLESS you "outsmart" the problem.

Nothing is impossible with *HyperStudio*. You just have to learn ways to work around certain apparent limitations.

Let's suppose you wanted to put Addy, her doghouse, and a bone on a detailed background—like, say, the "Tree" file included in the "HS Art" folder. If you were to place each of these items directly onto this background with the **rectangle selector** or **lasso**, you might end up with the following unsightly results.

With the **rectangle selector**, each piece of clip art has been placed on the background with an area of white around it. This looks like three poster board signs have been placed at the bottom of the tree. If that was your intended goal, then this would be okay. If your goal is to have a life-like scene of Addy coming out of her doghouse sniffing her bone (beneath the shade of a tree), then this would not look very good.

With the **lasso**, each piece of clip art is placed (without any pixels of white in it) on the background. The doghouse ends up partially transparent, Addy's eye turns blue, and she can hardly find her bone (which has now become camouflaged since it, too, is semi-transparent).

What can possibly be done to avoid these two undesired effects? that is what you are going to learn right now.

On Card 1, import the "Tree" from the "HS Art" folder as a background. Move to Card 2. On Card 2, import the "Addy" file as a background. (In fact, it does not matter which of the two cards has either background. That is really up to you. All that matters is that the "Tree" is on one card and "Addy" is on the other.) On the card with the "Addy" background, get the fill tool and select a neutral color.

A "neutral" color is some color from the palette that is not present in the "Addy" background itself. For example, purple is not used as a color anywhere in the "Addy" background. So, select purple as your fill color, and then click the fill tool anywhere in the white portion of the background. All of the empty white space should then become purple.

(To get rid of any remaining white spaces between Addy's legs, just click the **fill tool** there as well. You may want to work in fat bits if you find this difficult to do.) If you are successful, you will then have the "Addy" background with all of the empty white space filled in with purple. By using a neutral fill color, you have now made it possible to lasso the doghouse, Addy, and her bone without having any of the white

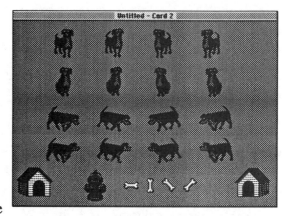

pixels in these selections becoming transparent. The **lasso** will shrink to each of these objects, but they will not become transparent.

Use the **lasso** to select each object one at a time. **Copy** (or **Cut**) the object, move to the other card, and then **Paste** it in place. In three fairly easy steps, you will end up with a scene that looks much more realistic than before. No see-through doghouse, no blue-eyed Addy, and no camouflaged bone. Just a contented little dog—and an equally contented user of *HyperStudio*.

There are other work-arounds for dealing with troublesome backgrounds and clip art. The best thing to do is experiment and see what works and what doesn't. The worst that can happen is that you may have to erase the background, load a new background, or add the clip art again. And mistakes are a way of learning, too. Don't forget that any artwork you or your students create can be **Exported Screens** (saved as disk files that can then be used as original background or clip art sources—as covered in detail in Lesson 2).

*HyperHint→When using the clip art selection dialog, you can select the entire art in the window by double-clicking on the **rectangle selector**. Why would you ever want to do this? Isn't getting the whole picture the same as loading it as a background? Yes and no. Yes, if you just add it to the card after selecting it. No, if you leave it selected after adding it to the card, and then **Scale** it down. That is how the miniature versions of the Book, Gazette, and USA map featured on page 43 were created. What do you suppose double-clicking on the lasso does? See if you can figure that answer out for yourself.*

One last thing you should do is explore the vast Media Library of art files included on the *HyperStudio* Resource CD. The easiest way to do this is to return to the Home Stack, and click on the "Media Library" button. This will take you to a Media Library information card.

One nice thing about the artwork contained in the

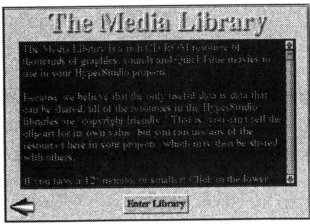

Media Library is that it is "copyright-friendly." It's intended for use in *HyperStudio* stacks. You violate no copyright law in doing so—provided you don't sell the artwork "for its own value." The copyright-friendly nature of Roger Wagner Publishing's art files can't be understated. A number of companies which supply clip art put too many restrictions and stipulations on how this art may be used—making the use of their art more trouble than it is worth. Many clip art suppliers, in fact, only authorize the use of their clip art in PRINTED documents (in other words, for use on paper). This is unfortunate since the definition of "print" has come to take on a whole new meaning with the advent of interactive multimedia. *HyperStudio* stacks can be printed to paper, but their true power can only be experienced when they are "printed" to a computer screen. Hopefully, more companies will come to share RWP's philosophy that artwork should be copyright-friendly for use in a variety of printed media.

When you get to the Media Library information card, just click on the **Enter Library** button, which will take you to a menu card from which you can explore the many categories and types of art included.

HyperHands-On!
Student Task Cards—Lesson 4
"Practice Importing Backgrounds and Adding Clip Art"

Step 1. Create a new stack.

Step 2. Bring in (or "import") an art file as a background.

Click on **File** and select **Import Background...** from the menu. This will bring up a dialog box from which you can choose the source for the art file. To locate the file you need, you first have to tell *HyperStudio* the method you want to use to get the art. For this lesson, select **Disk file** as your source. Selecting **Disk file** indicates that the art you want is already stored on a disk (floppy disk, hard drive, cartridge drive, CD-ROM, etc.).

Selecting **Disk file** brings up another dialog box in which you can choose the file you wish to import. *HyperStudio* automatically shows a folder called "HS Art." "HS Art" is provided as a basic starter kit of art files. You aren't limited to the files in this folder, however. For example, you could click on the **Desktop** button, and then select a file from a floppy disk or CD-ROM. *You could even locate and import an art file you may have saved during Lesson 2.*

Some very good backgrounds are included in the "HS Art" folder. These include a Book, Gazette, Tree, and USA Map.

HyperHint→*To select a file, you can either highlight it and then click the* **Open** *button, or you can double-click on the file name. Any buttons that appear with a double outline (like the "Open" button, for example) can also be activated by pressing the* **return** *or* **enter** *keys. You can locate a file by scrolling through the list, but a quicker way to locate a particular file is to press the letter key on your keyboard corresponding to the first letter in the file's name.*

Step 3. Make changes to the background if you wish.

Once you have imported a background, you can use any of the paint and selection tools to make changes to it. Or you can always import another file to replace it. **Just remember that importing a background means that the current background is completely replaced by the chosen art file.**

Step 4. Choose a file that you can use to add clip art to your background.

Click on **File** and choose **Add Clip Art** from the menu. *HyperStudio* will display the same dialogs you saw when you imported a background. This time, however, *HyperStudio* will not immediately place the file you select on your card. Instead, a "Clip Art" dialog box will be displayed. This dialog shows the top portion of the art file, a "scroll bar" along the right and bottom sides, a rectangle selector and lasso, a "Get another picture..." button, a "Cancel" button, and an "OK" button.

The **scroll bars** allow you to move up, down or across the picture to locate the portion you are interested in. If you accidentally choose the wrong file, or if you decide that this is just not the file you want, you can get another picture file. You can even cancel your decision entirely. If the file is the one you want, you need to select a portion of it before clicking on the **OK** button.

Some very good clip art files in the "HS Art" folder are Addy, Addy With Cars & Paws, Computer 1 & 2, Education 1 & 2, and Icon Library.

Step 5. Select some clip art to add to your background with the **rectangular selector**.

Remember the **rectangle selector** you used in Lesson 3? It "selects" a piece of art by placing a rectangular frame around it. Highlight the **rectangle selector** in the clip art dialog box, and then select something in your picture file. You should see the familiar "marching ants." Once you have selected it, click on the **OK** button (or press **return** or **enter** on your keyboard).

Step 6. Place the clip art on your background.

After you click on the **OK** button, *HyperStudio* will place the selected clip art in the center of your card. You can now place the clip art wherever you'd like on the card, resize it, flip it, etc. Since you used the **rectangle selector** to obtain this piece of art, you can apply any of the effects you used with this tool in Lesson 3. Remember, you need to leave the clip art selected to apply any changes to it, and you need to click off it to place it down on the background.

The **rectangular selector** can only select "rectangular" areas. When using the **rectangle selector**, you often end up selecting a part of the area around any clip art you select. You can always get the fill tool and fill in this extra area with a color that matches the background. This works fine as long as your background is one solid color, or has large areas of solid color on it. But if the background you place the clip art on is detailed, then this solution doesn't work.

Step 7. Select some clip art to add to your background with the **lasso**.

Repeat Step 4. Then, instead of highlighting the **rectangular selector** as you did in Step 5, highlight the **lasso**. Select something in your picture file, and then click on **OK**.

Step 8. Place the clip art on your background.

Do you remember what makes the **lasso** special? It shrinks to fit whatever you select. But it also ignores any color in the selection area that is the same as the color on which it is first clicked. The clip art files in the "HS Art" folder feature lots of little images surrounded by white. If the image you select with the **lasso** has any white in it, the white will become transparent. That is no problem if your background is white. But if your background has some other color on it, this color will show through the transparent parts of your clip art. And if the background you place lassoed clip art on is detailed or patterned, then this becomes an even more difficult problem to deal with.

Step 9. Outsmart the **lasso** (Part 1).

Suppose you wanted to put Addy, her doghouse, and a bone on a detailed background—like, say, the "Tree" file included in the "HS Art" folder.

Import the "Tree" from the "HS Art" folder as a background. Create a new card. On Card 2, import the "Addy" file as a background. Get the fill tool and select a neutral color. A "neutral" color is some color from the palette that is not used in the "Addy" background itself. For example, purple is not used as a color anywhere in the "Addy" background. So, select purple as your fill color, and then click the **fill tool** anywhere in the white portion of the background. All of the empty white space should then become purple. (To get rid of any remaining white spaces between Addy's legs, just click the **fill tool** there as well. You may want to work in magnified view if you find this difficult to do.) If you are successful, you will then have the "Addy" background with all of the empty white space filled in with purple. By using a neutral fill color, you have now made it possible to lasso the doghouse, Addy, and her bone without having any of the white pixels in these selections becoming transparent. The **lasso** will shrink to each of these objects, but they will not become transparent.

Step 10. Outsmart the lasso (Part 2).

Use the **lasso** to select each object one at a time. **Copy** or **Cut** the object, move to the first card, and then **Paste** it in place. Move back to Card 2, select the next object, and so on. In three fairly easy steps, you will end up with a very realistic scene. You will avoid getting a see-through doghouse, and Addy's eyes and the bone will stay white.

Lesson 5: Doing Things the "Write" Way

"Creating and making the best use of Painted Text and Text Objects"

HyperOverview:

In the mid-1400s, Johann Gutenberg revolutionized the power of the written word by simplifying the process of creating it. A renaissance of ideas emerged. Today, *HyperStudio* is transforming the written word into an interactive and engaging means of communication.

There are practically no limits to what you can do with text in a stack. In this lesson, you will learn the two basic ways of creating text with *HyperStudio*—painted text and text objects. (In Lessons 12 and 13, you will learn additional techniques to truly harness the power of text in your stacks.)

Using text in *HyperStudio* is a unique process. There are a number of excellent software programs on the market today that enable you to do incredible things with text. They combine powerful user interfaces and impressive screen layouts. But for all of their glitz and panache, they are, in many ways, just glorified typewriters. The end goal when using many desktop publishing programs is to print text onto paper. Such is not the case with *HyperStudio*. Although it has full printing capabilities, *HyperStudio* is designed to be used interactively, both by a stack's creator and its end users, directly on the computer screen. To print the text of a stack to paper is to lose part of its essence. As mentioned in the previous lesson, *HyperStudio* is redefining what it means to "print" information.

HyperPrerequisites:

- Experience using the paint and selection tools, and a basic understanding of how each tool functions (Lessons 2 and 3)

- Word processing/desktop publishing experience (helpful, but not essential)

HyperClinic:

HyperStudio provides two methods for adding text to a card. The first method involves putting text-shaped paint down on the background of the card. This method is referred to as "painted text." The second method involves creating a word processing field into which text can be typed. This is called a text "field" or "object." Each method has its inherent strengths and weaknesses. It's not only important to know how to create each type of text in a stack, but when to use one method versus the other. We will discuss the "when" at the end of this lesson. For now, let's take a look at the "how."

T In Lesson 2, you were introduced to each of *HyperStudio*'s paint tools. One of these tools, however, was just briefly mentioned. This is the **text tool.** The text tool is used for "painting" text onto a card's background.

It's basically a paintbrush that can adjust its size and shape to apply paint in the form of letters and numbers. Learning how to use it is quite simple. Start up *HyperStudio* and create a new stack. Select the text tool from the tool set. Notice the moment you move the tool over the card itself, it transforms into what resembles a capital letter "I" (often referred to as the I-beam pointer). You use this little pointer to decide where you want to start typing… er, um, painting. To actually apply the text, place the pointer where you want it and click once on the mouse button. A blinking vertical line will appear—just like the one you may be familiar with seeing in any word processing or desktop publishing program you have used. This blinking line (often referred to as the insertion point) indicates the point at which the text will begin to appear. So how do you make the text appear? that is easy… just start pressing keys on your keyboard. Notice that the blinking line moves as you type each character on the card. You can also press the **delete** or left-pointing arrow keys to erase characters.

Your text is kind of short, bold-looking, and black (assuming you did not select some other color in the color palette before starting to type). If you are using the Macintosh version of *HyperStudio*, you just painted with a text style (or font) known as "Chicago." In fact, you painted with Chicago (size 12, black, plain)—the same style used to create the sample sentence below.

I'm creating painted text with HyperStudio's text tool.

This is *HyperStudio*'s default text style. When you first start up *HyperStudio*, you are offered Chicago, size 12, black as your initial text style. You may accept or reject this offer. If you wish to reject it, you may easily select a different text style, size, or color.

Type a short line of text on your card, but don't click the I-beam pointer a second time. Once your text is typed, select **Text Style…** from the **Options** menu. A dialog box will appear. A scrolling list of fonts available on your particular computer is included. To see what a font will look like, just highlight it in the

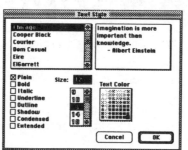

list. Below this list are a number of effects you can apply to the text. You can also highlight a size preference for your text, or type a size directly into the Size field.

HyperHint→Some fonts don't look very good at certain sizes. Without going into a lengthy discussion of why this is, here's a handy piece of advice. HyperStudio will display any suggested sizes at which your selected font will look its best. These sizes will always appear in "outline" form. You are free to choose from any "plain" sizes as well (or type in your own specific size), but you may find the results less than satisfactory on your card.

The text style dialog box also features a 64-color palette from which you can select a color for your text. A preview of what your font looks like is displayed in the upper right portion of the dialog box. When you are through making your selections, just click on the **OK** button (or press either the **return** or **enter** key).

The text style dialog box will disappear, and your card will return. Assuming you did not click the I-beam a second time after typing your text, your text will no longer be Chicago (size 12, black, plain). Its appearance will be the result of whatever you selected in the text style dialog box. The insertion point may have gotten bigger or smaller, depending on the size of the text you selected.

For the examples that follow, the word *"HyperStudio"* was painted five separate times (each time selecting a different font, size, and style). Black was the color choice, a different color could certainly have been chosen for each one. Notice that it is possible to select a number of style settings at one time.

HyperStudio
Chicago (Size 24, Italic, Outline)

HyperStudio
WindsorDemi (Size 36, Plain)

HyperStudio
Old English (Size 36, Bold, Condensed)

HYPERSTUDIO
Flintstone (Size 24, Bold, Outline, Shadow)

HyperStudio
Script MT Bold (Size 48, Underline)

You can also bring up the text style dialog box by double-clicking on the text tool. (**Note:** You can only double-click on a tool if the tool set is placed out on the card.) The text style dialog box is draggable. Just click on the lined bar at the top of the box, hold the mouse button down, and drag the dialog box to wherever you would like it.

If you have the font you want, but want to make a color change, you can do this a couple of different ways. While your text is still active (meaning you just painted it, the insertion point is blinking, and you haven't clicked the I-beam pointer on a new location), you can either select **Set Text Color...** from the **Options** menu,

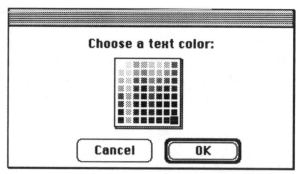

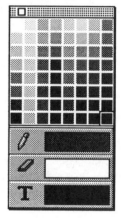

or just select the color you want from the color palette. If you use the **Set Text Color...** method, a little dialog box will pop up. Just select the color you want and then click **OK**. If you change your text color by accessing the color palette directly, you will notice that the 16 patterns are missing. This is because patterns are not available for creating text—well, not directly. Remember, with *HyperStudio* there is always a way to work around an apparent limitation. Keep reading.

While you are typing text with the text tool, your text remains active. This means that you can erase and retype a character(s), as well as make text style adjustments. However, the moment you click the I-beam pointer again, the text you were just working with gets turned into paint. It becomes a part of the background. When this occurs, *HyperStudio* no longer perceives it as text. It's paint—just as if you'd used one of the other paint tools to apply it. We will get to the negative aspects of this later on, but for now, let's look at the benefit of this result. Once your text is officially "paint," you can do anything to it that you learned to do with art in Lessons 2–4 (select it, fill it, resize it, copy and paste it, etc.). So, creating patterned text is possible—as are many other special effects.

Try three quick and easy ways to enhance painted text. This first way involves simply filling your text with a pattern. Use the text tool and type a word on your card. For effect, you might want to set its size

rather large—like 48, 72, or 96. Set it for shadow to give it a three-dimensional look. After typing the word, get the fill tool. (This will automatically set the word as paint on the card.) Select a pattern from the color palette and fill each letter. That is all it took to create the example shown here.

Now try this easy gradient text effect. Use the text tool and type a word on your card. To get a dramatic effect, pick a thick font and a size of at least 36 or 48 (depending on the font you select). The color you type it in does not really matter. Once you have the settings you want, click the I-beam pointer a second time to "paint" the text onto the background. Then, get the lasso and select the word. With the word selected, apply a gradient to it.

Here is a simple way to use overlapping text to create a three-dimensional effect. Use the text tool and create the same word on your card in three different shades (dark, medium, and light). Use the same font each time. Get the lasso, select the light version, and move it on top of the dark one (with the light version slightly higher and to the right of the dark version). Then, select the medium version with the lasso, place it on top of the other two versions (centering it between them), and click off to deselect it. Your text will appear to be raised slightly off the card, as if carved in bas-relief.

The three text effects described above do not even begin to scratch the surface of what you can do with painted text in *HyperStudio*. You would be amazed at the number of effects you can create with just a little bit of imagination and experimentation. *HyperStudio* is powerfully simple.

HyperHint→*The various fonts available to you for creating painted text depends on the number of different fonts you have installed in your computer's "Fonts" folder (located within the "System Folder" on your hard drive).*

The other method for creating text in a stack is to make a text "object." Unlike painted text, which becomes paint once it is placed on a card, a text object is a mini-word processing field. Text entered into one of these fields retains its identity as text. As such, it can be easily edited at any time. Another feature of a text object is that it "floats" over the background. Painted text becomes part of the background once it is no longer selected. But a text object occupies its own layer in front of the background. This means that changes made to a text object do not affect the background of a card. Later on, we will take a closer look at the pros and cons of painted text versus text objects. For now, you will just create a text object and learn more about it.

Select **Add a Text Object...** from the **Objects** menu. A dialog box will pop up telling you that a rectangle will appear on the screen to represent the text object. Click on **OK** to remove the dialog box after reading it. The text object rectangle will immediately appear.

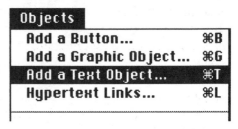

The text object rectangle is not a solid figure; rather, it resembles an area selected with the **rectangle selector tool** (it has the familiar marching ants). *HyperStudio* creates this rectangular area in the middle of the card. It behaves just as if you had used the rectangle selector tool. As the dialog box states, you can move and resize this text object rectangle. Try it. Notice that the arrow transforms itself into a four-pointed cross if placed inside the rectangle, a horizontal or vertical two-pointed line if placed on one of the sides, or a diagonal two-pointed line if placed on a corner—just like when you used the rectangle selector tool back in Lesson 3. Unlike an area selected with the rectangle selector tool, however, you cannot apply any of the **Effects** from the **Edit** menu. In fact, the moment you click anywhere outside the rectangle a "Text Appearance" dialog box will appear.

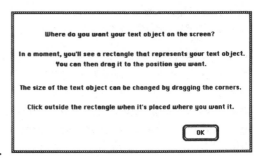

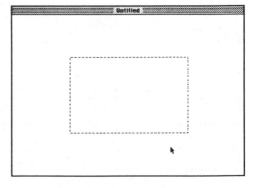

After moving and/or resizing the text object rectangle, click outside of it to bring up the "Text Appearance" dialog box. This dialog box allows you to set the characteristics of your text object. By default, the font will be Chicago, Size 12, Black (unless you have been using text before and have set the **Text Style...** for another font, size, color, etc.).

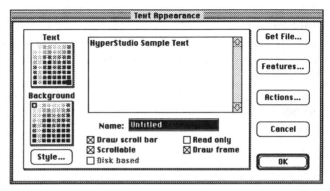

Because your text will be contained in a rectangular field, you can set both the color of the text and the color of the background. Let's avoid some confusion, though. The "Background" referred to in the "Text Appearance" dialog box is not the background of the card. It refers to the color of the rectangular field in which the text is contained. By default, your text object will be set for black text on a white background (as seen in the example above). But you can change these colors if you'd like. For instance, you could set the text object to display white text on a black background.

Clicking the **Style...** button performs the same function as selecting **Text Style...** from the **Options** menu. The "Text Style" dialog box you first encountered when creating painted text appears. However, it offers a few extra selection choices when used in conjunction with a text object. This dialog box only displays a "Text Color" palette for painted text, but includes a "Background" palette for text objects.

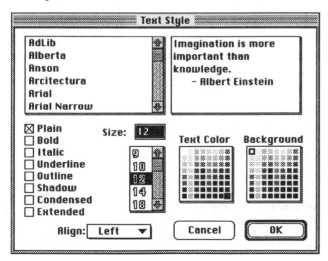

There is also a choice included allowing you to set the alignment of text within a text object. By default, it is set to align text along the left side of the field. You can change this to center the text in the field, or to align text along the right-hand side.

HyperHint→The alignment setting affects the entire text object. There is currently no way to have different alignment settings for various portions of text within the same text object. If, for example, you wanted to have a centered heading and a left-

```
Align: ✓Left
       Center
       Right
```

aligned body of text within the same text object, you would have to do this manually by using the space bar to move the heading over to center it in the field.

Clicking on **OK** in the "Text Style" dialog box will return you to the "Text Appearance" dialog box. In this box, you can also make choices about the structure of your text object. If "Draw scroll bar" is selected, *HyperStudio* will place a vertical bar along the right hand side of your text object, with up and down pointing arrows. Why would you need these? Well, if you have ever done word processing or desktop publishing, you know that fields of text often hold more text than is displayed on the screen at one time. These programs feature scroll bars that allow you to move up or down through the text. *HyperStudio* is no different. It allows you to create fields containing more text than can be displayed at one time. Scroll bars allow users to scroll the text up or down in the field. The up and down arrows will not become active, however, unless you actually enter more text into the object than the field can display in its area. Once activated, you simply click on either arrow to scroll through the text. If you wish to scroll through several lines, just click on the arrow and continue to hold down the mouse button until you reach the desired point in the field. Once the arrows are activated, the scroll bar will also feature a little draggable square. You can click on this square, hold down the mouse button, and drag the square up or down along the scroll bar. This will scroll through your text much more quickly than clicking on either of the two arrows. And even faster than dragging the square is to click on the bar itself. Try clicking on various points along the bar to see how much text is scrolled.

Obviously, if you select "Draw scroll bar" for your text object, you should also select "Scrollable." You can only scroll up and down through a text object if this choice is selected. So, if you ever want to give your text object a scroll bar, be sure you also make it scrollable. The **scroll bar** will still function if you don't set it to be scrollable; however, you will find that entering text in the object will be very difficult and cumbersome.

HyperHint→While you should always select "Scrollable" if your text object has a scroll bar, there are times when you may want a scrollable object without selecting "Draw scroll bar." We will explore this option later in Lesson 12.

"Draw frame" creates an outline for the text object. This outline is always black, and can't be changed using the "Text" or "Background" color palettes. If you click this selection off, then your text will still be in its rectangular field, but no outline will be drawn around it. Leaving this selection off can be an effective way to create text that appears to be painted, but which retains its identity as a text object. We will look at this in just a few minutes when we compare the pros and cons of each text option.

By default, "Read only" is not selected. The reason is quite simple. Selecting "Read only" makes it impossible to enter new text into the text object. So, if you select this option before actually typing into the field, *HyperStudio* will not permit you to enter any text. Don't worry if you ever accidentally select this while creating a text object. This option, along with all the other text object settings, can be changed later at any time, as we will explore next. For now, don't select this option. This is an option you will want to select after creating and typing into your text object. It basically prevents a user of your stack from accidentally adding or erasing text to your text object. Again, you can always go back at any time and choose new settings for a text object.

Before clicking on **OK** in the "Text Appearance" dialog box, there are a few more selections you can make. You can use the **Get File...** button to import a previously-saved text file. *HyperStudio* can import text files from any word processing/desktop publishing program as long as they have been saved in TEXT format. Most programs allow you to save text in a variety of commonly-used formats. So, you can type your text in your favorite word processing/desktop publishing program, save it in TEXT format, and then import it directly into a text object in *HyperStudio*.

HyperHorizons: Another reason you may want to type your text in your favorite word processing/desktop publishing program is that these programs often come with built-in spell checking capabilities. The current Macintosh 3.0 version of *HyperStudio* does not include built-in spell checking capabilities. The new Macintosh 3.1 version of *HyperStudio* will include a built-in spell checker. An option that is currently available, however, is to use the *Hyper Bee Spelling Checker* by Mike Westerfield of The Byte Works, Inc. This spell checker can be installed into the Extras menu of *HyperStudio* (covered in Lesson 9), from which it can be accessed to check the spelling and punctuation of text in text objects, object names, names of cards, etc. This extra works with Macintosh System 6.0.8 or better, *HyperStudio* 2.0 or better, and requires only 200K of free disk space.

The other choice available in the "Text Appearance" dialog box is to click on the "**Actions...**" button. This will take you to another dialog box from which you can select several interactive possibilities for your text object. For now, I recommend that you not make any action selections. We will explore these possibilities in great detail in the next chapter.

It's almost time to click on **OK**. But there is one more thing you should consider. Notice that you can give a name to your text object. *HyperStudio* provides the default name "Untitled." While you can just accept this name if you want to, it is recommended that you type in a new one. It's a good habit to get into since naming objects is important if you want to use some more advanced techniques, such as Hide and Show (discussed later in this tutorial). The name you type for your text object doesn't need to be long, but it should be something that relates to the material contained in the text object. For example, you could name it "My First Text" or "Introduction" or just "Text 1."

HyperHint➜*Whenever text is highlighted (such as the word "Untitled" in the "Text Appearance" dialog box), you can replace it simply by typing the word(s) you want to replace it with. Some people think they have to click off the highlighting, then use the "delete" key, and then type in their new text. But the easiest way to replace text is to highlight it (or leave it highlighted if it already is), and then just start typing the new text.*

Now click on **OK**. The "Text Appearance" dialog box will disappear, and your text object will appear on the screen. If you imported a text file, this text will be displayed in the object. Otherwise, your text object will be empty, with a blinking insertion point waiting for you to start typing. Believe it or not, the tool used for typing text into a text object is the **browse tool** (remember—the hand with the pointing finger). When you move the browse tool over the text object, it transforms into an I-beam pointer. Enter some text into your text object. Type enough text into the object to cause the scroll bar (assuming you selected this option) to become active. You can now use the scroll bar to move up or down through your text, or you can use the four arrow keys on your keyboard to move around.

After typing in your text, suppose you want to go back and make changes to the text object. Don't select **Add a Text Object...** from the **Objects** menu. This creates a whole new text object. To edit an existing text object, select one of two tools: the arrow tool or the text edit tool.

 The **text edit tool** is used exclusively for making changes to text objects.

 The **arrow tool** is used to make changes to any objects on a card. (To this point, you have only learned about text objects. There are two other objects, however, that can also be created with *HyperStudio*: Buttons (Lesson 6) and Graphic Object (Lesson 8).

Both tools are editing tools. Both tools have the appearance of a pointing arrow when moved over the card itself. Why have two tools that perform the same function and look the same when used on the card? Well, they don't actually perform the same function. As stated above, the **text edit** tool can only edit text objects. With only one text object on a card (like you have right now), you probably don't see what difference this makes. But suppose you had other objects (buttons or graphic objects) on the card, too. Using the **text edit** tool might be the better choice since it is more discriminating in what it will edit. But the **arrow tool**, because of its all-around versatility in being able to edit any objects, will probably become your editing tool of choice in most situations. In fact, even though you were not introduced to this tool until Lesson 5, it will probably end up being one of the top two tools that you will use most often on a regular basis from this point on—the other being the **browse tool**.

To be quite honest, the **text edit tool** is almost never used. The only times you will use it is when you have a number of various objects on a card. In such an instance, the text edit tool keeps you from wasting time by accidentally clicking on a button or graphic object—especially if you have several objects that are close to or overlapping each other. Using the arrow tool on overlapping objects can be a real nightmare.

It's really up to you whether you prefer to use the **arrow tool** or the **text edit tool** at this point. Regardless of which editing tool you choose, you can use it to make changes to your text object. To do so, place the tool on your text object and double-click on the mouse. (You can also place the tool on the text object, click on it once, and select **Edit this Text Object...** from the **Objects** menu.) The first method. It is faster and easier. It will cause the "Text Appearance" dialog box to reappear, and you can make any changes you would like.

If you want to adjust the size of the text object itself, get one of the two editing tools and click once on the text object to select it. You can now make your adjustments just as if this were selected with the rectangle selector. (But remember, you cannot use any **Effects** on it.)

If you just want to change the color of the text in a text object, a quick way to do this is to click on the object once with the editing tool, and then select your choice of color from the color palette. If you want to change the color of the background field, do the same thing while also pressing the **option** key on the keyboard.

If you forget to import a text file with the **Get File...** button in the "Text Appearance" dialog box, don't panic. Just click once on the text object with the editing tool, and then select **Import Text...** from the **File** menu. Normally, this menu item reads **Import Background...** (see Lesson 4). But when a text object (or a portion of it) is selected, this item changes.

Whenever you make changes to a text object with the editing tool, the changes are made to the entire text object. So how could you make one word, for instance, a different color than its surrounding text? Use the **browse tool**. Move the tool over the text object until it becomes an I-beam pointer. Click the pointer on the first letter of the word, hold the mouse button down, and drag the pointer across the word to highlight it. Once highlighted, select the color of your choice from the color palette.

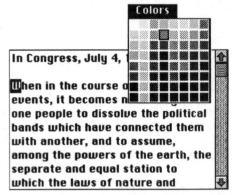

If you want to make a word or selected portion of text a different font and/or size than its surrounding text, highlight it as mentioned in the preceding paragraph. Then, select **Text Style...** from the **Options** menu. Then make your changes in the "Text Style" dialog box that appears.

If you want to delete an entire text object, click on it once with the editing tool and press the **delete** key. If you want to delete a portion of text within a text object, highlight it with the browse tool and press **delete.** The same is true for copying and cutting text. Using the editing tool copies/cuts the entire object, while using the browse tool copies/cuts the highlighted portion.

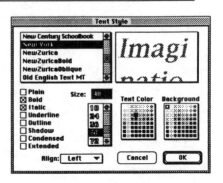

There are other ways to effect changes to text objects other than the ones just mentioned. Experiment on your own. *HyperStudio* provides various ways to reach the outcome you desire. In sum, remember that you need either the **arrow tool** or the text edit tool to make changes to the overall structure or appearance of a text object. You use the **browse tool** to type the text into the

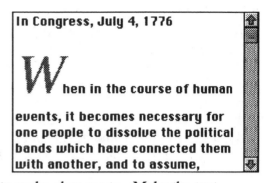

object, and to select portions of the text to make changes to. Make the text object "Read only" after you complete it to prevent accidental changes or deletions. "Read only" text objects no longer have the insertion point blinking on and off all the time either, which can get quite annoying after a while.

*HyperHint→There is a real quick way to move back and forth between the browse tool and the arrow tool. Press the **shift** and **tab** keys on the keyboard. If you are using the browse tool, this will make the arrow tool appear. If you are using the arrow tool, the browse tool will appear. It sure saves time over selecting each item from the tool set. There is a really quick way to get the rectangle selector tool, too. Just press **shift–control–tab** to go back and forth between the rectangle selector and the browse tool.*

If your text object features a word or phrase used on several occasions, or if you have several text objects throughout a stack, the **Find Text...** command in the Move menu will no doubt come in handy at some point. Such an occasion might be if you wish to replace each occurrence of a certain word or phrase with another. Or perhaps you want to locate each use of a word or phrase to double-check that it was spelled properly. Whatever the need, this command can help speed up the process. Using this command brings up a dialog box which allows you to conduct a search, based on variables that you set. However, this will only find the first occurrence of the word or phrase you enter in the search field. You will **need to press ⌘–shift–F to continue the search.** You might wonder at first why this command is located in the **Move** menu. *HyperStudio* "moves" through each text object, and from card to card, searching for the word or phrase you have indicated. Makes sense, huh?. You have now learned a little about painted text and text objects. But it pays to know a little something about the pros and cons of each. Discovering the advantages and disadvantages of each type is a continuous learning process.

Text objects are not part of the background on a card. This makes them very easy to edit. They can hold an incredible amount of text which can be scrolled. They can also carry out several actions (which we will learn about later). However, text in a text object is dependent upon the font(s) you have or don't have in your "Fonts" folder (within the "System Folder" of your computer). Text in a text object will only look good to a user of your stack if he/she has the same font(s) on his or her computer. When sharing stacks with others, therefore, it is a good idea to use standard fonts in your text objects. Standard fonts are fonts that are available on most every computer. These fonts are Chicago, Courier, Geneva, Helvetica, Monaco, New York, Times, and Palatino. Text objects can be moved around or layered on top of one another without disturbing the background. But, because text objects are not a part of a card's background, you can't use paint effects on them as you can with painted text (demonstrated earlier in this lesson).

Fonts

Painted text becomes part of the background once it is set in place. As such, it cannot be easily edited or moved like text in a text object. However, because painted text is no longer text once it is set in place, it does not matter whether or not users of your stack have the same font(s) on their computers. Painted text is paint in the shape of text. Therefore, painted text is the better choice when using non-standard fonts.

FONTS AVAILABLE ON OUR CLASS COMPUTER		
Albertus MT	*Alison*	ArielMTCondensed
Arquitectura	Athens	*BAZOOKA*
Benguiat Frisky		Bernhard Modern
Berliner Grotesk	Black Chancery	
Black Forest	Bodoni MT Ultra Bold	
Boulder	BUBBLE	
Calligrapher	Carmet 821	Casino
Castle Font	Charlie Chan	
Chaucer	Chicago	Cooper Black
Courier	Dom Casual	EIRE	El Garrett
FILLMORE	FLINTSTONE	Fresh Script
Futura Bold Condensed	Geneva	
Gill Sans Condensed Bold	Harrington	
Headliner Font	Heather	
Helvetica	Hobo Jester Klang MT	

If you or your students want to create fancy titles and headings in your stacks, using painted text is recommended. If you have information that you will need to edit easily, use text objects. Text objects offer a number of interactive advantages over painted text, which will be covered in upcoming lessons. Plus, in Lesson 7, you will learn how to create a "transparent" text object (a text object that mimics painted text). And in Lesson 8, you will learn how to create "Painted Text Graphic Objects" (painted text that behaves like objects). So, our exploration of the use of text in *HyperStudio* is far from over!

HyperHint➜*As a time-saving device, you might consider printing out a list of the fonts available on the computer(s) in your classroom for your students to refer to when planning their stacks. The example shown on page 66 is a list that was made using ClarisWorks. (There are a number of font utilities available that can do the same thing.) Type the name of each font using its actual typeface. Keep a list similar to this one in a special binder in your classroom, along with printouts of available clip art. Your students can use this binder as a handy reference guide as they plan for and design their stacks. On your list, print each font at the same size. That way, students can make comparisons. For example, size 36 of one font may be much larger or smaller than size 36 of another. You may want to have each of the standard fonts underlined, with instructions to your students that these are the only ones they may use in text objects.*

HyperHands-On!

Student Task Cards—Lesson 5

"Practice Making Painted Text and Text Objects"

Step 1. Create a new stack.

Step 2. Get the text tool (it looks like a capital "T") from the tool set.

The text tool is used for "painting" text onto a card's background. It's like a paintbrush that can change its size and shape to add paint to the background in the form of letters and numbers. Learning how to use it is pretty simple.

Notice the moment you move the tool over the card itself, it transforms into what resembles a capital letter "I" (often called an "I-beam" pointer). You use this little pointer to decide where you want to start typing... er, um, painting.

Step 3. Paint some text with the text tool.

To actually apply the text, place the pointer where you want it and click once on the mouse button. A blinking vertical line will appear—just like the one you may be familiar with seeing in any word processing or desktop publishing program you have used. This blinking line (often called the insertion point) shows the point at which the text will begin to appear.

So how do you make the text appear? that is easy... just start pressing keys on your keyboard. Notice that the blinking line moves as you type each character on the card. You can also press the **delete** or left-pointing arrow keys to erase characters.

Your text is kind of short, bold-looking, and black (assuming you didn't select some other color in the color palette before starting to type). If you are using the Macintosh version of *HyperStudio*, you just painted with a text style (or font) known as "Chicago." In fact, you painted with Chicago (size 12, black, plain)— the same style used to create the sample sentence below.

I'm creating painted text with HyperStudio's text tool.

This is *HyperStudio*'s default (or preset) text style. When you first start up *HyperStudio*, you are offered Chicago, Size 12, Black as your first text style (or "font"). You can either use it or pick something different. If you want something different, it is easy to select another font, size, or color.

Step 4. Change the text style, size, and/or color of your text.

Once your text is typed, select **Text Style...** from the **Options** menu. A dialog box will appear. A scrolling list of fonts available on your particular computer is included. To see what a font will look like, just highlight it in the list. Below this list are a number of effects you can apply to the text. You can also highlight a size preference for your text, or type a size directly into the Size field. There is also a color palette from which you can select a color for your text. A preview of what your font looks like is displayed in the upper right portion of the dialog box. When you are through making your selections, just click on the **OK** button (or press either the **return** or **enter** key).

The text style dialog box will disappear, and your card will return. If you did not click the I-beam a second time after typing your text, your text will no longer be Chicago (Size 12, Black, Plain). Its appearance will be whatever you selected in the text style dialog box. The insertion point may have gotten bigger or smaller, depending on the size of the text you selected.

Step 5. Fill your text with a pattern.

You can only use colors for painting text—not patterns. But once your text is painted, you can fill it with any patterns you like.

While you are typing text with the text tool, your text remains active. This means that you can delete and retype a character(s), as well as make text style changes. But the moment you click the I-beam pointer again, the text you were just working with gets turned into paint. It becomes a part of the background. When this happens, it is no longer text. It is paint—just as if you would used one of the other paint tools to make it. Once your text becomes "paint," you can do *anything* to it that you learned to do with art in Lessons 2–4 (select it, fill it, resize it, copy and paste it, etc.). So, creating patterned text *is* possible—as are many other special effects.

Use the text tool and type a word on your card. For effect, you might want to set its size rather large—like 48, 72, or 96. Set it for shadow to give it a three-dimensional look. After typing the word, get the **fill tool**. (This will automatically set the word as paint on the card.) Select a pattern from the color palette and then fill each letter. That is all there is to it.

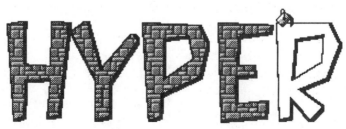

Ask your teacher to show you a few other neat things that you can do with painted text.

Step 6. Create a text object.

The other method for creating text in a stack is to make a text "object." Painted text becomes paint, but a text object is a mini-word processing field. Text in a text object always stays text. That means you can edit it at any time. Another feature of a text object is that it "floats" over the background. Painted text becomes part of the background once it is no longer selected. But a text object is in its own layer in front of the background. This means that changes made to a text object don't affect the background of a card.

Select **Add a Text Object...** from the **Objects** menu. A dialog box will pop up telling you that a rectangle will appear on the screen to represent the text object. Click on **OK** to remove the dialog box after reading it. The text object rectangle will immediately appear. *HyperStudio* creates this rectangular area in the middle of the card. You can move and resize this text object rectangle. Try it. Notice that the arrow transforms itself into a four-pointed cross if placed inside the rectangle, a horizontal or vertical two-pointed line if placed on one of the sides, or a diagonal two-pointed line if placed on a corner—just like when you used the **rectangle selector tool** back in Lesson 3.

Unlike an area selected with the **rectangle selector tool**, however, you can't apply any of the **Effects** from the **Edit** menu. In fact, the moment you click anywhere outside the rectangle a "Text Appearance" dialog box will appear.

Step 7. Make changes to the text in your text object.

After moving and/or resizing the text object rectangle, click outside of it to bring up the "Text Appearance" dialog box. Because your text will be contained in a rectangular field, you can set both the color of the text and the color of the field that it is in. Clicking the **Style...** brings up the **Text Style** dialog box you used earlier. Since you are working with a text "object" this time, there are a few extra things you can select from, including how you want to set the alignment of text within your text object. It's already set to align text along the left side of the field, but you can change this to center the text in the field, or to align text along the right hand side. *Whatever alignment you select will affect the whole text object.*

Step 8. Make changes to the text object itself.

Clicking on **OK** in the **Text Style** dialog box will return you to the **Text**

Appearance dialog box. In this box, you can also make choices about how your text object will behave. Select **Draw scroll bar** to make it possible to move the text up or down in the field using clickable arrows. These arrows don't become active unless you actually put more text into the object than the field can display at one time.

If you select **Draw scroll bar** for your text object, you should also select **Scrollable**. You can only scroll up and down through a text object if this choice is selected. So, if you ever want to give your text object a scroll bar, be sure you also make it scrollable.

Draw frame creates an outline for the text object. This outline is always black, and *can't* be changed using the **Text** or **Background** color palettes. If you click this selection off, then your text will still be in its rectangular field, but no outline will be drawn around it.

Selecting **Read only** makes it impossible to enter new text into the text object. Don't select this option until after creating and typing into your text object. It basically prevents a user of your stack from accidentally adding or erasing text to your text object.

Don't use the "Actions..." button at this time. Wait until you learn more about *HyperStudio* actions in the next lesson.

Before clicking on **OK**, notice that *HyperStudio* gives the name "Untitled" for your text object. While you can just accept this name if you want to, go ahead and type in a new one. It's a good habit to get into since naming objects is important if you want to use some more advanced techniques later on. The name you type for your text object doesn't need to be long, but it should be something that relates to what is in it. For example, you could name it "My First Text" or "Introduction" or just "Text 1."

Step 9. Type some text in your text object.

Now click on **OK**. The **Text Appearance** dialog box will disappear, and your text object will appear on the screen. Now you can type in it. Believe it or not, the tool used for typing text into a text object is the **browse tool** (remember—the hand with the pointing finger). When you move the browse tool over the text object, it becomes an I-beam pointer. Type enough text into the object to cause the **scroll bar** (assuming you selected this option) to become active. You can now use the **scroll bar** to move up or down through your text, or you can use the four arrow keys on your keyboard to move around.

Step 10. Edit your text object.

After typing in your text, suppose you want to go back and make changes to the text object. Don't select **Add a Text Object...** from the **Objects** menu. This creates a whole new text object. To change (or "edit") a text object, select one of two tools: the arrow tool or the text edit tool.

 The **text edit tool** is used exclusively for making changes to text objects.

▶ The **arrow tool** is used to make changes to any objects on a card.

Both tools are editing tools. Both tools look like a pointing arrow when moved over the card itself. Why have two tools that look the same and do the same thing? Well, they don't actually do the same thing. The **text edit** tool can only edit text objects. With only one text object on a card (like you have right now), you probably don't see what difference this makes. But suppose you had other objects (buttons or graphic objects—which you will learn about in later lessons) on the card, too. Using the **text edit** tool might be the better choice—since it only selects text objects. But since the **arrow tool** is able to edit any objects, you will probably use it most often.

Use either tool to make changes to your text object. Just place the tool on your text object and double-click on the mouse. (You can also place the tool on the text object, click on it once, and select **Edit this Text Object...** from the **Objects** menu—but the first way is a whole lot faster and easier.) The **Text Appearance** dialog box will reappear, and you can make any changes you would like.

Step 11. Make changes to just some of your text.

Whenever you make changes to a text object with an **editing tool**, the changes are made to the entire text object. So, how could you make one word, for instance, a different color than the rest of the text around it? Use the browse tool. Move the tool over the text object until it becomes an I-beam pointer. Click the pointer on the first letter of the word, hold the mouse button down, and drag the pointer across the word to highlight it. Once highlighted, select the color of your choice from the color palette.

If you want to make a word or selected portion of text a different font or size than its surrounding text, highlight it as mentioned in the preceding paragraph. Then, select **Text Style...** from the **Options** menu. Then make your changes in the **Text Style** dialog box that appears.

There are other things you can do with text objects. If you want to delete an entire text object, click on it once with the editing tool and press the **delete** key. If you want to delete just a part of the text, highlight it with the browse tool and press **delete.** The same is true for copying and cutting text. Use the editing tool if you want to copy or cut the entire object, and use the browse tool if you want to copy or cut the highlighted portion.

HyperHint→There is a really quick way to move back and forth between the ***browse*** *tool and the* ***arrow tool.*** *Press the* ***shift*** *and* ***tab*** *keys on the keyboard. If you are using the* ***browse tool****, this will make the* ***arrow*** *tool appear. If you are using the* ***arrow*** *tool, the* ***browse tool*** *will appear. It sure saves time over selecting each item from the tool set. There is a really quick way to get the* ***rectangle selector tool****, too. Just press* ***shift–control–tab*** *to go back and forth between the* ***rectangle selector*** *and the* ***browse tool.****

Lesson 6: A Tour of the Factory

"Saving Stacks, Button Types, Icons, Card Links and Sound"

HyperOverview:

You have learned quite a lot so far about what *HyperStudio* can do with art and text. Much of this information could be applied to other programs as well. For example, Adobe *Photoshop*®, MicroFrontier *Color It!*®, and Fractal *Design Painter*® can all do what *HyperStudio* does with art. And *ClarisWorks*®, *Microsoft Works*®, and a number of other desktop publishing programs can do what *HyperStudio* does with text. These programs feature drawing, text, selection and editing capabilities galore to rival (and in some cases exceed) those of *HyperStudio*. But what sets *HyperStudio* apart is that it combines the best art and text features into one program. And, what is more, *HyperStudio* adds a component many of these other programs lack—its end product communicates interactively.

This interactivity is achieved by assigning actions to objects. The primary focus of this lesson is the creation of buttons. Buttons have long been the interactive heart and soul of *HyperStudio*. With the advent of *HyperStudio* for Macintosh version 3.0, interactive capabilities became available for use with any objects (text objects, buttons, graphic objects), as well as with cards and stacks themselves. But this lesson spotlights the humble button—the preeminent feature that puts the "hyper" in *HyperStudio*.

The function of buttons in a stack, is reminiscent of the movie, *Willy Wonka & the Chocolate Factory*. Do you remember it? It first appeared in movie theaters in the early 1970's, and featured Gene Wilder as the imaginative Willy Wonka. Based on the book *Charlie and the Chocolate Factory* by Roald Dahl, this movie tells the story of a young boy who dreams of meeting the wondrous "candy man" Willy Wonka. Charlie is one of five children who are lucky enough to find golden tickets in their "Wonka Bars," allowing them the once-in-a-lifetime privilege of touring Willy Wonka's mysterious factory. All of the children succumb to moments of greed while at the factory, but only Charlie makes the effort to atone for his wrongdoing. For this act of selflessness, Charlie wins the respect of Willy Wonka, and is rewarded by becoming Willy Wonka's apprentice and future heir to the factory.

So what does any of this have to do with buttons? Good question. Willy Wonka takes the children through the factory one room at a time, from the first room to the last, like the pages in a book. As they begin the tour, Willy Wonka even states, "Oh, you can't get out backwards. Gotta go forwards to go back. Better press on." The only way to get back to where they start is by going in a room-by-room order. But in the end, Charlie is treated to a ride in Willy's "Great Glass Wonkavator." Unlike an elevator, which can only go up and down, the Wonkavator "can go sideways and slantways and longways and backways and squareways and frontways and any other ways that you can think of. It can take you to any room in the whole factory just by pressing one of these *buttons*... Just press a button—ZING, you are off!"

Like the Wonkavator, *HyperStudio* enables you to break out of linear constraints. With buttons, you can move from card to card if you want to, or you can skip whole sets of cards. You can move from a card in one stack to a card in another stack. You can move from a card in a stack out to another program. You can even jump out to the Internet.

Each room of Willy Wonka's factory featured some wonder of his imagination. Buttons can do this, too. For example, Willy Wonka had "Wonkavision." *HyperStudio* allows you to create and play movies. Willy Wonka had singing "Oompa Loompas." *HyperStudio* lets you create and play sounds and music. And these are just a few of the things you can do with buttons. As Willy Wonka would agree, buttons can help make "your dreams become realities, and some of your realities become dreams."

HyperHardware:

HyperStudio Program Resource CD (optional)

HyperPrerequisites:

A working knowledge of the material covered in Lessons 1-5

HyperClinic:

Create a new stack. Before going any further, it is time you learned how to *save* a stack. The first time you save a stack, you need to tell *HyperStudio* where you'd like the stack to be located, and what its file name will

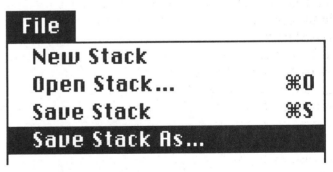

be. To save your stack, select **Save Stack As...** from the **File** menu. A dialog box will appear in which you can name your stack and select its location for saving. The procedure is practically identical to that for saving art files (described in detail in Lesson 2). Create another folder on your hard drive for saving your stacks. You might consider naming the folder something like

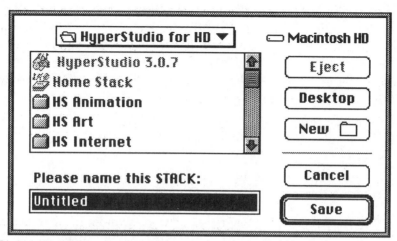

"Our Class Stacks." The name you choose for the stack itself should definitely *not* be left as "Untitled." Type a name that identifies what the stack is about. For this lesson, you might name your stack "Addy's Vacation." (Keep in mind that Macintosh file names can have up to 31 characters.)

HyperHint→*A word of advice: If at all possible, save the stacks you and your students create to a hard drive. Floppy disks, even the best on the market, can go bad. Time and time again teachers are frustrated because they or their students had lost days or weeks worth of work due to floppy disk failure. Hard drives can fail, too, but they tend to be a far more reliable location for saving stacks. Since having students save directly to the hard drive, stacks are seldom lost. Saving, saving, and re-saving stacks to floppy disks is risky at best. If students want copies of their stacks on disk to take home, consider having them save on the hard drive during the creation of their stacks. Then, at the very end, transfer the stacks to floppy disks. That way, you are only saving the stacks to disk one time.*

Another consideration is that information can be accessed more quickly from a hard drive than from a floppy disk. You will find your stacks will generally run more smoothly when saved to and run from a hard drive, especially if your stacks access other disk-based files, like sounds or QuickTime *movies.*

Once a stack has been saved, you will notice its name appears in the title bar at the top of each card in your stack (replacing the word "Untitled"). This is a default setting of *HyperStudio*. Unless you specify otherwise, the title bar will display the name of your stack and the card that you are currently on. (In Lesson 7, you will learn how to change this default setting.) As long as you don't intend to save the same stack under a different name or to a different location, you can select **Save Stack** from the **File** menu, instead of **Save Stack As.**

You will be saving your stack at various times during its creation, so you should become very familiar with the **Save Stack** keystroke. And because you never know when your computer might freeze or the power might suddenly go out, it is recommended that you save your stack every few minutes—that is, if the changes you have made to it are ones you want to keep. Students have been known to forget this advice, work on a stack for half an hour or more, and then experience the heart-wrenching feeling of loss as their computers froze. Saving every few minutes guarantees that, should something happen, you will never lose more than a small amount of the work you have put into your stack.

For this lesson, you will use buttons to create an interactive book about Addy's make-believe vacation. Start by importing the "Book" background from the HS Art folder onto Card 1 of your stack. Create a new card, and import the same exact background onto it. There is a handy shortcut for this. While on Card 1, click on **Edit** in the menu bar and select **Ready Made Cards**. Continue to hold down the mouse, and you will notice a branching menu. From this branching menu, select **Same Background**, and let up on the mouse. *HyperStudio* will automatically create a second card in your stack with the same exact book background. This is an easier and faster way to create cards which use the same background. (We will learn more about the Ready Made Cards menu later in this tutorial.)

Your stack should now contain two cards with identical backgrounds. Return to Card 1. On this card, let's create the beginning of our story. On the left hand page, create a text object introducing Addy's vacation adventure. On the right hand side, add some clip art to go along with the text. For the example shown here, a text

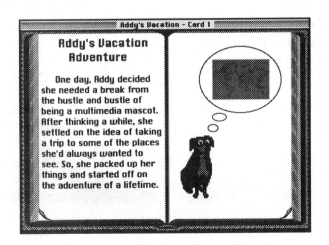

object was added without a scrollbar or frame to make the text look like it is written directly on the book. Leave about half an inch or so of space below the text object to accommodate a button we will be adding shortly. You could have just used painted text, but remember, it is much easier to go back and edit text in a text object than it is painted text. Chicago font (red, size 18 for the title and black, size 14 for the story) was used. For the artwork, use a picture of Addy sitting from the "Addy" file in the HS Art folder, scale it to 200% (twice its normal size). The HS Art "World Map" was clip art, and scaled to 20% its normal size. (**Remember:** Clip art stays selected until you click off it. While it is selected, you can make changes to it, such as scaling it, as was done here.) The oval tool was then used to draw a series of ovals to show Addy's thoughts.

Before moving back to Card 2, get the arrow tool and click once on the text object. While it is selected, copy it (select **Copy text object** from the **Edit** menu). Once on Card 2, paste the text object (**Paste text object** from the **Edit** menu). Not only does this save you time creating a whole new text object, but it pastes an identically-sized and positioned text object on Card 2 as the one on Card 1. While the text object is still selected after being pasted, you may want to reset your text style (in case the last choice you made was for a larger font size for the title on Card 1). To replace the actual text in the object, get the

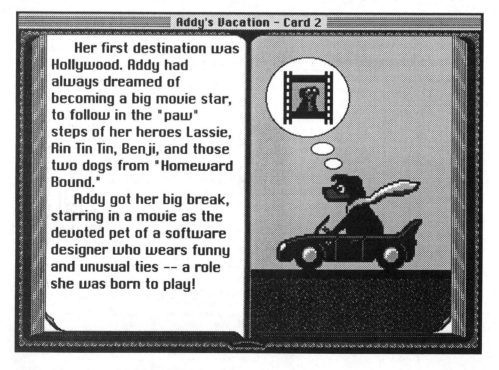

browse tool and highlight all of it. Leave it highlighted, and just start typing the next part of the story. Be sure to add some new artwork on the right hand side of the book. The example used clip art of Addy driving a car from "Addy With Cars & Paws" (scaled at 200%), along with a picture of Addy on film from "Button Art 2" (scaled at 150%)—both from the HS Art folder. Thought ovals (**oval tool**), a blue sky (**fill bucket** with light blue paint), road (**line tool** with large line thickness), and grass (**fill tool** with "grassy" pattern) were added.

Remember: Have you saved your stack in the last few minutes?

With the completion of your text and artwork on Cards 1 and 2, it is time to start making the book interactive. Return to Card 1. Select **Add a Button...** from the **Objects** menu. This brings up the "Button Appearance" dialog box. With this dialog, you can set the various attributes you wish to give your first button. There are eight types of buttons that you can create with *HyperStudio*. The top four button types are "visible" buttons—that is, their shapes are visible on the card. The bottom four types are "invisible" buttons—their shapes cannot

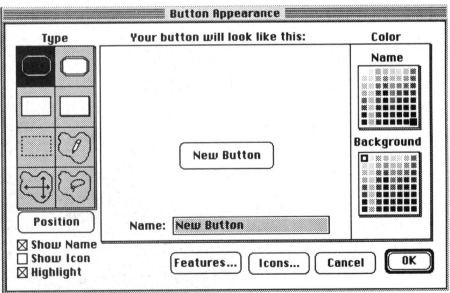

be seen on the card when using the **browse tool**. Each button type has its advantages, and, with time, you will learn the best occasions for using each type. For now, let's learn a little something about each type.

This is the rounded rectangle button. Use this button type if you want to create visible buttons with rounded edges.

This is the rounded **double rectangle** button. It is basically the rounded rectangle button with an extra outline.

*HyperHint→Notice that this button type resembles buttons with double outlines in dialog boxes. Well, not only does it resemble them, it behaves like them too. And as I pointed out in a HyperHint back in Lesson 4, any buttons that appear with a double outline can also be activated by pressing the **return** or **enter** key. Usually, buttons in stacks need to be clicked on to be activated. The **rounded double rectangle button**, however, can also be activated from the keyboard!*

This is, appropriately enough, called the **rectangle** button. It looks like a flat, two-dimensional rectangle.

This is the **drop shadow rectangle** button. It resembles a rectangle casting a slight shadow. The result is a button that looks three-dimensional, unless you place it against a black background—in which case it ends up looking like the rectangle button.

This is the **invisible** button. It is just like the rectangle button, except it is, well... invisible.

This is the **freehand area** button. When creating this button type, you use a pencil to draw the shape that you would like your button to be. It's great for creating odd-shaped button areas.

This is the **expanding area** button (or, what can be thought of as the "exploding" button). It is created very much like option-clicking the lasso tool, in that it expands outward to fill in an area of solid color.

Last, but not least, is the **lasso area** button. This button is created just like using the lasso tool. You select an area to which the button will cling or wrap itself. Keep in mind, however, that this button type is just as "discriminating" as its tool set counterpart. It ignores any pixels of color in the area you select that are the same as the color on which you first click.

And there they are, ladies and gentlemen... the "Eight Button Types of HyperStudio." They have tremendous potential, but require a creative soul to put them to good use. For "we are the music makers, and we are the dreamers of dreams."

Create an easy way for someone to move forward and backward through an interactive book, without needing to do so manually. Maybe some small hands pointing left and right to indicate page turns. With the "Button Appearance" dialog still showing, select the invisible button. This is a better choice than one of the visible buttons if our goal is just to show what is called an icon. Icons are little images that can be used on buttons. They are, however, not the same as clip art, backgrounds, or graphic objects. Icon files are created in a special format exclusively for use with buttons. Icons can be used with visible and invisible buttons, but for this page turn button, we just want the hands to show, and not a button outline as well (which is what we would get with one of the visible button choices). To get an icon on the first button, check **Show Icon** or click on the **Icons...** button. Either method will bring up the "Icons" dialog box. By default, this dialog allows you to scroll through the icon "Samples" provided. You can also see any icons you already have "In use," or choose other icons from "Disk Library...". The "Disk Library" option allows you to choose from other icon files that you might have.

Drop Shadow Rectangle
Button with Icon

Invisible Button
with Icon

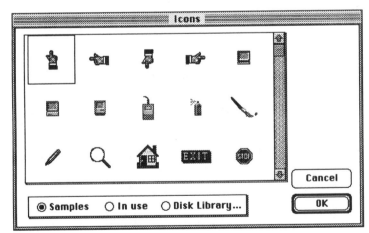

For example, there is a file called "Icon Library" already located in your HS Art folder from which you can select other icons. For now, choose the little hand pointing to the right. Just click on it once to select it, and then click on **OK.** This will return you to the "Button Appearance" dialog box.

While most *HyperStudio* users would know to click on a little pointing hand, let's go ahead and check "Show Name" as well. Use something simple like "Next page." You might also want to check "Highlight." This enables your button to blink on and off when clicked. The colors of the button are momentarily flashed in its opposite colors, giving the illusion of being pressed. A button does not need to highlight in order to work, but it provides a nice visual cue to someone that he or she properly clicked on it.

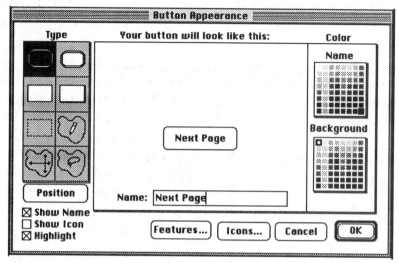

So, as seen here, the first button is invisible, shows an icon of a hand pointing to the right, shows the name "Next page," and is set to highlight when clicked on. (In fact, you can actually click on the button in the "Your button will look like this:" preview window to see it highlight!) You could also set the color of the text for the button's "Name" if you like. By default, it is set to black. Since this button is invisible, the "Background" color will not appear, so there is really no point in changing this selection.

HyperHint→Chicago, size 12 is the preset font for button names, and cannot be changed.

Now click on "Position" to place the button on the card. You will see a message telling you that you can use the mouse to drag the button where you'd like it on the card, and to resize it if you'd like. Since it has an icon and name on it, you won't want to resize it too small. The button is placed in the center of the card by default, selected with the familiar marching ants. You should be an old pro now at moving and resizing selected areas. Place the button near the bottom of the right-hand page.

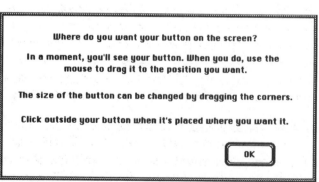

As the message stated, you simply need to click outside of the button area to place it. When you do so, *HyperStudio* will present you with the "Actions" dialog box.

```
┌──────────────────────────────────────────────────────┐
│▓▓▓▓▓▓▓▓▓▓▓▓▓▓▓▓▓▓ Actions ▓▓▓▓▓▓▓▓▓▓▓▓▓▓▓▓▓▓│
│                                                        │
│  ┌─ Places to Go: ──────┐  ┌─ Things to Do: ──────┐   │
│  │  ○ Another card...    │  │  ☐ Play a sound...   │   │
│  │  ○ Next card          │  │  ☐ Play a movie or video... │
│  │  ○ Previous card      │  │  ☐ New Button Actions... │
│  │  ○ Back               │  │  ☐ Play frame animation... │
│  │  ○ Home stack         │  │  ☐ Automatic timer... │
│  │  ○ Last marked card   │  │  ☐ Use HyperLogo...  │
│  │  ○ Another stack...   │  │  ☐ Testing functions... │
│  │  ○ Another program... │  └──────────────────────┘   │
│  │  ◉ None of the above  │   ┌──────────┐ ┌─────────┐  │
│  └──────────────────────┘   │  Cancel  │ │  Done   │  │
│                              └──────────┘ └─────────┘  │
└──────────────────────────────────────────────────────┘
```

You are in the heart of Willy Wonka's factory now. The sky's the limit. You can choose from a variety of "Places to Go" and/or from "Things to Do!" Each button you create can only have one selection from "Places to Go," but may have a combination of selections from "Things to Do."

HyperHint→Actions are the great temptation of HyperStudio. *But remember, each of the children in Willy Wonka's factory fell victim to his/her own temptations. Students, especially, have difficulty resisting the temptation to use as many actions as possible with each and every button they make. Your challenge as teacher is to help your students make appropriate action selections that are not only exciting, but which truly enhance the quality of the stack. Stacks communicate information. Careful selections of actions effectively communicate this information; careless selections obscure or detract from it.*

For now, we're going to resist the temptation. Our first button will simply lead to the next card. Select **Next card**. The "Transitions" dialog box will appear. This dialog allows you to set the manner and speed in which you would like to move from one location to another. By default, this is set on "Fastest" transition at "Fast" speed. Over 25 transitions are possible: Left to right, Right to left, Fastest, Bottom to top, Fade to black, Fade to white, Blocks, Diagonal right, Diagonal left, Blinds, Top to bottom, Bars, Rain, Dissolve, Barn open, Barn close, Mouth open, Mouth close, Iris open, Iris close, Zoom in, Zoom out, Razor left, Razor right, Bow ties, Diamond dissolve, and Fade to button color.

One thing you will want to teach your students is that transitions should not be distracting. Transitions should allow for a smooth movement from one location to another. They can also simulate animated actions. For example, you have begun creating an interactive book. Your "Next page" button should move from Card 1 to Card 2 in some manner that maintains the flow of the story. One very good transition choice for this would be "Right to left." Why? This transition will result in Card 2 replacing Card 1 from the right side of the screen to the left. In other words,

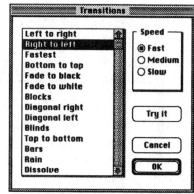

it will simulate actually turning to the next page—just like in a real book. Other transitions might look good, too. "Dissolve" would cause the words and picture on Card 1 to become small particles that fade away as the words and picture on Card 2 fill in to replace them—kind of like the transporter on the *Starship Enterprise*. What is neat about this transition is that only those parts of each card that are different will appear to dissolve into one another. The book itself does not appear to change, even though all of Card 1 is really dissolving into Card 2.

An example of a transition that would be distracting in this case would be "Fade to black" or "Fade to white." These transitions cause the entire card to fade to either a black or white screen, and then fade back to the next card. The effect is that the whole book disappears, and then reappears again. There may be times when this would be appropriate, but, in this case this effect would interrupt the flow of the story.

To get an idea of what each transition will do, just click on the **Try it** button. It is not a perfect representation of what the transition will actually look like in the stack, but it does give you a kind of preview of what to expect.

The speed of your transition is important, as well. Set it too fast, and it may happen too quickly to really be noticed. Set it too slow, and your user may get annoyed or impatient with the effect. "Medium" speed is generally a good option. That way, the transitions will not occur too quickly on a newer, faster computer—nor will they take too long on an older, slower computer. What looks good on one computer may not look as good on another. And you want to create your stacks for easy use on whatever type of computer your user may have.

So, for the "Next page" button in your book, select "Right to left" at "Medium" speed.

Click on **OK**. You will return to the "Actions" dialog. For this button, let's not assign any "Things to Do." We will do this later in the lesson. In the "Actions" dialog, click on **Done**. You will return to Card 1. With the browse tool, now click on the button you have made and watch your transition take place. Pretty exciting, isn't it?!

Now that you are on Card 2, follow the same steps and create a button that moves back to Card 1 (except choose "Previous card" in the "Actions" dialog rather than "Next card"). Create an invisible button that shows an icon of a hand pointing left, with the name "Previous page," that highlights, that uses a similar type of transition as your "Next page" button, and that is located in the bottom corner of the left hand page. Students will often want to create buttons with entirely new looks and actions. However, stacks look more professional when buttons for certain actions are similar in placement, design, and function. They are also easier to use. For my example, the button on Card 2 uses the hand pointing left

icon, says "Previous page," highlights, uses a "Left to right" transition (similar, but the opposite of, the first transition for the effect of turning back a page), and is placed in the bottom corner of the left hand page.

Move to Card 2. Copy the text object, and then create a new card. *Don't* use the **Same Background** command this time, as this will create a new card with the same look as Card 2 (including all the artwork now on Card 2). This demonstrates that **Same Background** is best to use when you want to establish a series of cards with identical backgrounds *before* adding any other clip art or paint to them. Paste the text object on Card 3, and import the book background.

HyperHint➔*New cards are always added to a stack immediately after the current card. So, if you were on Card 1 when you added the new card, it would have been added between Cards 1 and 2. In fact, the new card would have become Card 2, and the original Card 2 would have been repositioned and renamed as Card 3. If you ever create a card that you no longer want, you can select* **Delete Card** *from the* **Edit** *menu. You can also copy, cut, and paste cards. These can be very useful and powerful commands, since a card consists not only of backgrounds, clip art, or paint, but also any text objects, buttons, etc. that you have added.*

For the example of Card 3, the text in the text object was replaced with the next part of the story... a visit from Addy to a hardworking teacher writing a *HyperStudio* tutorial. What a fitting idea, don't you think?. Clip art of Addy driving in a limousine (from "Addy With Cars & Paws") flipped sideways and scaled 200% was added. A portion of the "USA" map as clip art (which was not scaled, since only a portion was selected).

Of course, this is only an example. You are free to create whatever you'd like. However, this example will teach you certain button types and actions. By at least adding a portion of the USA map to your card, you will be able to make good use of our button type—the expanding area button. The expanding area button "explodes" outward to fill in solid areas of color. That makes it the perfect choice for making interactive maps. So, after adding a portion of the map to your card, add a new button. In the "Button Appearance" dialog, select the expanding area button as your button type, and set it to highlight. Give the button a name (since, as said back in Lesson 5, naming objects is a good habit to get into if you eventually plan to use more advanced techniques), but don't check "Show name." Leave "Show Icon" unchecked as well. Then, click on **Position.**

Addy appears to let you know that you need to click inside the area you'd like to select for your button. You will then see the familiar four-pointed

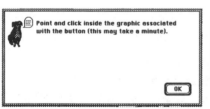

cross. In this example, the cross was placed over the state of Ohio, and then the mouse was clicked once. The button "exploded" outward to fill in the entire state, which is a solid shade of green. Immediately after this, Addy reappears to

say that the shape of the button has been defined. If you make a mistake, simply click on the **Try Again** button. If you are satisfied with the shape, click on **OK.**

Give this button the ability to play a sound. Check **Play a sound...** in the "Actions" dialog. You will be taken to *HyperStudio*'s "Tape deck." This amazingly interactive dialog box allows you to choose from a set of sound "Samples," to play sounds you might already have "In Use" by other buttons, or to get other sound files by choosing "Disk Library...." Selecting "Disk Library..." will first take you to the "HS Sounds" folder in the "*HyperStudio* for HD" folder on your hard drive. Like its sibling the "HS Art" folder, the "HS Sounds" folder contains a set of files to get you started.

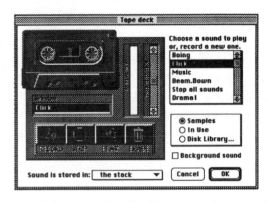

While the sample and "HS Sounds" files are small clips and sound effects, don't assume that is all *HyperStudio* will allow you to choose from. For example, the Program Resource CD contains a multitude of files in its Media Library. These files range from small clips and sound effects to full-length musical selections. As stated in the *HyperStudio* Reference Manual, "*HyperStudio* supports AIFF sound format, System 7 sounds (sound resource files), *HyperStudio* Apple IIGS sounds, WAV sound files (PC files) and Mod sounds (music files)."

HyperHint→ *Using the CD Play New Button Action, you can even play selections directly from CD-ROMs and audio CDs. We will take a closer look at this capability in a later lesson.*

The most exciting thing about *HyperStudio's* tape deck is that it enables you to record your own sounds. The only prerequisite is that your computer has a microphone (either built-in or externally connected to its sound-in port). To record a sound, simply press the green **RECORD** button. Don't be surprised if *HyperStudio* alerts you to the fact that your current sound input setting is not set for using the microphone. If this is the case, *HyperStudio* offers you the opportunity to reset it.

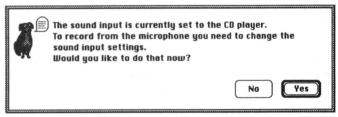

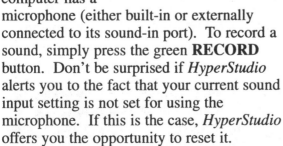

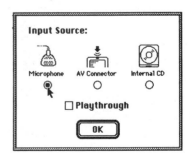

When you are finished recording, simply click the red **STOP** button. (Actually, just clicking the mouse again causes the recording to stop, as does pressing any key.) While you are recording, you should notice a green indicator in the "LEVEL" section of the tape deck. If everything is working properly, this indicator should move in response to the level of the input sound. You should also notice a moving bar in the "Selection" portion of the tape deck. This bar (or "gas gauge" as it is referred to in the reference manual) shows you how much memory you have used and how much you have left. According to the manual, "Digitized sound takes up about 5K for ten seconds."

To hear your recording, click the blue **PLAY** button. Don't be surprised if your sound is a little muffled or unclear. By default, *HyperStudio* automatically compresses your sound to cut down on the amount of memory required. Because it is compressed, the quality of the sound is lower.

HyperHint➔ *You can make clearer recordings by holding down the ⌘ key while recording. The tradeoff, though, is that while your sound is much clearer, it also requires about twice as much memory. Digitized sound, whether compressed or not, can take up quite a bit of memory if longer than just a few seconds in length. By default, your sound is stored as part of your stack, increasing the overall memory required by the stack itself. In the next lesson, you will take on the status of an "experienced user." Among other things, this will allow you the option of saving your recorded sounds as separate, disk-based files (which helps to cut down on the stack's memory).*

Require your students to limit their use of recorded sound to brief stack introductions or other short recordings throughout their stacks. When students wish to record longer sounds, have them use a sound editing program. Another option is to have them use the BlabberMouth New Button Action (which will be covered in Lesson 12). Having students write down and practice what they will be recording helps guarantee the sound will be as short as possible.

When you select a sound, its name appears in the "Selection" portion of the tape deck. If you record your own sound, by default it is given the name "Untitled" followed by a number. Again, it is recommended that you never leave anything named "Untitled." Give the sound a name that fits what it is. For example, if a student records an introduction to his/her stack, it could be called "Intro."

You can also adjust the "VOLUME" of your sound. Sounds should be set at a fairly high volume. You never know what the overall volume of a given computer will be set on. Setting a high volume for the sound in the button itself guarantees that it should be fairly audible on just about any computer.

For this example stack, record your own voice saying, "Addy, could you stop by for a visit?" for the expanded area button. Then click on **OK** in the "Tape deck," and then click on **Done** in the "Actions" dialog. It now plays your voice back whenever you click on Ohio. The problem, is, however, that the user would have no idea to click on Ohio. One drawback to using invisible buttons is that, because they are invisible, users may not know there are any buttons to click on—unless the button has an icon or name, like the ones you added to Cards 1 and 2. One possible solution for this is to include a small statement indicating where the button is. The example has a sentence just below the map stating, "Click on Ohio to hear a message." Painted text, Geneva font, size 10, red was used. It's big enough to be read by a user but small enough that it doesn't draw too much attention to itself.

Have you saved your stack in the last few minutes?

Create one last card, and again give it the "Book" background. For the example, the text object from Card 3 was copied and pasted on Card 4, and replaced the text to continue the story. The file "Animals" was added as clip art (scaling it at 40% its normal size). The border around it was erased after placing it on the card. A picture of Addy facing away 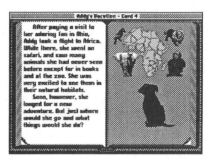 was also used from the "Addy" file. The fill tool was then used to fill in the rest of the page with light blue paint. This was done so that a lasso could be used to create buttons for each of the animals. (Some of the animals have white areas in them. Since the background of the book page was originally white, lassoing these animals would have left spaces where the buttons could not be clicked— which might frustrate a user of the stack. Filling in the background with a color not found in any of the animals will prevent this problem.)

Create a new button. Select the lasso area button type and check **Highlight**. Name the button, but *don't* check "Show Name" or "Show Icon." Then click on **Position**. Addy will appear telling you to use the lasso to select a portion of the background. Click on **OK.** Use the lasso that appears and select either Addy or one of the other animals. Once you have made your selection, Addy will inform you that your button's shape has been defined. As with the expanding area button, you can choose to make a new selection or keep what you have.

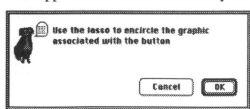

Check **Play a sound...** in the "Actions" dialog, and then select the appropriate animal sound from "Disk Library..." in the "Tape deck." The "HS Sounds" folder has sounds for each. For Addy, select "Small Dog." You should also find "Parrot," "Lion," "Elephant," and "Monkey" sound files. After selecting the right sound, click on **OK** and then **Done.** Then click on your button with the **browse tool.** The animal should highlight and make a noise.

It never ceases to amaze me that you don't need to know any computer programming to use *HyperStudio.* Creating buttons requires very little skill. It is mainly just making a series of choices from menus and answering basic questions. You call the shots, and *HyperStudio* does all the work.

If you are feeling inspired, create lasso area buttons for all of the animals on Card 4.

Well, we don't have a conclusion for "Addy's Vacation Adventure" story just yet, but that is okay. Go ahead and link the rest of the pages together. For example, we need "Next page" and "Previous page" buttons for Cards 3 and 4. There is a very easy way to do this. Move back to Card 1. Get the **arrow tool** and click once on the **Next page** button. This will select the button. With the button selected, choose **Copy** button from the **Edit** menu. Now move to Card 2. Paste the button. Just like the copies we made of our original text object, this button is identical to the one on Card 1 and in the same exact location too. Move to Card 3 and paste the button again. You cannot paste it on Card 4 because this is not another card to go to from there. (You can paste it on Card 4 if you want, but the next card will be Card 1.)

HyperHint➔Cards in a stack aren't in true linear order. They are actually in cyclical order. In other words, the next card after the last card is the first card. And the previous card to the first card is the last card.

Now make a copy of the "Previous page" button on Card 2, and paste it on Cards 3 and 4.

Move to Card 1. Put one final button in this stack, allowing a user to move from Card 1 to Card 4—completely skipping Cards 2 and 3. Choose any one of the four visible button types for this last button from the "Button Appearance" dialog box. Be adventurous and give it a name color other than black and a background color.

Position the button (Place it just below the text object), and then click off it. When you see the "Actions" dialog, select **Another card...** from **Places to Go**. Another dialog box will appear, allowing you to choose the card you want the button to move to. Click either one of the directional arrows until you locate Card 4. Then click on **OK.** The "Transitions" dialog then appears. Choose the same transition you used for the "Next page" button. Then click on **OK**, and then **Done** in the "Actions" dialog. That is it. Someone using your stack could now move to this portion of the story without having to read Cards 2 and 3. Do your students enjoy reading "Choose Your Own Adventure" or "Twist-a-Plot" books? You can easily create multimedia books of this kind using *HyperStudio*'s "Another card" button capability.

Well, we didn't create all of the types of buttons possible. We only used a few "Places to Go" options. The only action we assigned any button was "Play a sound..." But it is time to wrap this lesson up. We will use a number of the other actions in upcoming lessons, though.

By the way, have you saved your stack lately?

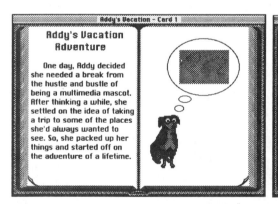

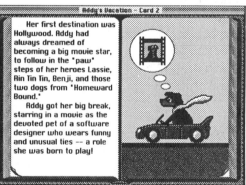

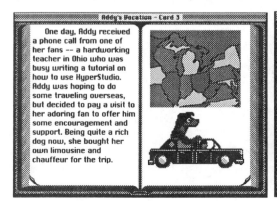

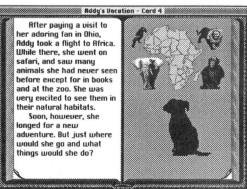

Here are some additional bits of information concerning buttons:

- Buttons are objects. That means they can be moved and edited without affecting a card's background. (If you want proof that buttons aren't part of a card's background, try looking at one with the **magnifying glass**, or erasing it with the **eraser** tool. Good luck!)
- You can edit any button by double-clicking on it with the arrow tool.
- You can resize **rectangular** buttons with the arrow tool.
- You can locate **invisible** buttons by pressing both the **option** and ⌘ keys.
- Use the browse tool to use buttons, and the **arrow** tool to edit buttons.

 HyperHint→The tool set includes a button edit tool and a sound edit tool. These tools are specifically for editing buttons. The button edit tool will edit any button, and the sound edit tool will edit any buttons that play sounds. As stated in the previous lesson, the arrow tool is almost always used for editing.

HyperHorizons: *The beta version of* HyperStudio 3.1 *for Macintosh does not include the sound edit tool in the tool set.*

HyperHands-On!

Student Task Cards—Lesson 6

"Practice Making Simple Buttons"

(Starting with this lesson, you might want to begin saving the stacks you make. Your teacher will probably have a preferred way for you to do this. So be sure to ask your teacher to show you the steps you need to know.)

Step 1. Create a new stack.

Step 2. Make a button.

Select **Add a Button...** from the **Objects** menu. This brings up the "Button Appearance" dialog box. With this dialog, you can set the design you want to give your first button. There are eight types of buttons that you can create with *HyperStudio*. The top four button types are "visible" buttons—that is, their shapes can be seen on the card. The bottom four types are "invisible" buttons—their shapes can't be seen on the card when using the **browse** tool.

This is the **rounded rectangle** button. Use this button type if you want to create visible buttons with rounded edges.

This is the **rounded double rectangle** button. It's basically the rounded rectangle button with an extra outline.

HyperHint→*Notice that this button type resembles buttons with double outlines in dialog boxes. Well, not only does it resemble them, it behaves like them too. Any buttons that appear with a double outline can also be activated by pressing the* **return** *or* **enter** *keys. Usually, buttons in stacks need to be clicked on to be activated. The rounded double rectangle button, however, can also be activated from the keyboard!*

This is, obviously, called the **rectangle** button. It looks like a flat, two-dimensional rectangle.

This is the **drop shadow rectangle** button. It's a rectangle casting a slight shadow. This button type looks three-dimensional, unless you place it against a black background—in which case it ends up looking just like the rectangle button.

This is the **invisible** button. It's just like the rectangle button, except it is, well… invisible. You can't see its outline when using the **browse** tool.

 This is the **freehand area** button. When creating this button type, you use a pencil to draw the shape that you would like your button to be. It is great for creating odd-shaped button areas.

 This is the **expanding area** button (or you can think of it as an "exploding" button). It expands outward to fill in an area of solid color.

 Last, but not least, is the **lasso area** button. This button is created just like using the lasso tool. You select an area, and the button will cling or wrap itself to it. Just like the **lasso** tool, this button type ignores any pixels of color in the area you select that are the same as the color on which you first click.

Select one of the first four "visible" designs for your button by clicking on it.

Step 3. Add an icon to your button.

There are little images (called "icons") that you can add to buttons. They are not the same thing as clip art. Icons can appear on buttons—clip art cannot.

To get an icon on your button, check **Show Icon** or click on the **Icons…** button. Either way will bring up the "Icons" dialog box. This dialog is already set to show you the icon "Samples" provided. You can also see any icons you might already have "In use," or choose other icons from "Disk Library…." The "Disk Library" option allows you to choose from other icon files that you might have. For example, there is a file called "Icon Library" already located in your HS Art folder from which you can select other icons. For now, choose the little hand pointing to the right. Just click on it once to select it, and then click on **OK**. This will return you to the "Button Appearance" dialog box.

Step 4. Add a name to your button.

While most *HyperStudio* users would know to click on a little pointing hand, go ahead and check "Show Name." Type a name like "Next page." You might also want to check "Highlight." Buttons that highlight blink on and off when clicked. The colors of the button are momentarily flashed in their opposite colors, so they look like they are really being pressed. A button does not need to be highlighted in order to work, but it helps make it obvious to someone that the button was properly clicked.

Step 5. Position your button.

Now click on **Position** to place the button on your card. You will see a message telling you that you can use the mouse to drag the button where you'd like it on the card, and to resize it if you'd like. Since it has an icon and name on it, you won't want to resize it too small. The button is automatically placed in the center of the card, and selected with "marching ants." You can place the button anywhere you want on your card. A good location might be near the bottom on the right hand side of the card.

Step 6. Set your button to go to the next card.

After positioning your button where you want it, click outside of it to place it. When you do this, *HyperStudio* will present you with the "Actions" dialog box.

Select **Next card**. The "Transitions" dialog box will appear. This dialog allows you to set the effect and speed (the "transition") in which you would like to move from one location to another. It is already set on "Fastest" transition at "Fast" speed. But more than 25 transitions are possible: Left to right, Right to left, Bottom to top, Fade to black, Fade to white, Diagonal right, Diagonal left, Blinds, Top to bottom, Rain, Dissolve, Barn open, Barn close, Mouth open, Mouth close, Iris open, Iris close, Zoom in, Zoom out, Razor left, Razor right, and Fade to button color.

To get an idea of what each transition looks like, just click on the **Try it** button. You will not see exactly what the transition will look like in the stack, but it does give you a good idea of what to expect. An important thing to remember is that you should not pick a transition for a button just because it looks cool. You should pick a transition that helps your stack flow from one card to another and creates a useful effect.

Step 7. Finish your button.

After setting the transition for your button, click on **OK.** You will return to the "Actions" dialog. Don't give it any "Things to Do." you will do this with the next button. In the "Actions" dialog, click on **Done.** You will return to your card. Don't click the button. You have not made the "next" card for it to go to.

Step 8. Import a background onto the card (or paint your own design).

Importing a background, or using the paint tools, has no effect on the button. That is because the button is not on the background. It is floating above it.

Step 9. Make a new card, and import a background onto it or design your own.

Step 10. Move back to your first card. Get the **browse** tool and click your button.

The first card will move to the second card using whatever transition you set the button for. Pretty cool, huh?!

Step 11. Make a button to return to the first card.

Follow the same steps and create a button that moves back to Card 1 (except choose "Previous card" in the "Actions" dialog rather than "Next card"). Make this button "invisible" with an icon of a hand pointing left, and name it something like "Previous page." Set it to highlight if you want and position it on the card (such as in the bottom corner on the left hand side). Then click off the button to place it.

Step 12. Make the button play a sound.

Instead of just taking you back to the first card, give this button the ability to play a sound. **Check Play a sound...** in the "Actions" dialog. You will be taken to *HyperStudio*'s "Tape deck," which allows you to choose from a set of sound "Samples," to play any sounds already "In Use" by other buttons or to get other sound files by choosing "Disk Library...." Selecting **Disk Library...** will take you to the "HS Sounds" folder in the "*HyperStudio* for HD" folder on your hard drive. The "HS Sounds" folder contains a set of sound files to get you started.

The most exciting thing about *HyperStudio*'s tape deck is that it enables you to record your own sounds. (Your computer will need a microphone in order for you to record a sound. Check with your teacher about this, as well as for further instructions on how to record sounds.)

Step 13. Finish your button.

Once you have selected a sound (either from the samples or one you recorded), click on **OK,** and then click on **Done** in the "Actions" dialog.

Step 14. Try out your button.

Click your button. It should take you back to the first card, and should play your sound at the same time.

The two buttons you have now made are very basic. Your teacher will introduce you to other more exciting ways to use buttons as your knowledge of *HyperStudio* grows. You have only just begun to experiment with ways to make your stacks "interactive."

Intermediate Level

Goal/Objectives/Final Project

Level Goal: While completing the lessons in the Intermediate Level of this tutorial, students will learn basic *HyperStudio* skills in using graphic objects, cookie cutter/copier art techniques, and auto-timed buttons necessary for the creation of a small 2–4 card stack.

Level Objectives: Throughout the Intermediate Level, the student will acquire the ability to...

- add and create graphic objects. (Lesson 8)

- utilize Extras such as Box Maker and EarthPlot. (Lesson 9)

- use cookie cutter/copier art techniques. (Lessons 10)

- create test response and/or auto-timed buttons. (Lesson 11)

- work with various sample New Button Actions, such as Hide/Show, RollCredits, GhostWriter, and BlabberMouth. (Lesson 12)

End-of-Level Project: Upon completion of the Intermediate Level lessons, the student will create a stack that...

- utilizes Beginner Level features as needed.

- includes the use of graphic objects.

- features examples of art or titling created with the cookie cutter/copier.

- incorporates test response and/or auto-timed buttons.

- makes effective use of New Button Actions.

Suggested topics include an interactive storybook stack, a literary analysis stack, a research stack with accompanying test items, or a self-running presentation or advertisement stack.

Lesson 7: That's Quite an Experience!

"The benefits of setting your Preferences to 'Experienced User' status"

HyperOverview:

Experience is perhaps the greatest teacher of all. Many things can neither be fully understood nor truly appreciated unless they've been experienced. *HyperStudio* is one of these. Simply reading about it is not enough. You have got to use it to know it. Once you acquire a certain degree of experience, you are able to take on greater responsibilities. *HyperStudio* provides a means to allow you and your students greater responsibility in the creation of your stacks.

HyperPrerequisites:

* "Experience" using the skills and information covered in Lessons 1–6

HyperClinic:

When you first start using *HyperStudio*, it is assumed that you are a beginning user. For this reason, the software provides many reminders and prompts as you are in the process of creating. It also limits your selection of choices. This is all to make learning *HyperStudio* easier and less overwhelming. But if you have successfully accomplished the goals and objectives at the beginner level, then it is time to move on to bigger and better things. It's time to increase your status.

 Start up *HyperStudio*. Select **Preferences** from the bottom of the **Edit** menu (if you are using *HyperStudio* 2.0 or earlier for Macintosh, or the Apple IIGS version, **Preferences** is located in the **Apple** menu). You will be presented with the "Preferences" dialog box, which enables you to modify certain program settings and stack characteristics. These modifications, in turn, are saved in a small "*HyperStudio* Preferences" file located in the Preferences folder of your hard drive's System Folder.

This file is updated whenever you make changes in the "Preferences" dialog box. Near the bottom of this dialog will be a place to check "I'm an experienced *HyperStudio* user." Do so now. That is it—you now have greater

Preferences

┌─ Stack preferences ─────────────
  Stack password: [   ]
  ☐ Lock stack
  ☐ Show card number with stack name
  ☒ Turn on Automatic Timers & HyperLinks
  ☐ Automatically save stack
  ☒ Presentation mode...
  ☒ Ignore extra mouse clicks

┌─ Program preferences ───────────
  ☒ I'm an experienced HyperStudio user
  E-mail address: [   ]

(Cancel) (OK)

power over *HyperStudio*. Or, to borrow a phrase from the classic *Star Wars* movies, "May the force be with you."

Making changes in the "Preferences" dialog does not make *HyperStudio* harder to use. In fact, it is actually easier to use. By now, you have probably gotten tired of the seemingly endless prompts and message reminders this software displays. As an "experienced user," *HyperStudio* will not present as many of these from this point on. For example, Addy will no longer appear the first time you create a new stack to tell you that "you have just created a new stack...." Face it, you only need to see that reminder a few times before it gets quite annoying. With your new status, the annoyances will be fewer.

HyperHint→Whenever you make changes in the "Preferences" dialog, HyperStudio *perceives these as stack changes. Therefore, if you try to quit the program or create a new stack,* HyperStudio *will alert you to the fact that you have made changes to your stack, and will ask if you wish to save it. Changing your user status is one of the "Program preferences" therefore, it takes effect whether you save the stack or not. However, all of the "Stack preferences" are stack-specific; any changes you make in this section of the dialog box only apply to the current stack. Therefore, if you make stack preference changes, be sure to save the stack.*

After setting your status to "experienced user," click on **OK** to close the dialog box. (we will take a look at some of the other

> In your new stack do you want the same card size and number of colors as in the current stack?
>
> No   Yes

"Preferences" choices at the end of this lesson.) Make a new stack. Addy still appears, but this time she's not reminding you of the obvious. Rather, she has an important question for you to answer. Unless you are an experienced user, your new stacks are always created in the same dimensions and number of colors as the stack that was being used before the new stack was created. Since you will often start up into the Home Stack itself, these dimensions will be the default size (512 x 342 pixels), as alluded to in a *HyperHint* in Lesson 4, and the number of colors available will be 256, as covered at the beginning of Lesson 2. This is assuming you are using the current Macintosh 3.0 or Windows 1.0 versions. If you are using earlier Macintosh versions, you are limited to 16 colors unless you are an experienced user. The Apple IIGS version is limited to 16 colors regardless of your user status (although you can work around this limitation using other paint software, such as *DreamGrafix* by DreamWorld Software.) If you want your new stack to be the same size and have the same number of colors available as the stack you are currently using, then answer Addy's question with a **Yes.** If you want the option to make size and color changes, then answer **No.**

If you click **No**, you will be presented with a dialog box from which you can select the number of colors and card size dimensions for your new stack. (The default selections will be the same as the stack you are currently using; therefore, making no changes is the same as answering "Yes" to Addy's original question.) A number of card sizes can be selected from, or you can set your own dimensions. Give your choice careful consideration. If you are designing your stack(s) to be usable on computers with various monitor sizes, the standard card size (or smaller) will actually offer you the most flexibility.

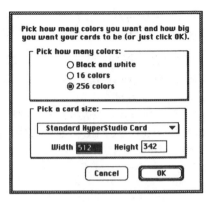

HyperHorizons: As mentioned in Lesson 2, the current color limitation for the Macintosh and Windows versions of HyperStudio *is 256 colors.* HyperStudio 3.1 *for Macintosh will break new ground by raising this limit to thousands or millions of colors—depending on the color capability of your particular computer setup.*

```
✓ Standard HyperStudio Card
  Current Screen Size
  Mac Classic 9" (512 x 342)
  Mac Hi-Res 12" (512 x 384)
  Apple Color RGB 14" (640 x 480)
  PowerBook (640 x 400)
  Full page (640 x 870)
  Two page (1152 x 870)
  Custom size
```

Assuming you have made your color and card size selection, your new stack should reflect these choices. If, later on, you decide you would like to change the number of colors and/or the card size of your stack, you will be relieved to know that you don't have to recreate it from scratch. You can simply select **About this Stack...** from the **Objects** menu (sorry, no keystroke shortcut for this one). This brings up an "About Stack" dialog box, a section of which includes a "Change # of colors or size..." button. Clicking this button brings up the same color/card size dialog box you

Number of colors:	256
Card width:	512
Card height:	342

Change # of colors or size...

were presented with when creating your stack. Make the changes that you want to make, click on **OK**, and then click on **OK** once again in the "About Stack" dialog box. *HyperStudio* will then convert your stack. Naturally, any reduction in the number of colors may result in an undesired graininess to any artwork. This is called "dithering." Dithering is basically the use of mixed pixels of various colors to simulate a color or colors that are not actually present in the current palette. Changing the card size may also result in similar undesired results—particularly if the card size is increased, in which case your artwork may end up looking chunky. This conversion cannot be undone, so be careful not to save your stack if you are dissatisfied afterwards. Just reopen the stack.

HyperHint→Not only are card backgrounds affected by converting a stack, objects are too. Buttons, text objects, and graphic objects (covered in the next lesson) are also adjusted in color and/or size.

Being an experienced user means far more than having greater control of stack colors and size, or getting fewer annoying messages and reminders. It also means that you have access to object "features," which we will explore in the next lesson. For now, let's take a look at some of the other items in the "Preferences" dialog.

- Locking a stack protects it from unwanted alterations. If you wish to lock a stack, set a "Stack password" and check "Lock stack...". This causes the other stack preference selections to become unavailable, and reduces the menu bar to display only three menu choices: **File Edit**, and **Move.** While there may be a few occasions when locking a stack would be necessary (such as a stack with testing functions, which we will learn about later), you are strongly discouraged from using it. For one thing, it is very easy to forget passwords, in which case even you, the stack's creator, could not make changes to it. Another reason is that it is very frustrating for those who use the stack(s). *Locked stacks prohibit investigation.* One of the best ways to learn new *HyperStudio* techniques is to use the arrow tool to double-click on buttons and other objects in people's stacks. Remember how double-clicking with an editing tool allows you to make changes to objects? Well, it is also a neat way to see what settings and actions someone else used in putting a stack together. Stacks can be "picked apart" allowing you to learn more about *HyperStudio* by doing and seeing what others have done. Of course, investigating someone else's stack does not mean that you have the right to change it and claim it as your own. Even if a stack is locked, someone who's determined enough will manage to find a way of unlocking it and pirating its contents. So use this capability sparingly. It usually brings more trouble than it is worth.

- Check "Show card number with stack name" if you want the title bar of your stack to display both the stack's name and the number of the card the user is currently on. If this is not checked, then only the stack's name will appear in the title bar.

- The capabilities available by checking "Turn on Automatic Timers & HyperLinks" will be explored in Lessons 11 and 13.

- If you check "Automatically save stack," your stack will be saved whenever you either quit *HyperStudio* or open another stack. I think the pros are outweighed by the cons on this one. The nice thing about this preference is that you don't get that annoying message reminding you that you have made changes to your stack, and asking whether or not you want to save it. However, your stack is saved regardless of whether you like the changes you made or not. If you are dissatisfied with changes made, having this preference selected would make you extremely nervous—A general rule, is that you refrain from using this preference.

- Use "Presentation mode…" to affect the way your stack is framed on the screen. If unchecked, the desktop shows around the borders of the stack. This allows you to click outside the stack to bring up the desktop, or some other application you may be currently using. This can be bothersome, though, if you *accidentally* click outside the stack. Checking this preference allows you to set a picture, color, or the desktop pattern itself as the stack's border. The *actual* desktop is covered, preventing the accident I just described from occurring. You can double-click on a color in the palette to bring up the full 256-color palette. Finally, you can choose whether or not to have the title bar show in your stack.

*HyperHint→Stacks often look more professional when the menu and title bars are hidden. Don't confuse the two. The **menu bar** runs across the top of the active screen area, and includes all of the menu selections. The **title bar** runs across the top of the stack itself, and at most only includes the name of the stack and card number. By the way, the title bar, like the bars at the top of many of the dialog boxes, is a "draggable" area. If you click on it and hold down the mouse, you can drag the stack around on the screen.*

- *HyperStudio* buttons need to be clicked on only ***once*** with the browse tool to be activated. The only time they should be double-clicked is with the arrow tool as a quick way to begin editing them. Check "Ignore extra mouse clicks" to prevent accidental double-clicks with the browse tool by users of your stack. For example, if you have a button on one card in the same location as a button on the card it moves to, double-clicking it with the browse tool will cause the first button to be activated, and the second click will activate the button on the second card. This is usually not something you will want to have happen. "Ignore extra mouse clicks" prevents the browse tool from registering two consecutive clicks.

Note: No hands-on application of this lesson is included for the students. It is recommend that you *not* allow students to access the "Preferences" dialog. Many potential problems can be avoided if you, the teacher, be solely responsible for making any preference selections.

Lesson 8: A Little Too Graphic

"Creating Graphic Objects/Setting Object Features"

HyperOverview:

A graphic object is clip art with an attitude. Clip art is lifeless. A graphic object is energetic. Clip art is flat. A graphic object is three-dimensional in nature.

When pondering the nature of graphic objects, one can be reminded of the graphic artist M.C. Escher. He is a master at combining elements of time, space and distance through his art in ways that truly push the limits of imagination and understanding. In a number of Escher's works, elements are shown breaking free from the constraints of two-dimensional space into the third dimension of depth. Escher's art has had a resurgence in popularity in the past few years. Perhaps you have seen such works as "Reptiles" or "Drawing Hands" in books or on T-shirts. "Reptiles" shows an open sketch book with a geometric tessellation design of interconnecting lizards on one of the pages. At the edge of the design, the lizards can be seen coming up out of the sketch itself onto other objects around the sketch book, and then back down into the sketch book to become a part of the design again. "Drawing Hands" shows two hands in the process of sketching each other on a sheet of paper. The hands themselves have come up out of the paper and are holding pencils. They are drawing each other's sleeve, which, in time, will no doubt become three-dimensional as well.

Like the images in M. C. Escher's works, graphic objects seem to come right out from the screen itself. While not truly three-dimensional, they can behave as such. Clip art stays on the background, and can be hard to move. Graphic objects (like buttons and text objects) occupy space in front of the background, and can be clicked on, moved around, dropped on buttons, used as animation or video overlays, etc.

HyperPrerequisites:

- "Experienced user" preference status

- Working knowledge of drawing and selection tools, clip art, painted text, text objects, buttons, and button actions

HyperClinic:

There are two ways to create a graphic object—*adding* it directly to a card, or selecting a part of the background and *converting* it to a graphic object. Create a new stack, or open one that you are currently working on.

HyperHint→*You can start up* HyperStudio *by double-clicking on the icon for your particular stack. Doing so will bypass the Home Stack and take you directly to your stack.*

On a blank card in your stack, import the same "Tree" background we used in Lesson 4. Add a picture of Addy as clip art and place it somewhere up in the tree. Next, add the same exact picture of Addy as a graphic object. To add a graphic object directly to a card, select **Add a Graphic Object...** from the **Objects** menu. A dialog exactly like the one for importing backgrounds and adding clip art will appear, from which you can choose the source for the art file you wish to use. As with backgrounds and clip art, you can choose from **Disk file, Video,** or **QuickTake camera** (if one is connected to your computer).

HyperHorizons: *Version 3.1 for Macintosh will feature a slightly different dialog for adding art. The first two choices will still be* **Disk file** *and* **Video,** *but the third choice will read* **Digital camera.** *This will allow users of either Apple's* QuickTake® *camera or Kodak's line of digital cameras to access images for use as backgrounds, clip art, and/or graphic objects.*

After selecting your source, another dialog will appear. Notice that it is almost exactly like the one for adding clip art (a "scroll bar" along the right and bottom sides, a "rectangle selector" and "lasso," a "Get another picture..." button, a "Cancel" button, and an "OK" button). The only difference is that the dialog title bar will read "Graphic Objects" instead of "Clip Art." The same limitations apply to the rectangle selector and lasso tools as discussed earlier in Lessons 3 and 4. But for now, just select the same picture of Addy with the lasso. After selecting the picture, you will return to your card. Place Addy somewhere up in the tree and then click outside the image. With clip art, this just deselects the image, but with graphic objects, clicking outside also brings up another dialog box. The "Graphic Appearance" dialog has several options to choose from. It is recommended you name your object rather than using the default "Untitled." You can frame your

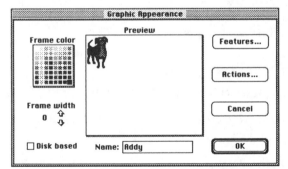

graphic object if you'd like, choosing both the color and width of the frame. If the object is selected with the **lasso**, the frame wraps to the image. If the object is selected with the **rectangle selector**, the frame wraps to the rectangular area. Frames are applied from the outside in.

Selecting "Actions" will bring up the same dialog we encountered when making buttons (see Lesson 6). So, graphic objects can act just like buttons in the sense that they can perform actions when clicked on. And remember, although you did not begin to explore "actions" until Lesson 6, you learned that the "Text Appearance" dialog allows for text objects to carry out actions as well (Lesson 5).

HyperHint➔A button does not immediately activate when clicked on. As long as the mouse button is down, the button on the screen does nothing. The user must click on the screen button, and then let up on the mouse button before any action(s) will take place. Graphic objects and text objects activate any action(s) the moment they are clicked on. Put more simply, buttons require a mouse down/mouse up combination to activate, while graphics and text objects activate immediately upon mouse down. (If the text object is not "read only," then clicking in the field itself requires a mouse down/mouse up combination. If the scroll bar is active, then clicking on it does not carry out any actions. This is a good thing. If actions occurred every time you scrolled through text, things could get quite annoying.) There are some exceptions to this information, however, as we will see later in this lesson.

The "Graphic Appearance" dialog contains two additional choices: a "Disk based" check box and a "Features..." button. (Unless your "Preferences" is set to "experienced user," these two choices will not be included in the dialog.) Checking "Disk based" causes *HyperStudio* to load the image for the graphic object from its file location. *HyperStudio* remembers where the image is and where you have placed it on the card. But why would you ever want to leave a graphic object "disk based?" Well, one good reason is that it can cut down on the stack's size in terms of memory. Graphic objects, especially large ones, can take up quite a bit of memory if saved within the stack itself. If the object is "disk based," then *HyperStudio* just accesses it from the actual disk file when it is needed, and you can save significant amounts of memory. There is a down side to this, however. You need to be careful not to change the object file's disk location or name; otherwise *HyperStudio* won't be able to access it.

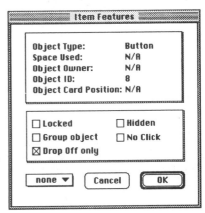

Clicking the "Features..." button brings up the "Item Features" dialog box. Here, you can make additional choices affecting the way a graphic object behaves. Checking "Locked" causes the graphic to be unmovable and uneditable. Trying to edit it later will result in a message from Addy reminding you that, "This message is currently locked and can't be edited."

Do you want to unlock it?" The "Group object" feature is one that we will discuss in Lesson 15. "Hidden" causes the graphic object to be unseen when using the browse tool. The object will *not* be hidden if you are using either the **arrow** or the **graphic edit tool**. Why would you ever want a hidden graphic? Well, imagine having objects that can appear and disappear in response to a user's input. Not only would this add some interest to a stack, but it would provide some interactive feedback for the user as well. In Lesson 12, you will explore this very possibility when you learn about New Button Actions, which includes the popular "Hide/Show" NBA. Checking "Draggable" makes it possible for the graphic object to be moved around the card with the **browse tool**. All objects (buttons, text objects, and graphic objects) can be moved around using the **arrow tool** (or their respective special editing tools). However, it is the **browse tool** that people need into order to *use* a stack. So, *HyperStudio* provides a feature that allows users to drag graphic objects around using the **browse tool**. Again, you may be wondering why someone would want to do this. Well, imagine being able to drag a graphic object onto a button and having some other action occur. Not only is this possible, but it is also quite easy.

So, make your Addy graphic "draggable." you will add some buttons later.

Before clicking **OK,** set one other remaining feature. Click on the button that says **none.** This displays a set of cursor alternatives for the **browse tool**. Normally, the **browse tool** resembles a hand with the index finger pointing up. However, this is only one of over twenty possible ways this tool can appear. This set of cursors is not only available as a graphic object feature, but is available for buttons, text objects, cards, and stacks themselves. To set a cursor design for a whole stack, select **About this Stack...** from the **Objects** menu, and make the choice from the "About stack" dialog. To set a cursor for a particular card, select **About this Card...** from the same menu, and make the choice from the "About Card" dialog. If you want the browse tool to change its design whenever it moves over a particular object, then make this choice from the object's "Item Features" dialog.

Like card transitions, cursors should be used with careful consideration to the overall effect. While having a multitude of different cursors on a card might be an exciting temptation, it could also be very distracting for the user. Effects in a stack should enhance its ability to communicate ideas and information—not detract from it. So go easy on the use of cursors. Since our Addy graphic object is draggable, an appropriate cursor would be the little "grabby" hand near the bottom of the menu.

Select this cursor, click on **OK** to close the "Item Features" dialog, and then click on **OK** once again to close the "Graphic Appearance" dialog. You should now have two pictures of Addy on your card. They may *look* the same, but they definitely won't *behave* the same. Try as you might, you will not be able to rescue the clip art Addy with the **browse tool** or the **arrow tool**. You could use the **rectangle selector** or **lasso tools** to select the clip art Addy and remove her from the tree, but you will end up moving part of the tree as well. You will leave a big hole behind, too. But you should have no problem using the **browse tool** to rescue the graphic object Addy from the tree. And wherever you move her, the background will be left unaffected. Further, the **browse tool** will become a "grabby" hand whenever it is over the graphic object Addy.

However, since Addy was added as a graphic object using the lasso tool, there is still the "undesired effect" we addressed back in Lesson 4. Because her eyes are partly white, they became transparent when Addy was selected. We could have selected Addy with the **rectangle selector**, but then she would have a big white rectangle around her. It's possible, though, to create a graphic object version of Addy without transparent eyes or a big white rectangle.

Begin by re-importing the "Tree" background. The clip art version of Addy will be replaced, while the graphic object version will remain untouched—clearly demonstrating that graphic objects are not part of the background. Now delete the graphic object Addy by clicking on it once with either the **arrow** or **graphic** edit tool, and pressing the **delete** key. Create a new card. On this card, import the entire "Addy" file as a background, and then fill in all the empty white space with some neutral color (remember doing this same thing back in Lesson 4?). Then, just as in Lesson 4, use the **lasso** to select one of the pictures of Addy, but don't copy it just

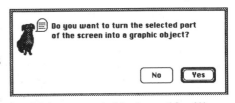

yet. After lassoing Addy, select **Add a Graphic Object....** Addy herself will appear asking if you want to convert the area you have selected into a graphic object. Answer "Yes," and follow the steps listed earlier in this lesson to make Addy a draggable graphic object. Then click once on the object with the **arrow** or **graphic editing tool**, copy it, and then paste it on the "Tree" card. Do the same thing with the doghouse and one of Addy's bones. Your "Tree" card should now look similar to what it looked like back in Lesson 4. The obvious difference, however, is that not only have Addy, the doghouse, and a bone been added to the card without any transparent areas, but they can also be moved around on the card without affecting its background. One minute Addy can be a typical dog with her doghouse at the foot of a big, shady tree and the next minute she can be the first dog on her block to have a treehouse.

Graphic objects make it very easy to create interactive scenes in your stacks, kind of like those children's toys that come with a series of background cards and removable stickers. But you can take this even further. There is a commercial multimedia product, called the *Family History Toolkit,* which can be used with *HyperStudio* to create interactive family genealogies. Included in this toolkit is a tutorial stack that demonstrates how to use graphic objects as part of an interactive keepsake box. It walks you through the steps necessary to create draggable graphic images of family heirlooms, which you can then actually take out of and put back in a wooden keepsake box. The box, along with open and closed drawers to use with it, are included as artwork with the toolkit.

As you add graphic objects to a card, you need to keep in mind that each graphic object (or any object) occupies its own layer. As an object is added to a card, it becomes one layer higher than the previously added object. So, if you added ten different objects to a card (whether they be graphic objects, text objects, or buttons), the last one added to the card would be nine layers higher than the first one added. You can test this idea of layers out for yourself right now using the scene you just created. If you added Addy to the card first, then the doghouse, and then the bone, you should be able to place the doghouse over Addy, and the bone on top of the doghouse. Since objects are layered based on the order in which they are added to a card, you should take the time to give some thought to the overall design and function of a card, rather than just randomly adding objects.

This is not to say, however, that you cannot adjust an object's layer if necessary. To do so, click on the object once with the **arrow tool** (or its particular editing tool) to select it. Then, use either the **Bring Closer** or **Send Farther** commands in the **Objects** menu. These commands adjust the layer of the currently selected object front or back by one layer position. So, depending on how far forward or back an object is in relation to the other objects on the card, you might have to use one of these commands several times in a row. If you want to adjust an object to be five layers closer, you'd have to select **Bring Closer** five times. (It is much easier to press the keystroke shortcut that many times in a row than it is to choose the command from the menu.) If you want to make an object move all the way to the front or all the way to the back, press the **shift** key while selecting the command. Remember, none of these commands will work unless you have an object currently selected with an editing tool.

HyperHint→*Graphic objects created with the **lasso tool** cannot be resized. Graphic objects created with the **rectangle tool** can be manually resized using either the **arrow** or **graphic edit tool**. Clip art can be converted to graphic objects, but there is no direct way to convert graphic objects back to clip art.*

(A workaround to this, however, would be to **Export the Screen** *(explained at the end of Lesson 2), which saves the entire card as an art file. This file could then be imported back into the stack as a background or added as clip art.)*

Try a few more things with graphic objects before bringing this lesson to a close. Back in Lesson 5 you learned to create painted text and text objects. In the course of that lesson, it was hinted that there was a possibility of creating a third type of text. The following paragraphs are taken from a tutorial stack, included as part of a commercial multimedia product called **The Multimedia Yearbook Toolkit,** which can be used with *HyperStudio* to create interactive class or school yearbooks.

It's possible to create a third type of text which maximizes the strengths of text objects and painted text, while minimizing each of their weaknesses. This third type is called a "painted text" graphic.

Because painted text is part of the background, it can be selected and converted into a graphic object. In fact, it can be selected, first used as a cookie copier (covered in Lesson 10) to take on a pattern or texture, and then converted to a graphic object. The reason for turning painted text into a graphic object is that graphic objects, like text objects, float in front of the background, and can be easily moved or layered.

Take another look at the scorecard...

"Painted Text" Graphic

Strengths: *Does not require user to have the same font(s) in his/her system folder as used by stack author. Ideal for use with non-standard system fonts. Can have patterns and textures. Can be moved and layered without disturbing the background. Can carry out several actions.*

Weaknesses: *Cannot hold large amounts of text like a text object. Is not scrollable.*

Converting painted text to a graphic object results in a type of text with a combination of strengths. It looks painted, can be moved and layered like a text object, and possesses actions and features because it is a graphic object.

Creating a painted text graphic is simple. Just follow these steps...

(1) Paint some text onto a solid-colored background using the text tool.

(2) Use the lasso tool to select the text.

(3) While selected, choose **Add a Graphic Object...** *from the* **Objects** *menu.*

That is it. As a graphic object, the text can now carry out several actions and can have a colored frame. If you are an experienced user, you can even assign special features to the text.

This tutorial stack goes on to demonstrate eight different effects that can be created using "painted text" graphic objects, including relief text, embossed text, drop-shadow text, gilt-edged text, or glowing text.

For our last activity in this lesson, let's teach Addy how to respond to her name. Copy the graphic object of Addy and paste it onto a new card you have created. Now make three visible buttons. Name one button "Addy" and the other two any other names you would like. As you make each button, you will no doubt notice that the "Button Appearance" dialog box now includes access to "Features" (unlike it did in Lesson 6, when you weren't an experienced user yet). Click on **Features** as you create each button. In the "Item Features"

Item Features	
Object Type:	Graphic
Space Used:	2 K
Object Owner:	1
Object ID:	2
Object Card Position:	1

☐ Locked   ☐ Hidden
☐ Group object   ☐ Draggable

[none ▼]   [Cancel]   [OK]

dialog, check "Drop Off only." As mentioned earlier, buttons usually require a mouse down/mouse up combination to be activated. **Drop Off only** buttons are an exception to this. A button given this feature will not activate until a graphic object is "dropped" on it. Since Addy is a draggable graphic object, making each button **Drop Off only** will enable it to respond if Addy is placed on it. Don't check any of the other button item features.

Give each button an action to play a sound. For the "Addy" button, have it play the "SmallDog" sound clip from the HS Sounds folder. Assign some kind of negative response sound to each of the other two buttons—such as "StairBonk" or "GlassBreak." Or, you could record your voice saying something like, "Sorry, that is not it." An easy way to get the same sound for each button is to assign the sound to one button, and then select "In Use" for the sound source of the other button. This allows a button to play a sound currently being used by another button. In other words, the sound is only added to the stack once (saving memory), and can be "borrowed" by other buttons when needed.

Now for the exciting part. Drag Addy onto one of the buttons. If you pasted Addy on your card before creating each of the buttons, then this will not be possible just yet. In fact, Addy will end up going underneath each of your buttons. Remember, each object occupies its own layer, and since Addy was added first, she is in the lowest layer. Select Addy with the arrow tool and press **shift+**. Then switch back to the browse tool, and drag away. Addy should now bark in response to her name, while the other two names should elicit negative feedback for the user. You could use this technique to create all kinds of simple word recognition games, especially for primary students.

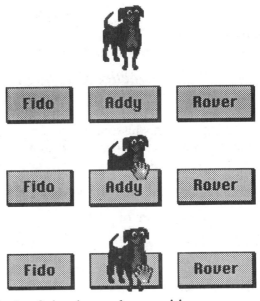

That is about it for this lesson. You are not quite done with graphic objects, or with objects in general. They will still play key roles in some of the upcoming lessons.

For more information about the *Family History Toolkit* or the *Multimedia Yearbook Toolkit,* contact Flecknology Innovations, 1235 Lomeda Lane, Beavercreek, OH. Ph/Fax (937) 427-0965. E-mail: tfleck@aol.com or timfleck@erinet.com.

HyperHands-On!
Student Task Cards—Lesson 8
"Practice Creating a Draggable Graphic Object and Drop Off Buttons"

(Beginning with this lesson, it is assumed that your teacher has set your copy of *HyperStudio* to "experienced user" status, and that you have either created a new stack, or you are working with a stack you have already started.)

Step 1. Import the "Tree" background from the HS Art folder onto a blank card.

Step 2. Add a picture of "Addy" as clip art and place it somewhere in the tree.

Step 3. Add a picture of "Addy" as a graphic object.

To add a graphic object to a card, select **Add a Graphic Object...** from the **Objects** menu. A dialog exactly like the one for importing backgrounds and adding clip art will appear, from which you can choose the source for the art file you wish to use. Select **Disk file.** (You can also select a piece of clip art or a part of the background, and then turn it into a graphic object using the same command.)

After selecting your source, another dialog will appear. It is almost exactly like the one for adding clip art (a scroll bar along the right and bottom sides, a "rectangle selector" and "lasso", a "Get another picture..." button, a "Cancel" button, and an "OK" button). The only difference is that the dialog title bar will read "Graphic Objects" instead of "Clip Art."

Step 4. Place the graphic object on the card.

After selecting the picture, you will return to your card. Place Addy somewhere up in the tree and then click outside the image. With clip art, this just deselects the image, but with graphic objects, clicking outside also brings up another dialog box.

Step 5. Set the appearance of the graphic object.

The "Graphic Appearance" dialog has several options to choose from. It is recommended you name your object rather than using "Untitled." Go ahead and name it "Addy." You can frame your graphic object if you'd like, choosing both the color and width of the frame. If the object is selected with the lasso, the frame wraps to the image. If the object is selected with the rectangle selector, the frame wraps to the rectangular area. A frame starts on the outside edge of a graphic object.

Selecting **Actions** will bring up the same dialog you used when making buttons in Lesson 6. So, graphic objects can act similar to buttons because they can perform actions if you click on them. For this example, don't set any actions for your "Addy" graphic.

Step 6. Set the features of the graphic object.

Clicking the **Features…** button brings up the "Item Features" dialog box. Here, you can make more choices about how the graphic object will behave. Check **Draggable**. This will make it possible for you to move "Addy" around the card with the browse **tool**. All objects (buttons, text objects and graphic objects) can be moved around using the **arrow tool** (or their respective special editing tools). But it is the **browse tool** that people need in order to *use* a stack. So *HyperStudio* provides the "draggable" feature to allow you to drag graphic objects around using the **browse tool**. Don't check any other features for this lesson.

Step 7. Drag your graphic object around on the card.

Click on **OK** in the "Graphic Appearance" window. With the **browse tool**, you should now be able to grab Addy and move her from place to place on the card. Notice that you can't move the Addy you added as clip art. And also notice that when you move the graphic Addy, nothing happens to the background.

Step 8. Teach Addy to bark at her name (Part 1).

Add three visible buttons to your card. Name one button "Addy" and the other two any other names you'd like. Set the "Features" for each button to "Drop Off only." "Drop Off only" buttons only do an action when a graphic object is "dropped" on them. Since Addy is a draggable graphic object, making each button "Drop Off only" will make it respond if Addy is placed on it. Don't check any of the other button item features for this lesson.

Step 9. Teach Addy to bark at her name (Part 2).

Give each button an action to play a sound. For the "Addy" button, have it play the "SmallDog" sound clip from the HS Sounds folder. Give a negative sound to each of the other two buttons—such as "StairBonk" or "GlassBreak." You could even record your voice saying something like, "Sorry, that is not the right name."

An easy way to get the same sound for each button is to assign the sound to one button, and then select **In Use** for the sound source of the other button. This allows a button to play a sound currently being used by another button. In other words, the sound is only added to the stack once (saving memory), and can be "borrowed" by other buttons when needed.

Step 10. Teach Addy to bark at her name (Part 3).

Before you can drag Addy onto any of the buttons, there is something you need to know. Every time an object is added to a card (whether it is a button, text object, or graphic object), it becomes the closest object (kind of like setting objects on top of each other on a desk). So, your buttons are closer than Addy is. If you try to drag Addy onto a button, she'll just end up going behind it. So, first select Addy with the arrow tool and press **shift+.** This is a keystroke command that will move Addy to the closest level.

Step 11. Teach Addy to bark at her name (Part 4).

Now, switch back to the browse tool and drag away. Whenever you drag Addy on top of the button with her name, she should bark. Whenever you drag her onto one of the other buttons, you should hear whatever negative sound you chose.

This is just one example showing how graphic objects can do much more than clip art can.

Lesson 9: Extra. Extra!

"Taking Advantage of HyperStudio's Extras"

HyperOverview:

Sometimes it is the little things that really count. After you work through this lesson *HyperStudio*'s little extras will be "headlining" a number of your future projects.

HyperHardware:

- NBAs & Extras folder (should be installed on hard drive)
- *HyperStudio* Program Resource CD

HyperPrerequisites:

- Working knowledge of drawing and selection tools, clip art, painted text, text objects, buttons, and button actions

HyperClinic:

By itself, *HyperStudio* is an absolutely incredible program. Using its Preferences dialog, you can customize *HyperStudio*'s performance to suit your needs. But not only can *HyperStudio* be customized, its performance can be expanded as well, by way of "extras." An "extra" is a small application, or add-on if you will, that expands *HyperStudio*'s capabilities, thus enabling the software to take advantage of new and innovative developments that come along. Extras are similar in function to the system extensions and control panels for your computer. In essence, they make it possible for *HyperStudio* to perform actions that were not originally a part of its built-in programming.

 When you installed *HyperStudio* on your computer, a folder containing "NBA's & Extras" was placed within the "*HyperStudio* for HD" folder, and some additional NBA/Extras files are located on the Resource CD. (we will explore the use of "NBA's" in Lesson 12.)

To actually use an extra, it must be a part of the **Extras** menu on the far right of the *HyperStudio* menu bar. A number of extras will be included in this menu already. However, to add or delete an extra(s) from the list, select the **Extra Manager**.

Extras
Box Maker
EarthPlot
Export WebPage
Extra Manager
LaserDisc Port Chooser
Menu Tamer
Message Box
Spell...
StoryBoard
Text Field Tamer
Tile It!
Title Card

To add an extra, click the **Add Extra...** button. Using the same basic steps for finding folders when Exporting Screens or Saving Stacks, locate the "NBA's & Extras" folder on your hard drive, or the folder by the same name on the Resource CD. Then simply select and open the particular extra you wish to add.

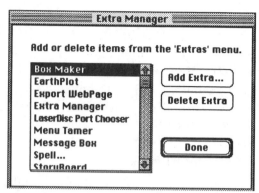

HyperHint→*Adding and deleting extras only affects whether or not they are available for use in the Extras menu. The files are not actually added or deleted from the hard drive or CD.*

Find out about some of the extras, most of which are included as part of the basic *HyperStudio* installation.

Box Maker can be used to create three-dimensional looking cubes. To use it, simply select it from the menu. *HyperStudio* will give you a tool in the shape of a cross. This tool will look familiar, since it is the same tool shape you get when using the **rectangle tool** (Lesson 2). Box Maker waits for you to draw a square or rectangle with this tool, which you do in exactly the same way as when using the **rectangle tool**. After you draw the shape and let up on the mouse, Box Maker extrudes it and provides you with a four-pointed cross, similar to the one you get when using any of the selection tools (Lesson 3). You can then set the depth or amount of extrusion for the "box" simply by moving the mouse. When you get a size and shape that you like, just click the mouse. That is all there is to it. Keep in mind that the box is painted onto the background. Its outline is always in whatever color is currently selected for the paint tools. It always draws in outline form, even if you have **Draw Filled** selected in the **Options** menu. However, you can affect the thickness of the outline by setting your **Line Size...** larger or smaller. Of course, you can always erase some of the lines and paint the sides with the **fill tool** or with a **gradient** after making the box.

HyperStudio has an interesting way to reinforce map skills with its **EarthPlot** extra, which enables you to create globes of the earth. By entering various coordinates into the EarthPlot dialog box, you can affect the size of the globe, and the viewpoint from which it is created. The current paint tool color determines the outline color of the continents, and the eraser color determines the

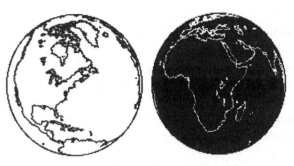

globe fill color. The globe on the left was created with the paint tool set to black and the eraser set to white. It shows the earth at 42°N latitude, 71°W longitude, from an altitude of 8 miles, and drawn at an earth width of 150 pixels. The globe on the right was created with the paint tool set to white and the eraser set to black. It shows the earth as viewed from 0° latitude, 30° E longitude, an altitude of 25 miles, and, like the first globe, at an earth width of 150 pixels. Globes can be easily recolored with the paint tools.

You will learn about the **Laserdisc Port Chooser** and **Export WebPage** extras in Lessons 17 and 18, respectively.

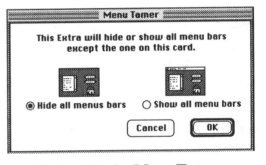

Menu Tamer is a handy little extra for hiding or showing all of the menu bars in a stack. As we learned in Lesson 7, you can use a command in the options menu to hide/show the menu bar on a card. But **Menu Tamer** lets you do this for all of the cards in one fell swoop (except for the current card). As stated in Lesson 7, one reason for hiding the menu bar in your stack is to give it a more professional look. **Menu Tamer** makes this a quick and painless process.

HyperHorizon: A spell checker extra will be included as part of HSMac 3.1 and HSWindows 3.0. Among its many other features, this spell checker will include the option of checking "painted" text, if the text is still active (see Lesson 5). **The Hyper Bee Spelling Checker** is an extra *now* available from The Byte Works, Inc. This spell checker extra features a host of options, and can even be used by people who still use HSMac 2.0. You can download a free demonstration version of the **Hyper Bee Spelling Checker** from the Macintosh StudioWare Library in the *HyperStudio* Forum on America Online.

Imagine seeing all of the cards in your stack at a glance. Imagine being able to change the arrangement of cards in your stack without having to copy and paste cards. Why imagine it when you can just *do* it. **StoryBoard** provides a convenient interface for viewing thumbnail sketches

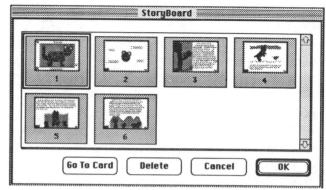

of all the cards in your stack. Deleting a card is as easy as selecting it and clicking on the **Delete** button. Swapping card positions is as easy as clicking on a card, holding down the mouse, and dragging the card to the position where you want it. You can select more than one card horizontally or vertically by holding the **shift** key as you click on each card. You can select any number of cards by holding the **shift** key while clicking on each card. If you want to move to a particular card after using StoryBoard, just select it and then press the **Go To Card** button. If you are satisfied with the changes you have made, click on **OK**. Otherwise, you can always **Cancel** what you have done.

HyperHint➔Depending on the types of card links you have made in your stack, you may have to reassign some of these links in your button actions after using StoryBoard.

Text Field Tamer is an extra that can definitely increase your productivity. Making text objects "Read only" helps prevent accidental changes, and makes your stack more presentable. Normally, you have to edit each text object in order to turn its "Read only" setting on or off. But with Text Field Tamer, you can do this for all the text objects on an entire card or in a stack at one time. Created by Ken Kashmarek and Bill Lynn, Text Field Tamer works with HSMac 2.0 or higher. It first appeared as part of the *HyperStudio* Journal (Volume 2.3) by Simtech Publications, and is currently available from the ***HyperStudio Journal*** Library of Feature Stacks for the Macintosh" at http://www.hsj.com/feature.html#tamer.

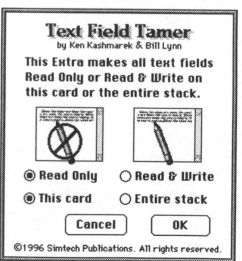

there is no law that says you have to work on the cards in your stack in order. As we saw with the StoryBoard extra, you can always go back and reposition how cards are arranged. As it is description states, **Title Card** makes turning the card you are currently on into the first card of the stack as easy as pushing a button.

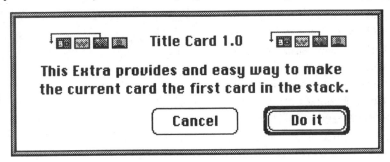

Well, that is a brief look at many of the extras currently available. No doubt more will enter onto the scene as *HyperStudio* continues to develop and evolve as the world's premiere multimedia authoring solution.

Take the HyperChallenge:

Let's do something a little different with this lesson. Try this challenge. The box and globe below were each created in a matter of minutes. Besides the **Box Maker** and **EarthPlot** extras themselves, the only tools used were the **eraser** and the **lasso**. The only menu commands used were **Replace Colors** and **Gradients**. Can you or any of your students figure out how to create objects similar to these?

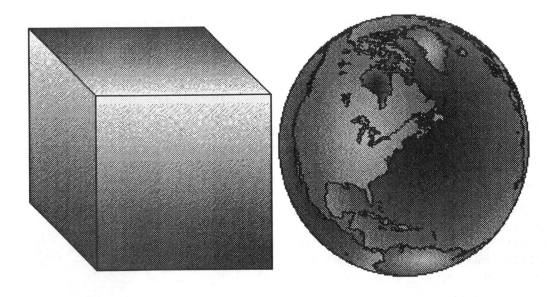

HyperHands-On!

Student Task Cards—Lesson 9

"Practice Using Some Extras"

Step 1. Practice using the **Box Maker** extra.

Box Maker can be used to create three-dimensional looking cubes. To use it, simply select it from the **Extras** menu. *HyperStudio* will give you a tool in the shape of a cross. This tool will look familiar, since it is the same tool shape you get when using the **rectangle tool** (Lesson 2). Box Maker waits for you to draw a square or rectangle with this tool, which you do exactly the same as when using the **rectangle tool**.

After you draw the shape and let up on the mouse, Box Maker makes your shape three-dimensional (it "extrudes" it) and provides you with a four-pointed cross, similar to the one you get when using any of the selection tools (Lesson 3). You can then set the depth (or amount of extrusion) for the box just by moving the mouse. When you get a size and shape that you like, just click the mouse. That is all there is to it.

The box is painted onto the background. Its outline is always in whatever color is currently selected for the paint tools (paint brush, pencil, etc.). It always draws in outline form, even if you have **Draw Filled** selected in the **Options** menu. You can affect the thickness of the outline by setting your **Line Size...** larger or smaller. Of course, you can always erase some of the lines and paint the sides with the fill tool or with a **gradient** after making the box.

Step 2. Practice using the **EarthPlot** extra.

You can increase your map skills with the **EarthPlot** extra. It allows you to create globes of the earth within seconds. You just enter various "coordinates" into the EarthPlot dialog box to affect the size of your globe, and the view from which you are looking at it.

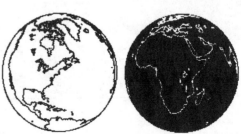

The current paint tool color determines the outline color of the continents, and the eraser color determines the globe fill color. The globe on the left was created with the paint tool set to black and the eraser set to white. It shows the earth at 42°N latitude, 71°W longitude, from an altitude of 8 miles, and drawn at an earth width of 75 pixels. The globe on the right (previous page) was created with the paint tool set to white and the eraser set to black. It shows the earth as viewed from 0° latitude, 30° E longitude, an altitude of 25 miles, and, like the first globe, at an earth width of 75 pixels. You can easily recolor a globe with the paint tools.

Step 3. Practice using other extras.

Check with your teacher to find out what other extras are available for you to use. Here are some very handy extras you should practice using:

Menu Tamer is an extra that will let you quickly hide or show all of the menu bars in a stack at one time.

The **StoryBoard** extra lets you see miniature versions of all of the cards in a stack at one time. Deleting a card is as easy as selecting it and clicking on the **Delete** button. Swapping card positions is as easy as clicking on a card, holding down the mouse, and dragging the card to the position where you want it. You can select more than one card across ("horizontally") or up and down ("vertically") by holding the **shift** key as you click on each card. You can select any number of cards by holding the **shift** key while clicking on each card. If you want to move to a particular card after using **StoryBoard**, just select it and then press the **Go To Card** button. If you are satisfied with the changes you have made, click on **OK**. Otherwise, you can always "Cancel" what you have done.

The **Title Card** extra lets you turn whatever card you are currently on into the first card of the stack at the push of a button.

Step 4. Take the HyperChallenge.

Let's do something a little different with this lesson. Try this challenge. The box and globe below were each created in a matter of minutes. Besides the **Box Maker** and **EarthPlot** extras themselves, the only tools used to make them were the **eraser** and the **lasso.** The only menu commands used were **Replace Colors** and **Gradients.** Can you (or your teacher) figure out how to create objects similar to these?

(Here is a clue: Ask your teacher about *option-clicking* the lasso.)

Lesson 10: A Cut Above the Rest!

"Cookie Cutter/Copier Techniques"

HyperOverview:

It's a holiday, and you are going to bake a batch of cookies. What do you need? Some eggs, some flour, some sugar… and your cookie cutters. You can't bake cookies with *HyperStudio* (not yet, at least), but you can use selected areas as cutouts or stencils to create some exciting, but simple, artistic effects in your stacks.

HyperHardware:

• *HyperStudio* Program Resource CD (Optional)

HyperPrerequisites:

• Working knowledge of drawing and selection tools, clip art, and painted text

HyperClinic:

You can be really adventurous in this lesson and make use of some artwork and photographic images from the Media Library folder on the Resource CD. Give Addy a rest.

Create a new stack in 640 x 480 card size. (If your computer monitor is too small for this size, that is fine. Go ahead and create your stack in the standard card size. You can just resize any background files you import if necessary.) Let's import a photo background for which we could do a really neat titling effect, such as the "Thunderbirds" photo (Figure 1) on the next page. The file path is *HyperStudio* CD: Media Library: Photo Gallery: Transportation by Air: Thunderbirds. Once you get your image, click on **Colors**. Notice something odd? What happened to all those nice colors that used to be in the color palette? Don't worry, nothing's wrong. It was mentioned back in Lesson 2 that each card can have its own set of 256 colors from the millions that are available. This particular photo has been imported with its own custom palette of colors. The photo appears its best when used with this set of colors. However, if you'd like, you can always convert an image to *HyperStudio*'s standard palette. To do so, just select **Standard Colors** from the **Options** menu. Don't be surprised if your screen temporarily displays a weird psychedelic array of colors. This is just *HyperStudio* at work remapping and dithering colors in the image to convert it to the standard palette. The final converted image probably won't appear as smooth as the original, since, it looks its best with its own custom set of colors.

*HyperHint→Backgrounds are always imported with their own custom palettes. Clip art is always added to match the palette. There is a way, however, to prevent a background from bringing in its custom palette. Select **About this Card...** from the **Objects** menu. Check **Lock colors** under **Card settings:** in the **About Card** dialog. So, if you were using the standard palette, you could lock the card's colors before bringing in the "Thunderbirds" photo. The photo would be imported already mapped to the standard palette. In effect, "Lock colors" converts a background as it is being imported, and Standard Colors converts the background once it is already on the card.*

Go ahead and convert your photo to the standard palette. Create a new card and erase it in a color other than white or black. Then use the text tool to paint the phrase "Go Thunderbirds!" onto the background. Select a thick font and a large font size for painting this phrase with. Paint the phrase three times: once in black, once in white, and the third time in whatever color you want, even black or white—it does not matter (Figure 2). With the lasso, select the white version of the phrase and move it on top of the black version, offsetting the two versions (Figure 3). Lasso the third phrase and cut it from the card. Move back to the first card and paste the phrase onto the background. Be sure to leave it selected. Paste it just below the Thunderbird jets (Figure 4).

Now for the exciting part. While the text is still selected, it is time to "cookie copy" the background. What this means is that we're going to copy a portion of the background up into the letters themselves. This is the "cookie copier" command. By using this command, the text becomes filled with any portion of the background beneath it. This can be thought of as the "soaker upper" command, because the result is that the background is soaked up into the text (Figure 5). The opposite command, is called the "cookie cutter" command. This command removes a portion of the background in the shape of the selected area.

Move back to the second card and paste the "cookie copied" text. There is no need to copy the text before leaving the first card—since the effect itself has been copied as part of the command. While it is still selected, move it on top of the black-white offset text you created. This will give it the look of having a shadow and highlight to it (Figure 6). Deselect the text to place it. Then use the lasso again and select all of the text on the card (Figure 7). Cut the text, move back to the first card, and paste it. Move it to the position you'd like, and deselect it to place it (Figure 8). The result will look like a portion of the clouds are in raised relief text.

HyperHint→*Before pasting the final text into place, you could always convert it to a "painted text" graphic object. That way, you would be able to adjust its placement later on if necessary without affecting the background.*

Now you are going to try a somewhat more spectacular effect. In the Resource CD Photo Gallery, You will find a picture of Bill Clinton. Use this to create an eye-catching screen as the opening to a make-believe interactive campaign stack.

To create this mock campaign screen, first make a new card and import the "President Clinton" art file from the Resource CD (Figure 9). The file path is *HyperStudio* CD: Media Library: Photo Gallery: People: President Clinton. Convert the image to the *HyperStudio* standard color palette to avoid having to deal with different palettes from card to card. Create another card and import the

"USA" background from the HS Art folder. We are going to jazz up the "USA" file by using it as a cookie cutter.) If the card size of your stack is 640 x 480, Addy will appear asking if you want to resize the image. ***Don't*** resize it.

HyperHint→There are 640 x 480 versions of all your favorite HS Art files on the HyperStudio Resource CD. Just follow this path to use any of them: HyperStudio CD: Media Library: HyperArt: HS Art 640 x 480.

Use the **pencil** or another paint tool to get rid of the frames around Alaska and Hawaii, and fill in all the blue around the states with some neutral color not found in the map itself (Figure 10). Use the **lasso** and select the USA. Cut the states from the card. Return to the Clinton card, paste the USA, and center it on top of Bill Clinton (Figure 11). Leave it selected and use the "cookie cutter" command. This will make a cutout from the photo in the shape of the USA (Figure 12).

Make a new card. Get the rectangle selector, select the top third of the card, and apply a blue to white vertical gradient. Select the bottom third of the card and apply a white to red vertical gradient. The result will be a card with an overall red, white, and blue gradient (Figure 13). Then paste the Clinton-USA cutout and center it how you'd like on the card. Add a little bit of painted text and you have got a professional-looking campaign screen (Figure 14).

Imagine how hard it would be to frame the Clinton photo by hand in the shape of the United States. But with the cookie cutter, it is practically effortless, and the final product takes only minutes to create.

We have only looked at two effects that can be achieved with cookie cutting/copying. But the capability to use selected pieces of art as "cutouts" or "frames" for other other pieces of art opens up an endless variety of possibilities for you and your students to experiment with.

HyperHorizons: *In the new updates to HSMac and HSWindows, the cookie cutter will be added as a selection in the Effects menu. Naturally, cookie cutting/copying will still be possible using the keystroke shortcuts as well.*

HyperHands-On!

Student Task Card—Lesson 10

"Practice Cookie Copying/Cutting"

Step 1. Import a background onto a card.

This can be any background you would like (something from the HS Art folder, the Media Library folder on the *HyperStudio* CD, etc.)

Step 2. Add a piece of art to a new card.

This art can be an image you add directly as clip art, a figure you draw with the paint tools, or a word(s) you make as painted text. If you paint some text, use a thick font (such as Chicago), and make it a large size (such as 48, 72, or 96).

Step 3. Select your piece of art using the lasso.

Remember: Any color in your piece of art that is the same as the color you start the lasso in will be ignored (Lessons 3 and 4). So, make sure the surrounding color is something different than any colors used in the artwork.

Step 4. With your piece of art selected, copy it.

Step 5. Move to the card with the background you chose.

Step 6. Paste your piece of art onto the background. Be sure to leave it selected.

Step 7. Make a cookie copy.

With your art still selected, use the "cookie copier" command. By using this command, your art becomes filled with any portion of the background beneath it. The opposite command, is called the "cookie cutter" command. This command removes a portion of the background in the shape of the selected area.

Step 8. Return to the other card, or make a new card.

Step 9. Paste your cookie copy.

You don't have to copy something once it has been cookie copied or cut because the commands do this automatically.

Step 10. Move the cookie copy where you want it, and then click off it to place it.

Neat, huh?. Experiment some more, and have your teacher show you some other exciting possibilities.

Lesson 11: Standing the Test of Time

"Using Buttons as Test Responses and Automatic Timers"

HyperOverview:

How many times have you heard someone say that computers will eventually run our lives, or that computers seem to have a mind of their own? TV and movies do a lot to fuel anxiety based on this misconception. The fact that computers can perform certain functions more accurately and more efficiently than people does not make them a threat. On the contrary. If anything, this provides people with more time for creativity and recreation. As an example, the draft of this tutorial is being created using a computer and desktop publishing software. All of the editing is done on screen before ever printing to paper. You don't waste nearly as much time (or paper) as you would if you were writing this tutorial by hand, or typing it on a typewriter. And while a lesson is printing, you can focus your attention on other tasks or activities.

Computers don't complain (well, not usually) about work. They patiently await our input while serving our needs. They keep track of operations and statistics, they organize files, and they can synthesize all of this information within moments upon request. But it is still people who program these operations, and who determine how best to make use of the information.

The human brain will never be eclipsed as the ultimate computer. It can signal the release of chemicals and the flow of blood, respond to a myriad of stimuli, and monitor and control the function of organs—all without the need for conscious effort—and still allow us to ponder the very meaning of life if we so choose. Imagine if each of these bodily functions required our constant, conscious effort. We would spend all of our time struggling to stay alive, with no time left over to enjoy it. Computers can provide us with time. They can take care of a host of difficult or burdensome tasks, allowing us to focus our energies and efforts into more meaningful pursuits.

HyperHardware:

HyperStudio Program Resource CD (Optional)

HyperPrerequisites:

A good understanding of creating buttons and text objects, and accessing files

HyperClinic:

In this lesson, we will look at two ways *HyperStudio* can save you some time and effort. Of course, as you have no doubt realized, creating stacks does take an initial investment of time and effort. But that factor is inherent in any creation, with or without technology.

This first time an effort saver is primarily for you, the teacher, and involves using *HyperStudio* to create interactive tests or quizzes. Back in Lesson 8, it was demonstrated how you could create a series of buttons, each of which would respond with a sound effect when a graphic of Addy was placed on it. That was one way of creating a simple testing interface to provide immediate feedback to the user. Often, however, immediate feedback could interfere with the validity of a test. With *HyperStudio*, it is possible to create tests that keep track of student responses in a separate file. Each student's performance can be monitored, but the correct/incorrect answers to each question need not be divulged during the actual taking of the test itself.

Create a new stack (Use 640 x 480 card size if possible). Before actually doing any work in the stack, save it. *Follow the steps outlined in Lessons 2 and 6 for creating a new folder into which the stack will be saved.* Let's call the folder "My HS Test Folder," and the stack itself "Moon Test."

HyperHint→Back in Lesson 6, the recommendation was made that you should save your stacks in folders. Let's reiterate this point, and add that this will prevent problems if you ever transfer your stacks from one computer to another. Don't save stacks, or any disk-based files they access, directly to the hard drive. First, create a folder on the hard drive, and then save the stack and its files into this folder. If you create a series of stacks that are linked together, the entire series of stacks should be saved into the same folder location. Saving stacks, and the files they access, directly *to the hard drive can result in some troublesome headaches down the road.*

"Moon Test" will end up being a small, 4-card testing stack about the moon. On the first card of this stack, import "Astronaut on moon." The file path is *HyperStudio* CD: Media Library: Photo Gallery: Space: Astronaut on moon. Then, create a text object for the first test question, and place it about an inch from the bottom. Make it almost as long as the card is wide, and about a half inch tall or so.

"Astronaut on moon" is such a great photo that it seems a shame to create a text object on it. But if we use painted text for the question, we won't be able to edit it or move it very easily later on. It sure would be nice if there was a way to create text that was both easy to edit (as in a text object) and was not framed in a field of color (like painted text). Well... you guessed it... there is.

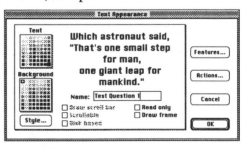

Now that you are an experienced user, you will notice a new button is available to you in the "Text Appearance Dialog." As with buttons and graphic objects, it is the **Features...** button. Click on it. This will bring up the "Item Features..." dialog. In this dialog is the option to make your text object "Transparent." This enables the background of the text object to be hidden, while only the text itself can be seen. The text object becomes like a see-through pane of glass with writing on it. When you check **Transparent**, Addy will immediately appear to tell you

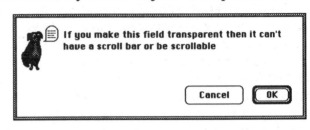

that it is not possible for a transparent text object to be scrollable or have a scrollbar. This is one of the current limitations of transparent text objects. However, this will not pose any problem in your case, since you are only entering one question in the text object. Just click on **OK.**

By making our text object transparent, the question we type will look like it is actually printed on the photograph itself. But because it is an object and not painted text, we can always go back and edit the text, reposition it, etc. To truly make the text look as if it is on the background, do *not* check "Draw Frame." For this example, Chicago, black, size 18 was used for the text itself. The text was also center-aligned in the "Text Style" dialog.

HyperHint➔Remember, it is a good idea to get in the habit of naming each of your objects. This text object was named "Test Question 1." Never leave something called "Untitled." Plus, in the next lesson, we will learn about some actions that actually take advantage of named objects.

Type the following statement in the text object: Choose the astronaut who said, "That is one small step for man, one giant leap for mankind." we will make the text object "Read only" at the very end.

Now it is time to create a set of response buttons. Unlike the buttons we made in Lesson 8, these buttons will not provide any user feedback. When any one of these buttons is clicked on, it will simply record the student's choice, and then move right on to the next card. Create the first button. This example uses the

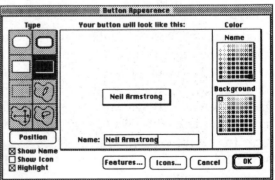

drop shadow rectangle button type (black text on a white background). Name the button "Neil Armstrong" (make sure **Show Name** is checked). You should also check "Highlight." Click on **Position** or **OK** to place the button on the card. Place it just below the question, and toward the left hand side of the card. Click off the button to bring up the "Actions" dialog. In the "Actions" dialog, check **Testing functions…**. This, in turn, brings up the

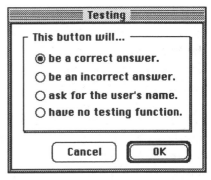

"Testing" dialog, which enables you to set whether a button represents a correct or an incorrect answer. It can also be used to get the user's name (which we will do a little later). The default setting is for a button to have no testing function. Check "be a correct answer," and then close the dialog by clicking on **OK**.

Don't close the "Actions" dialog just yet. Select **Next Card** under **Places to Go**. (In this example, the button was given a "Fade to black" transition at medium speed.) That is all it takes. "Neil Armstrong" is now a testing button and, if clicked on, will register a correct response and then move right on to the next card, giving the user only one opportunity to choose his/her answer. Don't try out the button just yet. Resist the temptation until we finish the stack.

Figure 1

Create two more buttons similar to this one. Give one the name "Edwin Aldrin" and the other "Michael Collins." Make sure each is set to move to the next card (Use the same transition and speed). Unlike the "Neil Armstrong" button, each of these needs to be set to register an incorrect answer. Your final card should look something like Figure 1.

Create a new card, and import the "Moon" background from the same folder on the CD. The previous card used a multiple choice format. Let's do a true/false format on this one. As in Figure 2, create a transparent text object that reads, "Only one side of the moon ever faces the earth." Then, create a "True" button and a "False" button. Do you know which one should be set as the correct response? That is right. Since the moon's periods of rotation and revolution are the same, only one side ever faces

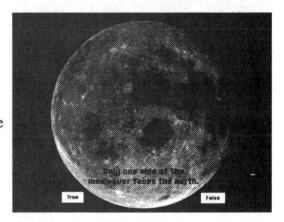

Figure 2

toward the earth. (Remember the fear everyone felt when Apollo 13 went out of radio contact as it orbited around the "dark" side of the moon?) As on the previous card, make sure each of these buttons is set to move to the next card. Speaking of which, have you saved your stack in the last few minutes?

Create a third card, which could be used to restart the test for the next user. On this card, import the "Earth from moon" photo. Create a large, transparent text object from the top of the card down to the edge of the moon's surface (see Figure 3). Since most of the card is very dark, use white type. At the top of the object, write "It is now time to head back to earth. I hope your mission has been a successful one." Return several lines to the bottom of the text object and write the instruction "Click on planet earth

Figure 3

to return home." To make the instruction less pronounced than the message at the top, highlight this line of text, and make it a smaller font size (the example uses size 14). One way to be able to click on "planet earth" to return home is to

Figure 4

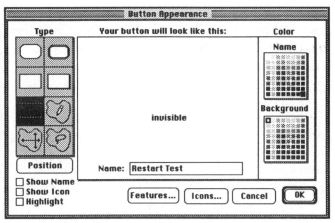

place an invisible button on top of it. As in Figure 4, create an invisible button just large enough to cover the earth in the photo. In this example, the button is named "Restart Test." The name, icon, and highlight options were left unchecked, however. In this case, options would be distracting, and would take away from the impact of the card itself. As with all of the previous buttons, set this one to move to the next card. Don't assign it any testing functions.

Create the fourth and last card. Import the "Launch shuttle clear" photo for the background. Sure it was the mission of the Apollo program—not the Space Shuttle—to land on the moon. But there aren't any pictures of a Saturn V rocket in the Photo Gallery folder.) Let's use this card to start the test. Huh?. To start the test? How can that be? This is Card 4. Ah, yes, but remember, with *HyperStudio*, it is not necessary to create cards in order, since buttons have the capability to take you anywhere (remember the "Wonkavator" analogy in Lesson 6?). In this case, however, we're going to let a few extras we learned about in Lesson 9 help us reorganize everything.

Make a transparent text object and type, "You are about to begin a mission of understanding. Your destination: the moon. Click on the space shuttle to get underway." Set the font color for white, and set the alignment for centered text. Highlight the space shuttle instructions and set the font size smaller to make it less pronounced. (See Figure 5.) As on the previous card, an invisible was created, which, in this case, was placed over the space shuttle. Set the button to move to the next card. Give the

Figure 5

card some personality by setting the button to also play a sound when clicked. One possibility is the sound "Rocket" (file path *HyperStudio* CD: Media Library: Sound & Music: Button Sounds: Rocket). The button needs one more very important action. Check **Testing functions**. Remember, the "Testing" dialog allows you not only to set a button for a correct or incorrect response, but can also get the name of the person using the stack. Check **ask for the user's name**.

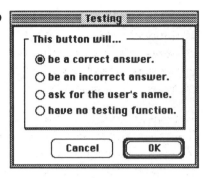

Exit the "Testing" and "Actions" dialogs. The button is complete. Don't click on it just yet. The temptation is practically overwhelming. Save the stack, and keep telling yourself that it is going to be really cool when it is all done.

Although there is no requirement that a stack's cards must be created in order, attention to order is still an important consideration. Barring certain exceptions, a stack always opens up to its first card. So, as this stack stands right now, a student would first encounter two cards-worth of questions, then a card to restart the test, and finally a card allowing him/her to register to take the test he/she just took and restarted. That would be pretty confusing.

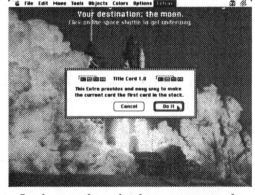

While on Card 4, select the **Title Card** extra, and click on **Do it**. Instantly, Card 4 becomes Card 1 (Figure 6). The original Card 1 becomes Card 2, and so on. Let's say, though, that you wanted Card 3 to come before Card 2. Get the **StoryBoard** extra. Click on Card 3 and drag it onto Card 2. Card 3 will become Card 2, and Card 2 will become Card 3.

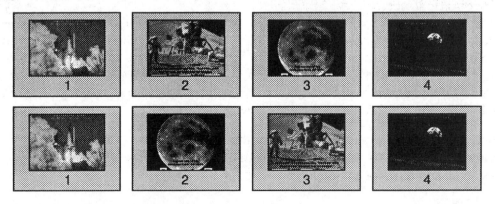

Our test is nearly complete. When it is, our initial investment of time and effort will pay off. Not only could it present an engaging testing environment for students, but it will record the name of each student who uses it, along with the answers he/she chooses. It will do all the grading. Just be patient for a few more minutes. This would be a good time to save your stack.

Here is another time-saving capability that can be incorporated into the stack. There are a few ways to make actions occur on their own on a particular card without requiring someone to click on a button. One method is to select **About this Card** from the **Objects** menu. This brings up a dialog that allows you to set an action(s) to occur upon arriving at, leaving, or clicking on a card. This presents some advantages over creating a button(s). The card itself acts like an object. Perhaps we will use these advantages in a future lesson. But for now, let's incorporate into the test the ability for one of the cards to play a sound without having to be clicked on. We don't want it to play upon leaving the card; instead we would like for it to occur shortly after the user arrives at the card. This is easy enough to do upon arriving at a card, but the only choice would be for the sound to begin immediately. In order for an action to occur on its own after a set period of time, it must be placed in either a button, graphic object, or text object. You will be sticking with buttons.

HyperHint→*Remember, with HSMac 3.0, any objects can be assigned to carry out actions—not just buttons. We have been using buttons in this lesson because they are easy to create, and, for those people using earlier versions of* HyperStudio, *they represent the only way to carry out actions.*

On Card 3, create a button that will play Neil Armstrong's famous words. Make an invisible button. Position it up at the top left corner of the card so that it is out of the way, and size it rather small. Select **Automatic timer...** in the "Actions" dialog. This dialog allows you to have an action(s)  occur immediately upon arriving at a card, to set a certain amount of seconds to go by before the action(s) occur, and to have the action(s) repeat over and over again. Set the sound to begin playing two seconds after the user arrives at the card. Don't set it to repeat. Click on **OK.** Then check **Play a sound...** and in the "Tape deck" dialog select **Disk Library**.

It is possible to extract sounds directly from other stacks to use in your own. There is an excellent set of stacks covering **The Apollo Program** (produced by students and staff for the Edgewater High School Engineering, Science, &

Technology Magnet Program) on the Resource CD. One of these stacks includes the use of a recording of Neil Armstrong's comment as he stepped onto the surface of the moon. To add it to the auto-timed button on Card 3, follow this file path after clicking on **Disk Library** (*HyperStudio* CD: Sample Projects: At School: Apollo Program *f*: The Apollo Project: Stacks: Exit). Open the "Exit" stack, and the tape deck will show the sound "Step." Now just close the "Tape deck" and "Actions" dialogs. The recording will start playing a few seconds later, and anytime someone comes to this card.

HyperHint→Auto-timed buttons can sometimes be a nuisance while creating a stack. If you don't want a button(s) to automatically activate while you are working on a stack, just uncheck the option "Turn on Automatic Timers & HyperLinks" in the "Preferences" dialog. Remember to check it again when your stack is finished.

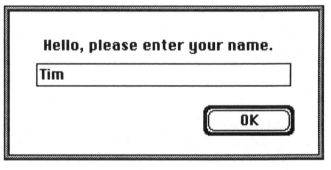

Now for the moment you have been waiting for. After saving the stack, return to Card 1. Click on the space shuttle. A message box will appear. Type your name in the space provided and click on **OK**. The rocket sound should play as the stack moves to Card 2. Click either answer on Card 2. The stack will move on to Card 3. A few seconds after reaching Card 3, you should hear the recording of Neil Armstrong. Click any one of the answer buttons. The stack will move on to Card 4. (Click on the earth and the stack returns to Card 1).

Okay, you got to take your interactive test, but your enthusiasm remains unsatisfied because *HyperStudio* did not tell you the results. Well, actually, it has. You see, while you were busy taking the test, *HyperStudio* was busy creating a little text file in your test folder. Create a new stack, and save it immediately as "Moon Test Results." Then, create a text object. Go with the default settings in the "Text Appearance Dialog" (scrollable, scrollbar, frame). Click on **Get File**. Locate your test folder, and you will find a file called "HS.Test.Results." Open it.

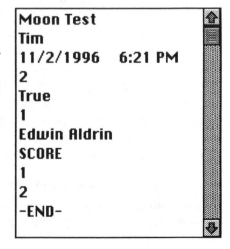

In the "Text Appearance" dialog, check "Disk based." This will make it possible to see the latest results without always having to reopen the "HS.Test.Results" file. Each time someone takes your test, the results file will be updated. And, because the text object in your "Moon Test Results" stack accesses this as a disk-based file, you will always have a convenient way of checking the results.

As seen in the example on the previous page, *HyperStudio* created a file while you took the test that...

    (a) recorded the name of the testing stack

    (b) recorded the name of the person who took the test

    (c) recorded the date and time at which the test was taken

    (d) recorded the names of the buttons clicked on, and

    (e) calculated the overall score

HS.Test.Results

Because the "HS.Test.Results" file is a text file, you can also open it with any word processing program—even TeachText or SimpleText. This file can be printed out as well, even from within *HyperStudio*. If the file already exists for your test, then *HyperStudio* will update it whenever the test is used. The original file is not replaced, so you don't need to worry about losing earlier results. *HyperStudio* merely continues adding to the list of information. If you would like, you can drag the "HS.Test.Results" file to the trash can to delete it. The next time the test is used, *HyperStudio* will create another results file.

With testing functions, *HyperStudio* enables you to create engaging evaluation stacks to use with your students. You may want to consider locking such stacks to prevent "inquisitive" students from editing buttons to figure out answers, etc. Make sure you remember the password. If you have access to several computers, you can save your stack(s) onto each one, thus making it possible for several students to test at the same time. Each test will produce its own results file.

Even more exciting than having students use *HyperStudio*-created tests is to allow them to create their own. In fact, student-created multimedia tests are excellent evaluation tools.

Auto-timed buttons are one way of enabling actions to occur without user intervention. With them, you can create self-running stacks. Imagine having a stack that welcomes parents to Open House. Each card could display something about the classroom or school, wait for several seconds, and then move to the next card. Such a stack would require an initial investment of your time to be created, but would leave you free to meet with parents and students during the event itself.

HyperHands-On!

Student Task Card—Lesson 11

"Practice Making an Automatic Timer Button"

An automatic timer button allows an action or combination of actions to happen (or "activate") without someone having to click the button with the **browse tool**.

Step 1. Make an invisible, automatic timer button.

Position it in a corner of the card so that it is out of the way, and size it rather small. Select **Automatic timer...** in the "Actions" dialog. The "Automatic Timer" dialog allows you to set an action(s)...

> **Automatic Timer**
>
> ○ Do these actions as soon as card is shown
> ● Do these actions after card is shown
>   activate after `3` seconds.
>
> ☐ Repeating (activate actions again and again)
>
> [Cancel] [OK]

- to occur immediately upon arriving at a card
- to occur after a number of seconds go by, and
- to have the action(s) repeat over and over again

For this practice, set the "timer" to activate after three seconds. Don't set it to repeat. Click on **OK** to return to the "Actions" dialog.

Step 2. Set the button to play a sound.

Check **Play a sound...** in the "Actions" dialog, and in the "Tape deck" select **Samples** or **Disk Library** (or record your own sound if your computer has a microphone).

Step 3. Exit the "Actions" dialog to complete the button.

Step 4. Move to another card.

Step 5. Make sure that "Turn on Automatic Timers & HyperLinks" is checked in the "Preferences" dialog.

Only use the "Preferences" dialog with your teacher's permission.

Step 6. Move back to the card with the automatic timer button.

After three seconds, you should hear the sound you selected or recorded.

Lesson 12: Playing in the NBA

"Using New Button Actions"

HyperOverview:

Without a doubt there are students in your class who idolize basketball players such as Michael Jordan, and who dream of one day playing in the NBA. But the reality is that very few children ever grow up to be NBA stars.

There is another reality, though. Children learn *HyperStudio* very quickly, and, given regular opportunities to use it in challenging ways, can become quite skilled at it.

HyperStudio has its own NBA—New Button Actions. With you as the coach, your students can not only play, but become NBA stars. Introduce your students to new button actions, and Michael Jordan won't be the only name topping their list of idols.

HyperHardware:

- *HyperStudio* Program Resource CD (optional)

- A computer with speech capability (if using the BlabberMouth NBA)

HyperPrerequisites:

- A good understanding of creating, naming, and assigning actions to buttons

- A good understanding of creating, naming, and setting features for graphic and text objects

HyperClinic:

This lesson will provide you with a brief introduction to four of *HyperStudio*'s sample New Button Actions: **HideShow**, **GhostWriter**, **RollCredits**, and **BlabberMouth**. Like the Extras described in Lesson 9, NBA's expand *HyperStudio*'s capabilities, and enable it to take advantage of new and innovative developments that come along. Although the name implies that they are new "button" actions, users of HSMac 3.0 can actually use NBA's with any objects, and/or with HyperText Links or entire cards or stacks (Lesson 13).

Create an interactive stack based on Edgar Allan Poe's "The Raven." Especially if you are a language arts teacher, this stack should convince you of the power of NBAs to bring literature to life. After this, you will doubt "nevermore."

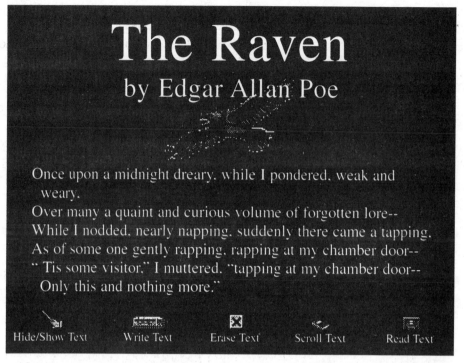

The Raven
by Edgar Allan Poe

Once upon a midnight dreary. while I pondered. weak and
   weary.
Over many a quaint and curious volume of forgotten lore--
While I nodded. nearly napping. suddenly there came a tapping.
As of some one gently rapping. rapping at my chamber door--
" Tis some visitor." I muttered. "tapping at my chamber door--
   Only this and nothing more."

| Hide/Show Text | Write Text | Erase Text | Scroll Text | Read Text |

"The Raven" stack will consist of only one card. Yet this card will enable you to
hide and show the poem, magically write it, erase it, scroll it automatically, and
have the computer read a portion of it. We will do all of this with just five
buttons, two text objects, and one graphic object.

Start by creating a new stack. A 640 x 480 card size was used, and, to establish
an ominous look befitting the poem, the background was erased in black. The
HS Resource CD has a terrific drawing by Ted Nicholas of a raven on it. If you
don't have the CD,
you could always
create your own using
the paint tools,
possibly locate a
similar image on
another CD, or
simply do without.
You might be quite
surprised to even find
a picture of a raven
on the CD.

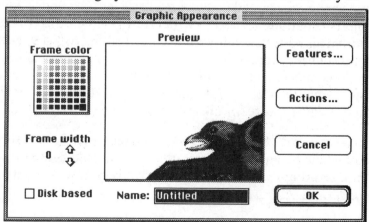

If you have the CD, add the raven to the card as clip art using the **lasso tool** (the file path is *HyperStudio* CD: Media Library: Animal Kingdom: Birds: Raven). Once you get it on the card, *don't* click off it. Leave it selected and scale it down in size. You may want to scale the raven by 50%. After scaling it, convert it to a graphic object. Give it a dark gray frame (one pixel wide), and name it "Raven."

Create a text object for the title. The example was made as wide as the card, and about an inch and a half tall. This would accommodate any text added, and would guarantee that the text could be perfectly centered. The object was made transparent with no frame, since a portion of it was on top of the raven's wing. "The Raven" was written in Palatino, white, size 72, center-aligned. In the text object itself, a return was put in after the title, and "by Edgar Allan Poe" was typed. The phrase was selected with the **browse tool**, then **Text Style** was selected, and the text was set to size 36. The text object was double-clicked on with the **arrow tool** and made to read only.

Create a second text object for the poem itself, and name it "Raven Text." This object was made about two inches tall, and about as wide as the card itself. The text color was set to white, and the background color to black. Don't make the object transparent. Transparent text

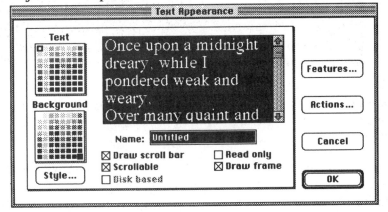

objects cannot be scrolled, and two of the NBA's we will be using require that the text object have the ability to scroll. Check **Scrollable**, but leave all the other options unchecked.

*HyperHint→If you check **Draw scroll bar**, you need to check **Scrollable** in order for it to function. However, a text object can be **Scrollable** without having a scroll bar. A scroll bar simply makes it easier to scroll the text. In a text object without a scroll bar, you can still scroll through the text using the up and down arrow keys on the keyboard (assuming you don't make the object "Read only"). Another way to scroll text without a scroll bar is to use the Roll Credits NBA, which we will be learning about shortly.*

In order to scroll, there must be more text in a text object than can be displayed in the field at one time. So, to make sure you have enough text to scroll (but to save time as well), type just the first three stanzas of "The Raven" in the object. Set the text style for Palatino, size 20. If you are working through this example, the first three stanzas read as follows. Be sure to add enough returns after the third stanza to ensure that the text will be able to scroll completely out of sight.

Once upon a midnight dreary, while I pondered, weak and
weary,
Over many a quaint and curious volume of forgotten lore —
While I nodded, nearly napping, suddenly there came a tapping,
As of someone gently rapping, rapping at my chamber door —
" 'Tis some visitor," I muttered, "tapping at my chamber door —
Only this and nothing more."

Ah, distinctly I remember it was in the bleak December;
And each separate dying ember wrought its ghost upon the floor.
Eagerly I wished the morrow;—vainly I had tried to borrow
From my books surcease of sorrow—sorrow for the lost Lenore —
For the rare and radiant maiden whom the angels name Lenore —
Nameless here for evermore.

And the silken, sad, uncertain rustling of each purple curtain
Thrilled me—filled me with fantastic terrors never felt before;
So that now, to still the beating of my heart, I stood repeating
" 'Tis some visitor entreating entrance at my chamber door; —
This it is and nothing more."

Create your first button. This button will be used to cause the text of the poem to disappear and reappear. The example used the invisible button design, set to show the button name ("Hide/Show Text" in white), to show an icon (a hand holding a magic wand from the icon samples), and to highlight. The button was positioned near the bottom left hand side of the card. In the "Actions" dialog, **New Button Actions**, was selected, and was presented with the "NBA" dialog. The **HideShow NBA** was selected, which brought up yet another dialog box.

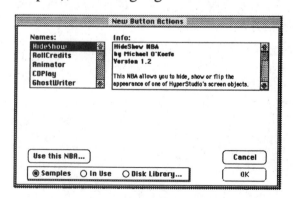

This NBA is very easy and fun to use. In the "HideShow dialog," simply enter the exact name of the object you wish to hide and/or show, which, in this case, is the poem in the "Raven Text" text object. Check **text field** for the kind of object, and **flip** for what to do with it. "Flip" gives you the most flexibility with this NBA by allowing you to hide the text if it is showing, and show it if it is hiding. The result is that the text can

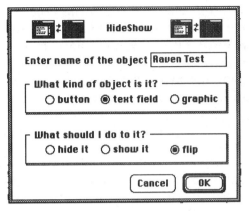

be turned on and off repeatedly. Click on **OK** and try it out. Click the button and your text should disappear. Click the button again and the text should reappear. This is a very popular NBA with students. It is a lot of fun to use, and makes it possible to display text on a card only when it is needed. Adding a sound (like a click) to a button that uses this NBA can enhance the effect.

Okay, okay. Stop playing with your hide/show button. It is addicting, but we have got more creating to do. Make a second button. This button will magically write the text of the poem letter by letter, as if a ghost is typing at the keyboard. Use an invisible button design again, show the button name ("Write Text" in white, show an icon the keyboard from the icon samples was used here), and set it to highlight. Position it a little to the right of the first button. Select **New Button Actions** again, and in the "NBA" dialog select the **GhostWriter NBA**. As with all of the NBA's, GhostWriter includes "Info" text fully explaining its use. In sum, GhostWriter allows you to specify the name of the text object, the speed at which the text is typed, and the actual text to be typed. The text object name and speed setting must each be enclosed in a set of curly brackets: { }. You don't need to leave a space between the name and speed, nor do you need to leave a space between the speed and actual text to be typed. The brackets are sufficient. Something to keep in mind: GhostWriter cannot enter text into a text object that is read only.

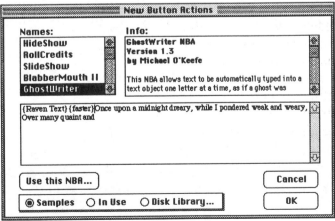

HyperHint→An easy way to enter the text you want typed by GhostWriter is to copy it from the text object itself and paste it into the GhostWriter text area. Better still, select and **cut** *the original text from the text object, and then paste it into GhostWriter. This not only saves you time having to retype the text for GhostWriter to use, but also leaves the original text object empty. GhostWriter enters text into the object* after *any text that is already present. Cutting the original text of the poem is not only a time saver for entering it into the GhostWriter dialog, but will also guarantee an empty field into which GhostWriter can type.*

Since the text in "Raven Text" is set to white, you won't see any of it when you first paste it into GhostWriter. Don't worry about it. It's still there. Now just exit the "NBA" and "Actions" dialogs. Click on your button. Is that amazing or what?. Text that appears to be typing itself.

The problem is, you have to cut or delete the text from the object before each time you want to use GhostWriter. This can become annoying really fast. One easy solution is to create a button for erasing the text. Create a third button and name it "Erase Text." Design it just like the two previous buttons—The example has an "X" sample icon—and place it next to the "Write Text" button. This third

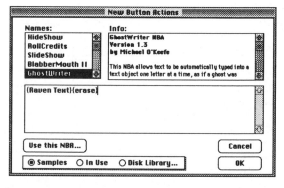

button will also use GhostWriter. GhostWriter not only has the ability to type text, but to erase it as well. Get to the "New Button Actions" dialog, but don't select GhostWriter. This time, click first on the button called **In Use**. This gives a list of any NBAs already "in use" by the stack. From this list, select GhostWriter. The information text describes a couple of different options for erasing text with GhostWriter, the easiest of which is to simply enter the name of the text object and the command "erase." Make sure each is enclosed in curly brackets. That is it. Exit the dialogs and try out the button. It should instantly erase all the text in the object.

HyperHint→Don't confuse "hiding" the text with "erasing" it. When the HideShow NBA hides a text object, it simply puts it out of sight. The text of the field is not removed. When the GhostWriter NBA erases text, it leaves the text object in sight, but removes any text from within it.

Time for the next button. Again, create an invisible button, set it to highlight, show name, etc. The example was named "Scroll Text," give it a sample icon of a book, and positioned it next to the "Erase Text" button. From the "Samples" in the NBA dialog, select the **RollCredits NBA**. This NBA performs automatic scrolling of text, and, like its description indicates, is great for creating rolling credits like on TV and in the movies. In order for this NBA to work, the text object you want to scroll must have more text in it than can be displayed at one time in the field. The object itself does not actually have to be set as "scrollable."

In the "RollCredits NBA" dialog, enter the name of the text object you want to scroll. To have RollCredits scroll all the way to the end of the field, leave the number of steps set at 0. Adjust the number of steps per second to set a scrolling speed you are satisfied with. Leave yours at the default rate of 20. You can also set the text to scroll by lines or by pixels. Lines scroll much more quickly; pixels scroll much more smoothly. Set RollCredits to scroll "Raven Text" by pixels, and set the amount of each step at 1 pixel. To get a good idea of how your particular settings will affect the scrolling of your text, just click on the **Test Speed** button. The only real way to judge for sure, though, is to exit the dialog and try it out. So, make your settings and try out your button. If you are not satisfied, you can always edit the button.

*HyperHint→To edit a button containing an NBA, you need to uncheck the little box next to **New Button Actions...** in the "Actions" dialog, and then immediately check it back on again. Don't exit the "Actions" dialog after unchecking "New Button Actions...." You must use an uncheck/recheck combination to get to the "NBAs" dialog. An easy way to get to the "Actions" dialog when editing a button is to press the ⌘ key while double-clicking the button with the **arrow tool** (or the **button editing tool**).*

Since we added several returns after the third stanza of the poem, the text should scroll until it is out of sight. Another neat thing to do is have text start out of sight and suddenly appear as it is scrolling. To do this, just make sure you precede the text with several returns as well.

You may be wondering how to reset the text after it is been scrolled. Since it is not read only, you can always click in it with the **browse tool**, and then press the up **arrow** on the keyboard to move back to the beginning. This can be time-consuming, though, especially if the object contains numerous lines of text. Another option is to click two separate times on the "Hide/Show Text" button you made. This resets the text almost immediately, but is only a good option if you have such a button handy. A third option is to use **shift–tab** twice.

Remember, **shift–tab** is the easy way to switch between the browse and arrow tools. Use **shift–tab** to get the arrow tool. This will immediately reset the text. Then, press **shift–tab** again to get the browse tool back so that you can click the button again if you wish.

It is time to make the fifth and final button for this lesson. This button will only work, though, if your Computer has the Speech Manager extension installed in your System folder. If you have an "AV" Macintosh (such as a Quadra 660AV or 840AV), a PowerMac, or another model of Macintosh introduced since 1994 (such as a newer Performa or LC model), or if you are computer has some version of System 7.5 on it, chances are pretty good that you have Speech Manager available.

If you have Speech Manager, create your fifth button in the same style as the previous four. Name yours "Read Text" and give it a sample icon of an audio cassette. In the "New Button Actions" dialog, select the **BlabberMouth II NBA**. The "BlabberMouth" dialog will then appear, and is quite easy to use. A number of speaking voices should be listed on the right hand side. These voices correspond to the Voices folder that should also be installed in your System folder (in the same Extensions folder as the Speech Manager). Choose the speaking voice. Of course, a "Vincent Price" voice for Speech Manager would be the ultimate choice. You can set whatever voice you choose to speak at a faster or slower rate, as well as at a higher or lower pitch. The only other thing needed is to either type in the name of the text object you want BlabberMouth to read text from, or to type in the specific text you want read. BlabberMouth currently has a 250-character limit in the amount of text it can read. Each letter, punctuation, and space counts as a character. BlabberMouth will only be able to read to the end of the fourth line in the first stanza. So, select this amount of

text, copy it, and pasted it into the text area of the BlabberMouth II NBA. You can always type the text in, or just enter the name of the text object and let BlabberMouth read as far as it can.

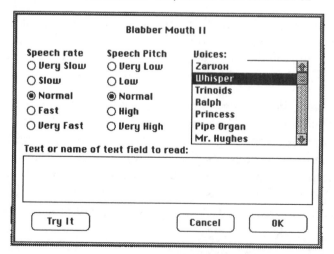

Some voices are better than others. Some are of higher quality, and do a much better job of pronouncing letter combinations correctly. However, no voice is perfect. You may have to type some words phonetically in the BlabberMouth text area. For example, "Victoria" (a very high-quality voice) pronounces *HyperStudio* as "hipperstudio." If you type the word "hiyperstudio," Victoria pronounces it correctly.

Well, you should now have a one-card stack that brings some extra excitement to Poe's classic work. And that was with just four NBAs. In later lessons, we will cover a few other NBAs. Imagine what this poem would be like if some spooky music were also playing in the background. Well, save your stack, and when we learn about the CDPlay NBA, this is something you just might want to do.

 This lesson covered some of the sample NBA's that are listed in the "New Button Actions" dialog. The "NBA's & Extras" folder within your "*HyperStudio* for HD" folder contains additional NBA's, as does the "More NBA's" folder in the "HS Utilities" folder on the HS Resource CD.

HyperHorizons: HSMac 3.1 and HSWindows 3.0 will both include a new HideShow 2 NBA. This new version of an old favorite will allow for transition effects when hiding and showing objects.

Don't forget we made the raven itself a graphic object. You might want to go back and edit it. Give it the BlabberMouth NBA, and have it quote "Nevermore."

HyperHands-On!

Student Task Cards—Lesson 12

"Practice Using Some Sample NBA's (New Button Actions)"

Step 1. Make a text object.

Don't make this text object transparent. Transparent text objects cannot be scrolled, and two of the NBA's we will be using require that the text object have the ability to scroll. Check **Scrollable**, but leave all the other options unchecked. Be sure to give the text object a name. Remember this name, and exactly how to spell it.

HyperHint→If you check "Draw scroll bar," you also need to check "Scrollable" in order for the scroll bar to work. However, a text object can be "Scrollable" without having a scroll bar. A scroll bar just makes it easier to scroll the text. In a text object without a scroll bar, you can still scroll through the text using the up and down arrow keys on the keyboard (if you have not already made the text object "Read only"). Another way to scroll text without a scroll bar is to use the Roll Credits NBA, which you will be using in a few minutes.

Step 2. Type some text into the text object.

In order to scroll, there must be more text in a text object than can be displayed in the field at one time. So, make sure you type enough text to be scrolled, and be sure to add enough returns after the last line for the text to be able to scroll completely out of sight.

Step 3. Make a button to make the text object disappear and reappear.

Create your first NBA button. You can make it any design you would like. In the "Actions" dialog, select **New Button Actions**. Then, in the "NBA" dialog, select the **HideShow NBA**.

This NBA is very easy and fun to use. In the "HideShow" dialog, just type the exact name of your text object. Check **text field** for the kind of object, and "flip" for what to do with it. "Flip" allows you to hide the text if it is showing, and show it if it is hiding. The result is that the text can be turned on and off repeatedly. Click on **OK** and try it out. Click the button and your text should disappear. Click the button again and the text should reappear. Adding a sound (like a click) to a button that uses this NBA can help add to the hide/show effect.

Step 4. Make a button to write the text in the text object letter by letter.

Select **New Button Actions** again, and in the "NBA" dialog select the **Ghost-Writer NBA.** Be sure to read through the instructions that are shown when you select this NBA. GhostWriter allows you to specify the name of the text object, the speed at which the text is typed, and the actual text to be typed. The text object name and speed setting must each be enclosed in a set of curly brackets: {}. You don't need to leave a space between the name and speed, and you don't need to leave a space between the speed and actual text to be typed. The brackets are enough. For example, you could type:

{name of your text object}{fast}The actual words in your text object.

Something to keep in mind: GhostWriter cannot enter text into a text object that is read only.

HyperHint→An easy way to enter the text you want typed by GhostWriter is to copy it from the text object itself and paste it into the GhostWriter text area. Better still, select and cut the original text from the text object, and then paste it into GhostWriter. This not only saves you time having to retype the text for GhostWriter to use, but also leaves the original text object empty. GhostWriter enters text into the object after any text that is already there. Cutting the original text of the poem is not only a time saver for entering it into the GhostWriter dialog, but will guarantee an empty field into which GhostWriter can type.

Now just exit the "NBA" and "Actions" dialogs. Click on your button. Is that amazing or what? Text that appears to be typing itself. If you are not satisfied with the speed you set for GhostWriter, just go back and edit the button.

Step 5. Make a button to erase the text from the text object.

The problem with GhostWriter is that you have to cut or delete the text from the text object before each time you click the button. That can get annoying really fast. One easy solution is to create a button for erasing the text. Create a third button, calling it "Erase Text."

This third button will also use GhostWriter. GhostWriter not only types text, but can erase it too. Get to the "New Button Actions" dialog, but *don't* select GhostWriter. This time, click first on the choice called **In Use**. This gives a list of any NBA's already "in use" by the stack. From this list, select **GhostWriter**.

The information text describes a couple of different ways to erase text with GhostWriter. The easiest way is just to type the name of the text object and the command "erase." Make sure each word is enclosed in curly brackets.

{name of your text object}{erase}

That is all you have to do. Exit the dialogs and try out the button. It should instantly erase all the text in your text object.

HyperHint→Don't confuse "hiding" the text with "erasing" it. When the HideShow NBA hides a text object, it just puts it out of sight. The text of the field is not removed. When the GhostWriter NBA erases text, it leaves the text object in sight, but removes any text inside of it.

Step 6. Make a button to automatically scroll your text.

For your fourth button, select the **RollCredits NBA** from the "Samples" in the NBA dialog. This NBA is great for creating rolling credits like on TV and in the movies. In order for this NBA to work, your text object *must* have more text in it than can be displayed at one time in the field.

In the "RollCredits NBA" dialog, enter the name of your text object. To have RollCredits scroll all the way to the end of the field, leave the number of steps set at 0.

Adjust the number of steps per second to set a scrolling speed you like.

You can also set the text to scroll by lines or by pixels. Lines scroll more quickly, but pixels scroll much more smoothly. To get a good idea of how your particular settings will affect the scrolling of your text, just click on the **Test Speed** button. The only real way to know for sure, though, is to finish the button and try it out. If you are not satisfied, you can always edit the button.

HyperHint→To edit a button containing an NBA, you need to uncheck the little box next to "New Button Actions..." in the "Actions" dialog, and then immediately check it back on again. Don't exit the "Actions" dialog after unchecking "New Button Actions...". You need to use an uncheck/recheck combination to get back to the "NBAs" dialog to make any changes.

Step 7. Reset the text in your text object after it is been scrolled.

One way to reset the text is to click in the text object with the **browse tool**, and then press the **up arrow** on the keyboard to move back to the beginning. This can take time, though, especially if your text object has several lines of text. Another way is to click two separate times on the "Hide/Show Text" button you made. This resets the text almost immediately. A third way is to press **shift–tab** twice. **Shift–tab** is the shortcut way to switch between the **browse** and **arrow tools**. Use **shift–tab** to get the **arrow tool**. This will immediately reset the text. Then, press **shift–tab** again to get the **browse tool** back so that you can click the button again if you want to.

Step 8. Make a button to speak your text.

Before making this button, check with your teacher to find out whether or not your computer has *Speech Manager* installed. It has to be installed in order for this button to work.

If you do have *Speech Manager*, create your fifth button. In the "New Button Actions" dialog, select the **BlabberMouth II NBA**. The "BlabberMouth" dialog will appear and is very easy to use. A number of speaking voices should be listed on the right hand side.

You can set whatever voice you choose to speak at a faster or slower speed (or "rate"), as well as at a higher or lower tone (or "pitch").

You can either type in the name of the text object you want BlabberMouth to read text from, or type in the exact text you want it to read. BlabberMouth can only read up to 250 characters. Each letter, punctuation mark, and space counts as one character.

Some voices are better than others. Some are of higher quality, and do a much better job of pronouncing letter combinations correctly. However, no voice is perfect. You may have to type some words how they sound (or "phonetically") in the BlabberMouth text area. For example, Victoria (a very high-quality voice) pronounces "*HyperStudio*" as "hipperstudio." If you type "hiyperstudio," Victoria will pronounce it correctly.

Complete the button and try it out. Not only is it exciting to hear the computer speaking your text, but it also takes a lot less computer memory to use BlabberMouth than it does to use recorded sound.

Lesson 13: Word Up!

"HyperText Links"

HyperOverview:

Creating objects is not the only way to get things to happen in a stack. Whole cards can behave as if they are objects, as can entire stacks. One of the most effective ways to generate actions in a stack, however, is to assign them to individual words and phrases. Text can get really *hyper* with *HyperStudio*.

HyperPrerequisites:

- A good understanding of assigning actions to objects
- A good understanding of creating and working with text objects

HyperClinic:

Actions are actions are actions. You can add actions to any object in a stack—a button, graphic object, or text object. An action will occur no matter what object it is assigned to. Each kind of object adds its own unique set of strengths to a stack. Deciding which one(s) will carry out a certain action(s) depends on the effect you are going for in the stack—a sixth sense that comes from time and experience creating with *HyperStudio*.

With the introduction of HSMac 3.0, it became possible to add actions to text—a technique called **hypertext links**. This technique is not the same as adding actions to an entire text object. With hypertext links, actions can occur when a single character, word, or phrase within a text object is clicked. This simply was not possible before. The only way to come close to this was to place invisible buttons over a portion of text. And if this portion of text was in a scrolling text object, then the word and button wouldn't always line up. With the option to create hypertext links, this crude method is no longer necessary. If you have ever "surfed the Internet," then you have probably used hypertext links. Perhaps you have moved from web page to web page by clicking on portions of colored text. If so, you have used hypertext links. In fact, the standard web developing language *HTML* stands for *HyperText Markup Language*. *We will* explore some of *HyperStudio*'s Internet capabilities in Lesson 18. But you don't need to be connected to the Internet to use hypertext links in *HyperStudio*.

You already have some working knowledge of using actions. So, rather than walk you through the creation of a stack for this lesson, a few examples have been highlighted that will demonstrate effective use of hypertext links. In the first case we will see how students might create an interactive class yearbook. Each section of the yearbook is designed as its own stack, and all of the stacks are saved into a common folder. Finally a "table of contents" stack can be created, which is used to move to any of the other stacks. This stack uses one text object, in which each topic is made a hypertext link to a particular stack. To create a link to "Class Activities," for instance, the phrase itself was highlighted with the **browse tool**. We then use **Hypertext Links...** in the **Objects** menu. The phrase appeared at the bottom of the "Hypertext Links" dialog. We click the **Add link** button to add it to the list of links. The "Action..." button provided access to the "Actions" dialog, where **Another stack...** and **Play a sound...** is checked. The appropriate stack in the yearbook folder was selected. To give the impression of turning the page to move to this stack, give it a "Right to left" transition at medium speed. The "page turn" sound can be made by recording the actual turning of a book page with the microphone. When you finish with the link, exit the "Actions" dialog, and then click on **Done** in the "Hypertext Links" dialog. The other links can be created in the same manner.

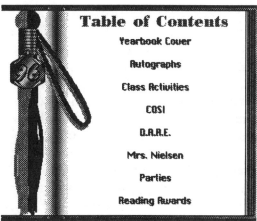

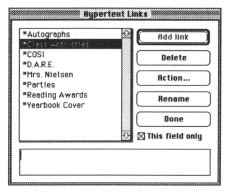

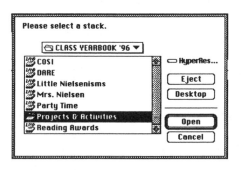

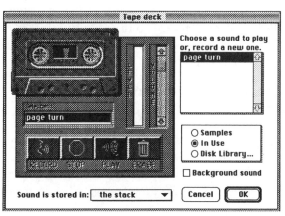

Issue 2.3 of the ***HyperStudio Journal*** featured a stack on the *Titanic* by two students, Michael Mukai and Jonathan Youngman. This stack was created as part of a research project called **Stack Attack!** (included among the school sample stacks on the HS Resource CD). *Titanic* is well-designed, and features a wealth of information, original artwork, and *HyperStudio* techniques. One card in this stack features a quiz on action verbs, which Michael and Jonathan created using hypertext links. The card itself was created to resemble an old-fashioned mail room. Each mailbox handle is a graphic object, which, when clicked on, uses the HideShow NBA to display a text object with a sentence about the *Titanic* in it.

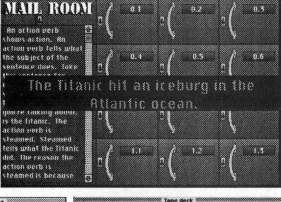

The boys selected various portions of each sentence, and created hypertext links which played sounds to indicate whether or not these

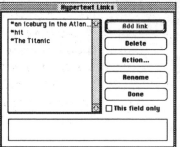

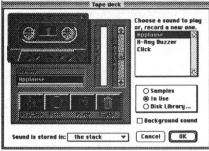

portions were action verbs. When the stack was presented in class, other students could come forward to take the quiz. If a student correctly identified the action verb in a given sentence, *HyperStudio* would play an "Applause" effect. If the student was incorrect, *HyperStudio* played a "Buzzer" sound.

Like the rest of *HyperStudio*'s capabilities, hypertext links are powerfully simple to use.

HyperHint→*Active hypertext links can sometimes be bothersome while creating a stack. If you don't want any links you have created to activate while you are working on a stack, just uncheck the option **Turn on Automatic Timers & HyperLinks** in the "Preferences" dialog. Remember to check it again when your stack is finished.*

Lesson 14: Multimedia in Motion

"Creating Frame and Path-Based Animations"

HyperOverview:

The art of animation is an old one. It had its humble beginnings in such early moving picture devices as the thaumatrope, the phenakistoscope, the zoetrope... and "tropes" and "scopes" of all kinds. No doubt you have seen and/or made your own flip books. Each of these objects simulates motion by flashing a series of still images at a high speed. The images are displayed so quickly one after the other that our brain perceives motion. Even a modern day film or video is nothing more than a series of still images played at high speed.

More and more, the computer is being used as an animation tool. As audiences have come to expect greater realism in action scenes, the computer has begun to replace crude miniature models and figures. In fact, these days it is quite common to see commercials and cartoons (and now full-length movies) created entirely by computer animation.

The great animation studios of today are successful for two main reasons: (1) they employ dedicated artists who work many hours to produce quality images, musical scores, etc., and (2) they carefully select and develop the stories and messages they choose to bring to life. *HyperStudio* has made the basic tools of animation development available and affordable to the masses. But just having the tools is not enough. Motivation, dedication, and application are all essential ingredients in creating animations that not only make an impact, but convey information.

HyperPrerequisites:

- A good understanding of assigning actions to objects

- A good understanding of using the paint and selection tools

- A good understanding of exporting screens, importing backgrounds, and adding clip art

HyperClinic:

HyperStudio enables you to create two types of animation: frame animation and path-based animation. Each has its own advantages and limitations. Frame animation involves creating a series of still "frames" or cells that change slightly from one to another. It is basically the same method that professional animators use. Because this type of animation often requires the creation of several individual frames, it can also require a great deal of time. Frame animations can require a lot of memory, too. Path-based animation is generally easier to create, and simply involves moving a graphic through a "path" on the screen. This path is recorded, and can then be played back. For animations that simply require something to move through a path—such as a fish swimming in a bowl, or an airplane flying across the sky—path animation is the more efficient way to go. However, no actual movement can be shown in a path animation. For example, it would not be possible to show a fish swimming in a bowl *while* moving its fins. This could only be accomplished with frame animation. Knowing a little about each type of animation will help you make the best use of each.

You will be starting with frame animation. When you installed *HyperStudio* on your computer, a starter "HS Animation" folder was created within the *HyperStudio* for HD folder. Let's make use of one of the sample sets of frame animation images included in this folder. Create a new stack (standard card size). Since the sample animation images are already created, we simply need to add a button (or any object, for that matter) to animate them. But before doing that, let's take a few minutes to study a set of images to get an idea of how the overall animation will be achieved. On Card 1, import "Addy.1" from the "Addy" folder within the HS Animation folder as a background (file path *HyperStudio* for HD: HS Animation: Addy: Addy.1). Create a new card. On Card 2, import "Addy.2." Continue this process for a total of seven cards. Addy will appear to sit up and jump through a hoop. In fact, she does this from two directions at the same time. Hmmm… wonder if Addy has a secret twin. Actually, each file includes two animation frames so that you could either play a sequence from right to left or left to right.

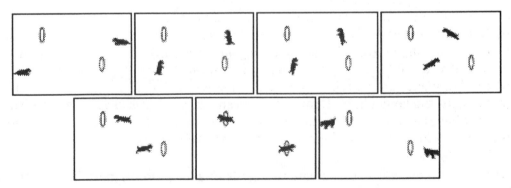

Notice that the hoops never move. Addy, however, changes both in her position on each card and in her body design—giving the illusion of movement. This sequence is clearly intended for use in a frame animation.

But moving back and forth from card to card is not a very efficient way to run an animation. Create a new card. On Card 8, just create a very basic button. You could name it something like "See Addy's trick." Position it somewhere near the bottom of the card, and then click off it to place it. Select **Play frame animation...** in the "Actions"

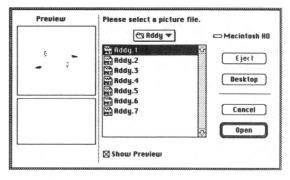

dialog. A dialog box will appear. (It is identical to the one you see when importing backgrounds and clip art.) This dialog normally defaults to the HS Art folder. However, since you just imported each of the files from the Addy folder,

that is the folder that should appear open on your computer at this point. If you ever need to get to the HS Animation folder, just move out one level from the HS Art folder, and it should appear among the listed folders in the *HyperStudio* for HD folder.

From the Addy folder, open any one of the numbered Addy files. Any one of the files in the sequence can be selected. *HyperStudio* takes care

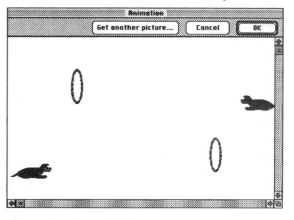

of animating them in the right order.) *HyperStudio* will display a window, similar in design to the one for selecting clip art. Unlike selecting clip art, however, this window only allows you to select a rectangular area. It is important to keep in mind that you need to select the entire area in which the animation will take place. So, make sure you select an area all the way from the end of Addy's tail to well past the hoop itself. Remember that in the last frame, Addy lands on her feet beyond the hoop. Make sure you select enough vertical area as well. In this sequence, Addy never goes higher than the hoop, nor lower than her reclined position.

After selecting the area you want, click on **OK** (or press either the **return** or **enter** key, remember?). *HyperStudio* will place the selected animation frame area in the middle of the card. This is by default. If you want, you can position the animation elsewhere on the card. Make sure you click inside the area to move it. Click outside the area to indicate to *HyperStudio* that the animation has been placed where you want it.

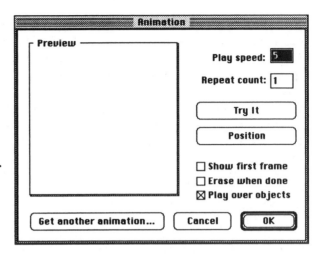

The "Animation" dialog will then appear. This dialog provides a number of controls and features to make adjustments to your animation. "Play speed" sets the rate at which the frames are animated. This rate is in 60ths of a second. The default value of five represents 5/60ths of a second. This is equivalent to 12 frames per second, which is quite fast. At this speed, Addy would jump through the hoop in just over half a second. A value of 15 would be equivalent to four frames per second. At this rate, the Addy would take just under two seconds to perform her trick. A value of 30 would be 30/60ths of a second, or two frames per second. At this rate, Addy would require just under four seconds to display her talent. You get the idea. Just keep in mind that the lower the number, the higher the speed. Set your speed for a value you like, depending on how energetic you think Addy is. The "Repeat count" establishes the number of times you want the animation to play. Set it too high and you will wear poor Addy out. Check **Show first frame** if you want the first frame of the animation to appear when the user arrives at the card. This is good to check if you don't want the animation to appear out of nowhere. The first frame looks as if it is clip art on the card, that is until the animation occurs. "Erase when done" makes the animation disappear after it has run its course. So, if you check this setting for the Addy animation, Addy will perform her stunt and then disappear. "Play over objects" enables the animation to play over any buttons, text objects, or graphic objects that might be located where it is playing. You can use the "Try it" button to see a preview of how the animation will run. If you need to adjust the position of the animation, just click on the **Position** button. And you can always change your mind and "Get another animation...". When you are satisfied with everything, click on **OK**. If you ever decide later to make changes, simply edit the button (or whatever object the animation is added to).

HyperHint→While frame animations will not play over objects unless you check this item in the "Animation" dialog, they will play over any preexisting clip art. Without careful planning, this can result in an undesired side effect. Always try to size and position a frame animation so that it appears as a natural part of the card.

Using a pre-made animation sequence is fun, but it is not nearly as exiting as creating your own original frame animation. While it may take time and planning to create the actual frames, the overall method is quite easy. Back in Lesson 2, you learned how to save cards as picture files—a command known as "Exporting the screen." To create a frame animation, you simply need to export a series of picture files. Just like the Addy files were saved in a folder, it is strongly recommended that you save your own animation files in folders. In order for *HyperStudio* to play the files back, they must all be named and numbered in a consistent format.

Make your own quick animation sequence. Create a new card. Draw a simple smiling face on it. Then, export the screen as "Face.1," and save it in a folder that you will call "Face Animation." Use the paint tools and slightly edit the face to give it less of a smile. Don't move the face—just adjust its features slightly. Export the screen again, calling it "Face 2." Change the face a little more, and export it as "Face.3." Create as many frames as you want in this manner until you get the face with a frown on it. Then, either erase the card, or create a new one. Add a button on the card, and select one of the "Face" files from your folder. Follow the steps outlined earlier in this lesson. Within minutes, you will have a basic animation of someone smiling and frowning.

The more you work with frame animations, the more ambitious you will become. Frame animations can be as simple or as stunning as you are willing to make them. Keep in mind, that frame animations can require a lot of memory. This can be a result of the number of frames involved, the number of colors used, and/or the animation area required.

Path-based animations are created using the **Animator NBA.** While path-based animations are limited in that they cannot show moving or changing parts, there are still numerous special effects that you can create with this NBA.

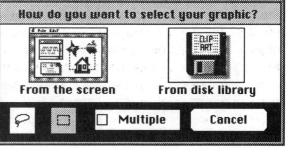

Since we seem to have rediscovered the true multimedia wonders of Addy, let's have her finish out this lesson with a feat of daredevil driving. Create a new card. Paint the word "ADDY" in very large text onto the background. Use a font with a stenciled design to it if you have one. The example on the previous page uses Steamer, size 190. We are going to convert one part of each letter into a graphic object. If you don't have a stenciled font like Steamer, that is okay. You can just make every other letter a graphic object. Before converting parts of the letters to graphic objects, fill each letter with a pattern if you would like. The example uses the brick pattern. Then, lasso one portion of each letter and convert it to a graphic object. Don't bother to give it any features or actions.

After this, create a button. In the "Actions" dialog, choose **New Button Actions**, and then **Animator** from the list in the "NBA" dialog. A dialog will appear asking you to select the piece of art for your animation, along with a choice of the **lasso** or the **rectangle selector**. The art can come directly from the card itself, or from a disk file. Click on the **rectangle selector** and choose **From disk library**." Then select the file **Addy With Cars & Paws**. When the art is displayed, select one of the pictures of Addy driving. Your card will return, along with the image you just selected. The Animator NBA is waiting for you to create a path.

To create a path, you simply move the image around on the card while holding the mouse button down. When you let up on the mouse, the Animator stops recording. However, it still waits for you, in case you want to record some more of the path. If you press the **shift** key, the image will move in a straight path. Place the car to the right of the letters and just off the screen. Press **shift**, hold down the mouse, and then drag the car in front of the letters, all the way to the far left hand side of the screen. To let Animator know that you are done recording your path, press **return**.

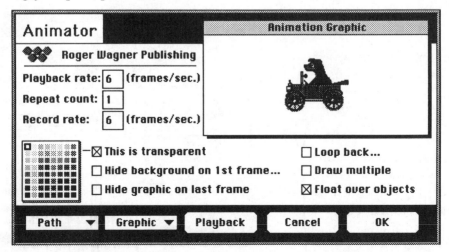

The "Animator" dialog appears, in which you can set a host of characteristics for your animation. As with frame animations, you can set the speed and repeat count. You can even adjust the record rate, resulting in smoother, less jerky paths. In this dialog, the speed number represents frames per second; therefore, the higher the number, the faster the animation. Since we selected the picture of Addy with the "rectangle selector," make sure **This is transparent** is checked on, and the color white is chosen. "Float over objects" enables the animation to play on top of buttons, text objects, and/or graphic objects. Uncheck this option. That way, Addy's car will not be able to drive in front of any of the portions of the letters we converted to graphic objects. The result will be Addy weaving in and out between the letters.

HyperHint➔Whenever you are creating a path-based animation, it always plays over any objects, whether or not "Float over objects" is checked. When the animation is created and the button is done, the path behaves according to the chosen settings.

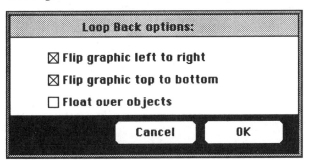

"Loop back..." allows the animation to play in reverse after it is completed. In this example, Addy is driving back in the direction she came from while upside down. You can use the "Loop back..." options dialog to toggle between floating and not floating over objects. That way, Addy could weave between letters as she drives from right to left, and then in front of all the letters when she goes back left to right.

"Draw multiple" draws each position the image was in during the creation of the path. In short, the picture is drawn multiple times. In Addy's driving animation, this setting does not produce a very desirable result.

You can always edit the path or create a new one. You can also select a new graphic, and/or make horizontal or vertical adjustments to it.

Finally, with the animation completed, you can click on the button (or other object to which it is assigned) while the animation is being run. By clicking the animation button every few seconds you can get three Addy triplets to drive across the screen.

This lesson has been but a brief introduction to marvels of multimedia in motion. As with a number of other topics addressed in this tutorial, entire books could be written just on the art of *HyperStudio* animation tricks and techniques alone.

HyperHorizons: HSMac 3.1 and HSWindows 3.0 will introduce a new type of animation capability which merges frame and path-based animation.

Lesson 15: Stacking Things in Your Favor

*"Increasing Productivity with Ready Made Cards &
Group Cards"*

HyperOverview:

Written by Frank Gilbreth, Jr., and Ernestine Gilbreth Carey, **Cheaper by the
Dozen** is the true, and very humorous, story of Frank and Lillian Gilbreth and
their 12 children. Frank Gilbreth was an efficiency expert, and a pioneer in the
field of motion study. He was a consultant for businesses and factories, teaching
them methods to speed up production by reducing wasted motions. He also
brought his work home with him. Frank Gilbreth believed that motion study
could and should be applied to the raising of children. This led to some amazing,
but often hilarious, results. Upon his untimely death, his wife carried on the
work and became one of the foremost experts in the field.

One barrier to getting teachers to use *HyperStudio* is that it requires work. It
takes time and effort to create stacks. It's much easier just to go out and buy
some prepackaged piece of software. But this software is not tailor-made to your
particular classroom needs, nor do you get to experience the satisfaction of
creating your own programs from scratch.

Veteran users of *HyperStudio* take advantage of as many techniques as possible
to save time and disk space when developing stacks. They experience the thrill
of creating, while reducing the amount of effort required. Throughout this
tutorial, numerous techniques have been presented that can help you to be a more
productive user of *HyperStudio*. This lesson covers a few more techniques that
you will find invaluable. So let's carry on the great Gilbreth tradition.

HyperPrerequisites:

A good understanding of backgrounds and objects

HyperClinic:

Perhaps you have used a word processing or desktop publishing program that
allows you to create and save documents as stationery files. Stationery files serve
as templates that you can use over and over again to create new documents. For
example, if you produce a weekly newsletter, you can create a stationery version
that has all of your font, spacing, margins, tabs, and other document settings
already preset. The stationery file could even have the newsletter name and logo

already in place. Then, when it is time to create the next newsletter, you can just open a copy of this stationery file and start typing immediately. You can focus your time and attention just on the information, since the stationery opens with all of your preestablished settings. Why create the newsletter from scratch each time? This would be an inefficient use of your time. Establish the settings once, save the document as a stationery template, and then reuse it.

 HyperStudio allows you to work with stationery templates, too. In the *HyperStudio* folder on your hard drive is a "Ready Made Cards" folder. All of the sample stacks located in the Ready Made Cards folder contain just one card each. Ready made cards are one-card stacks that can be used in other stacks as if they are cards. That is right. Stacks that can be used as cards!

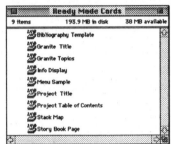

Suppose you create a card design for a project, and you want to reuse this card in the future. It contains artwork, text objects, buttons, etc., that you have carefully planned out and designed, and you would like to use this card as a template in other projects. No problem. Just save it as a one-card stack into the Ready Made Cards folder.

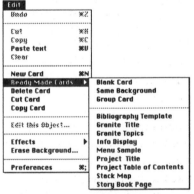

To access a ready made card from within *HyperStudio*, just select **Ready Made Cards** in the **Edit** menu, and then select the particular one you want from the submenu. When students create research stacks, require that they include bibliographies listing their various sources for information, graphics, sound files, etc. Recommend that they use the "Bibliography Template," since it is already prepared for this very purpose. They can devote their time to accurately listing their sources, rather than worrying about the design of the card itself. This also gives them more time to spend on the rest of the stack, which is as it should be.

Like new cards, ready made cards are added to the stack immediately after the card you are currently working on.

HyperHint→*If you save a stack to the Ready Made Cards folder, it will not be available in the Ready Made Cards menu until the next time you use* HyperStudio. *So, don't be alarmed if you save a stack but don't see it listed in the menu. The stack was saved, but will not appear in the menu list until you quit* HyperStudio *and restart it, since the list is created as* HyperStudio *starts up.*

Create a new stack in standard card size. Import the "USA" background from the HS Art folder that we have used a few times before. Then, use the **Same Background** command from the **Ready Made Cards** menu. This command is similar to the New Card command, with the added bonus of creating the new card with the same background as the previous card. This command is a faster way to add multiple cards with identical backgrounds to a stack than having to use New Card and Import Background each time.

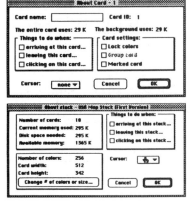

Use the **Same Background** command another eight times, until you have ten USA map cards. Then, select **About this Card...** from the **Objects** menu. The "About Card" dialog will appear. Don't make any selections in it, but do pay attention to the memory required. *HyperStudio* will report the memory used by the background, as well as the entire card. Since we haven't added anything to the card, the amount of memory used by both should be identical—which is 29K. Close the dialog and select **About this Stack...** from the **Objects** menu. Again, just pay attention to the memory report.

The "About Stack" dialog shows the memory currently being used by the stack, as well as the disk space required to save it. Since we have created ten cards in all, these two memory numbers should be approximately ten times larger than that reported for one card about 295K.

Each card in this stack is contributing 29K to the overall stack memory. That is not too bad, but many backgrounds that you will use in your stacks will require much larger amounts of memory. The USA map is at standard card size, and uses a limited number of colors. Try importing some of the images from the HS Resource CD (especially the photos) into your stacks.

Now create a new stack. (You don't need to save the first one unless you want to.) This new stack should also be in standard card size, and, as before, import

![USA Map Stack (First Version) - Card 2]

![USA Map Stack (Second Version) - Card 2]

the "USA" map as a background on the first card. Now, add nine more cards to the stack. This time, however, use the **Group Card** command in the Ready Made Cards menu to create each additional card. The first thing you might notice is that, in the title bar of your second stack, the card number is separated from the stack name by a bullet (•). It is that little dot you can make by pressing **option 8** on the keyboard. Normally, the card number is separated from the stack name by a dash. You can always identify a group card by this trademark difference.

The title bar of any grouped card will show the stack name and card number separated by a bullet.

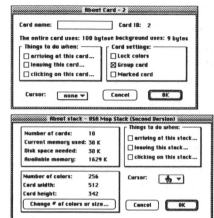

The differences between "normal" cards and group cards don't end there, though. When you used the **Same Background** command in your first stack, each additional card added another 29K to the overall stack memory. Believe it or not, in your second stack, only Card 1 is using 29K. The other nine cards are using almost no memory at all. Don't believe me? Check the card and stack dialogs. Each card 2–9 is using only 100 bytes of memory. That is one-tenth of 1K. The total stack memory is 30K. That is a tenth of the memory the first stack required. How is that possible? The two stacks look virtually identical, except for the difference in the title bars.

While the stacks may look identical, they are not behaving as such. In your first stack, the USA background was used ten times. In your second stack, the background was only used once—on Card 1. Cards 2–10 were each borrowing this background. In other words, the map was imported one time, and then shared among the members of the group. This resulted in dramatic savings in terms of stack memory. If you wish to create stacks in which several cards require the same background, then grouping the cards is the way to go. In fact, you can have any number of different groups within the same stack. In your current stack, create a new card using the **New Card** command. Import a different background on this card, and then use the **Group Card** command to add some more cards. The USA cards will all be grouped to each other, and the other cards you just created will be part of another group. You can even use the Storyboard Extra to rearrange and intersperse the cards. They will still retain their group identities.

If grouping cards seems too good to be true as a means of saving memory in stacks when duplicate backgrounds are used, then what is the catch? Well, the catch is that whatever you do to the background of *one* card in the group, you do to *all* the cards in the group. Scribble all over one of your USA map cards with a paint tool. Then move to another card in the group. It is scribbled on too. Remember, group cards share one background. If you add a piece of clip art to the background, then it, too, will show up on every card in the group.

Well, not really. That is just the way it is. In order to save on memory, the background has to be shared. But, as with most things in *HyperStudio*, there is always a way to work around an apparent limitation. In the case of group cards, the work around is to add things as objects. Instead of adding clip art, add graphic objects. Instead of adding painted text, add text objects. Since objects aren't part of the background, they won't show up on all the cards in the group unless you want them to. That includes buttons as well. The only way to get an object to show up on every card in a group is to check **Group object** in its "Item Features" dialog. This makes it very convenient to show a common object on each card in the group. Just create the object once, set it as a group object, and it will appear on every card in the group. Remember, objects require memory too. Creating one object and then grouping it is both efficient in creation time as well as overall stack memory used. And if you want a certain object on only one card in the group, then just don't make it a group object.

Here is a practical application of ready made cards, group cards, and objects that are for use in the classroom. Have each of your students bring in some leaves at the beginning of the school year, which we scanned on a flatbed scanner and saved as art files. At the conclusion of a unit on plants, have the students work in small groups to create interactive leaf collections using *HyperStudio*. Each group in charge of a certain category of leaves (e.g., lobed leaves, compound leaves, toothed leaves, etc.). Combine all of the stacks into a final "HyperLeaf Collection," by creating a ready made card template to establish a consistent stack design. This one card stack can be composed of an open collection book background, informational text objects, and previous/next card buttons. Save it to the Ready Made Cards folder.

Each group begins its stack by using the "HyperLeaf Template" for the first card. Each additional card is added by using the **Group Card** command. Each card in the stack will feature a different leaf, so have your students add each leaf as a graphic object. The leaves are not made group objects since we only wanted one leaf per card. The nine cards shown here make up one student stack created. The card size of the stack is 640 x 480. The "HyperLeaf Template" required 60K of memory. Each leaf averaged another 30K apiece. The total stack memory came to 344K. To have created this stack without group cards would have required a minimum of 540K of memory for all of the backgrounds, and about another 300K for the leaf graphic objects—nearly 900K altogether. Students achieved the same results for one-third the memory. If Frank Gilbreth were here he would surely jump "six and nine-tenths inches" in his joy at the efficiency of their work.

Lesson 16: Follow the Script

"Learning HyperLogo with the HyperLogo Reference Guide/Tutorial"

HyperOverview/HyperClinic:

To teach everything that HyperLogo offers would require a whole other book. Fortunately, such a book already exists—the **HyperLogo Reference Guide** that came with your copy of *HyperStudio* 3.0. The reference portion was written by Mike Westerfield, and the reverse side (a tutorial called **Exploring HyperLogo**), was written by Bill Lynn. For the HyperClinic portion of this lesson, work through Bill's tutorial. Bill's explanations are concise, easy-to-understand, and spiced with humor to keep your interest. You will be amazed at how quickly your students can learn it, too!

HyperLogo is a programming language with which you can create scripts to increase *HyperStudio*'s capabilities. It was developed by Mike Westerfield, who runs his own software company called Byte Works, Inc.®

Bill Lynn has his own software development company called Simtech Publications, and specializes in creating switch adaptive multimedia software. He also publishes the **HyperStudio Journal**, a bimonthly multimedia resource of artwork, sound clips, tutorials, utilities, feature stacks, and late-breaking news and information.

Both are regular contributors of ideas and suggestions to questions posted in the *HyperStudio* Forum on American Online, and have made available numerous tutorial and example stacks on the use of HyperLogo.

For more information about the **HyperStudio Journal**, Contact: Simtech Publications, 134 East Street, Litchfield, CT, 06759. Phone number (860) 567-1173. Web site: http://www.hsj.com. E-mail: HSJournal@aol.com

Lesson 17: Lights. Camera. Action!

"Using Audio and Video Sources with HyperStudio"

HyperOverview:

Turn your classroom into a multimedia production center with *HyperStudio* and some fairly inexpensive and accessible audiovisual components.

HyperHardware:

- Computer computer with video input/output capability—an "A/V Mac"
- *HyperStudio* Program Resource CD (Optional)

HyperPrerequisites:

- A good understanding of Macintosh system software and *HyperStudio*

HyperClinic:

This lesson is based on my original *Making Multimedia Magic* tutorial stacks (located in the Macintosh StudioWare Library of the *HyperStudio* Forum on America Online). Additional information can be found in the two "A/V Mac" stacks (located on the HS Resource CD). From the Home Stack, just follow the button path indicated below to locate the stacks. Another source of information is the "VCR as a Printer" section of the Appendix of the

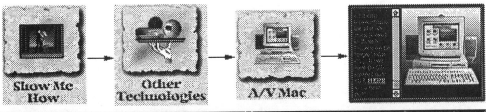

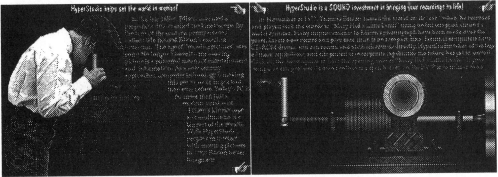

HyperStudio Reference Guide. This section is an excellent supplement to this lesson and lists the Radio Shack part numbers for some of the cable connectors and adapters pictured below.

This lesson shows ways to send and receive audio and video signals to and from a computer. You can use this information to assist you in recording student *HyperStudio* projects to videotape, and incorporating live and digitized video directly into your stacks. To take advantage of this information, you will need an A/V-equipped Macintosh of some type. Apple Computer, manufactures some Macintosh models with built-in AV capabilities. If your computer is not an AV model, then you will need to purchase a video board or peripheral device to enable it to send out and/or digitize video signals. For example, Apple Computer sells its own TV/Video System, which includes a tuner, remote control, video card and *QuickTime* movie editing software. The term "A/V Mac" will be used throughout the remainder of this lesson to refer to any Macintosh computer with full "audio/video in" and "audio/video out" capabilities.

Connectors and Adapters

Pictured below are some of the various types of cable plugs and adapters that will enable you to connect your AV Mac to various audio and video equipment.

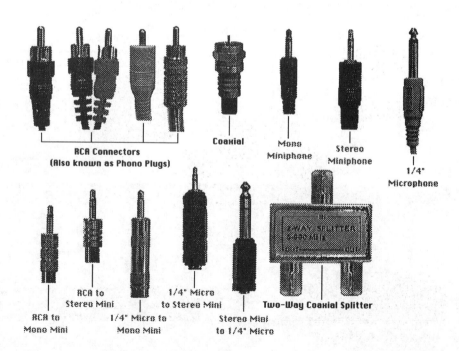

RCA Connectors
(Also known as Phono Plugs)

Coaxial

Mono Miniphone

Stereo Miniphone

1/4" Microphone

RCA to Mono Mini

RCA to Stereo Mini

1/4" Micro to Mono Mini

1/4" Micro to Stereo Mini

Stereo Mini to 1/4" Micro

Two-Way Coaxial Splitter

They've been pictured and named so that you can easily identify them. You probably have some of these at home or at school already, and those you don't can be purchased very inexpensively from Radio Shack.

Options Galore for Adding Pictures to Your *HyperStudio* Stacks

With an AV Mac, the possibilities are virtually endless when it comes to adding pictures and video to your *HyperStudio* stacks. Whenever you load a background, add clip art, or add a graphic object, *HyperStudio* presents you with a dialog box from which you can choose the source for the art file. If you choose **Disk file,** you have the option of getting a picture from the hard drive, a floppy disk, or CD-ROM. As if that weren't enough, though, *HyperStudio* will allow the AV Mac user to get an image from Video. If you select Video, a window will be displayed showing the image you can digitize. You can click on **OK**, or **Freeze** the image before selecting it. After digitizing the image, another window will be displayed, giving you the opportunity to use the **rectangle selector tool** or **lasso** to bring in all or part of the digitized image.

Shown below are some of the devices you can connect to your AV Mac. Of course, you will not be able to connect them all to the computer at the same time—at least not without some type of switcher box. Your AV Mac will have a video input port(s) for composite video and/or S-video. Either of these ports may be used, depending on the type of input device you are using.

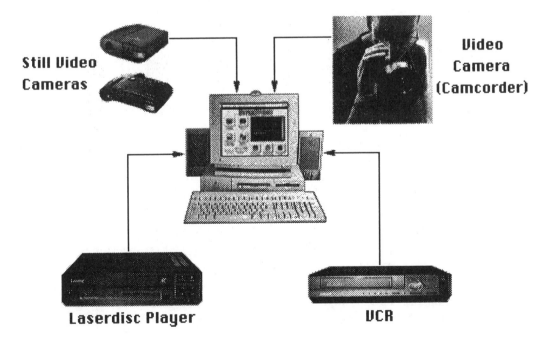

Still Video Cameras

Video Camera (Camcorder)

Laserdisc Player

UCR

Viewing a Stack on the TV With the Option of Recording It to Videotape

In order to view a stack on the TV, you need to connect your AV Mac, VCR, and TV. Here is one possible way to do this. Each connection identifies the name of the plug (and adapter if necessary) and the name of the connection port.

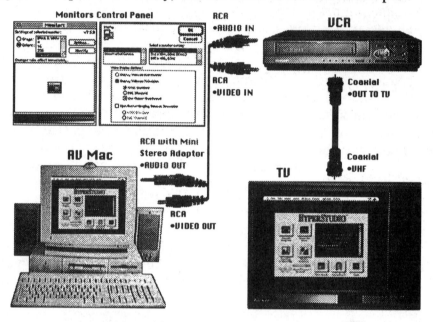

If you are using one of Apple's AV Macs, you will probably need to use the **Monitors** control panel after connecting the equipment. In the control panel, click on **Options**, and you will be presented with choices for monitor type and video display. You will need to set it to display the video on TV. If your VCR has a tape in it, you can then begin recording your stack.

Creating stacks that you wish to view on the TV in the standard card size (512 x 342). This will ensure that no parts of your stack will be cut off from view when displayed on the TV.

Mixing Multiple Sound Input Sources in the Recording of Your Stack

Don't let this next complicated affair scare you. This set of connections spotlights the use of the *Multimedia Recording Kit* from Roger Wagner Publishing. This kit comes with a Multimedia Sound Mixer, microphone, a set of headphones, cables and adapters, and enables you to integrate a variety of sound sources in the recording of your stack. With the exception of the RCA to RCA and Coaxial to Coaxial cables, all of the cables pictured in this diagram come with the Multimedia Recording Kit. For this reason, the Multimedia Recording Kit is really a much better deal than any other sound mixers on the market. (Contact RWP at 1-800-*HYPERSTUDIO* for more information.)

This diagram is essentially the same as the one for viewing and recording a stack on TV. The only difference is that this one shows how to use multiple sound input sources and a mixer to enhance the presentation of your stack. Instead of a stereo, you could also use a tape recorder or CD player. (**Note:** If your AV Mac has a CD-ROM drive, you already have the capability to play audio CD's without the need for a CD player. Check out the CDPlay NBA.)

Here is the name of the connection plug and the port where they are connected. To conserve space, the "/" is used to separate the Out and In plug names and port locations. For example:

> **Dual RCA/RCA**
> **MASTER OUT (Mixer)/AUDIO IN (VCR)**

Dual RCA/RCA means that the cable has two RCA plugs on one end and one RCA plug on the other. **MASTER OUT (Mixer)** means that the corresponding plug (the Dual RCA) is connected to the Sound Mixer at the **MASTER OUT** port. **Audio IN (VCR)** means that the single RCA plug of the cable should be

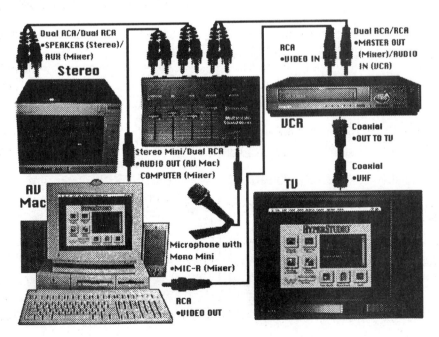

attached at the **AUDIO IN** port of the VCR. Sorry if this seems a little confusing. It really isn't, though. The Multimedia Recording Kit comes with a booklet to help you, filled with detailed descriptions and diagrams.

If you were to connect the hardware as pictured here, you would have the capability to see your stack on TV, narrate it, hear any sound effects in your stack, and have music playing (either from the stereo or CD-ROM drive—or both). Not only that, but you could record all of it onto videotape. Amazing, isn't it?

Using *HyperStudio* and the AV Mac to Create Multimedia Video Productions

With *HyperStudio* and an AV Mac, you and your students have the basic ingredients needed to create stacks using real-time video. This capability can be applied to the creation of video newsletters, live school news broadcasts, video portfolios, and a video yearbook.

In the "Actions" dialog, select **Play a movie or video...** You will then have to

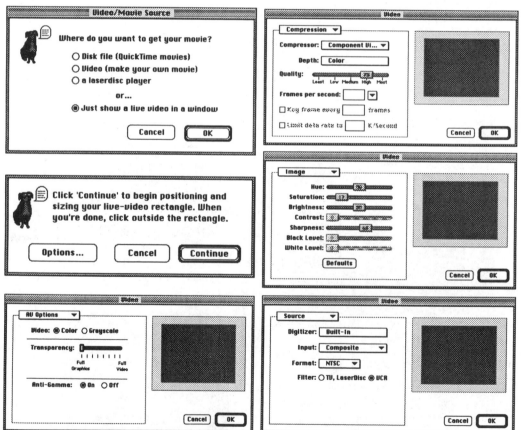

access a laserdisc or display a live video window. If you select live video, *HyperStudio* will enable you to position and size the live video window, and to make any adjustments you want to the color, hue, saturation, brightness, contrast, video source, etc.

By choosing live video, you can use a video camera to display students on the screen as part of a stack. In this way, students can appear in their own stacks, or even be anchors for a video news broadcast. Perhaps the students could create and star in their own interactive class play or video storybook. The options are unlimited.

To do a school-wide, live news broadcast, you would need to use a Two-Way Coaxial Splitter. One coaxial cable would then feed out of the splitter into your TV so that the news team could watch the program as it is being aired. The other coaxial cable would need to connect into your school's cable drop. This technique can be used to produce live news programs.

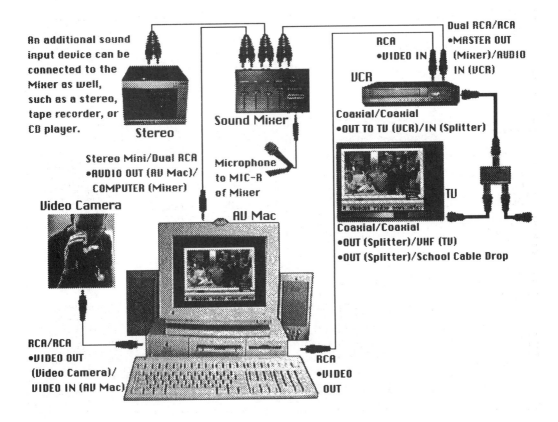

Lesson 18: Cruisin' the HyperHighway

"An Introduction to Using HyperStudio with the Internet"

HyperOverview:

It's beginning to sound cliché, but the Internet can be likened to an information highway. Internet service providers allow us access to this highway, and browser applications are the vehicles with which we travel. But you know, it is not the highway that is important—it is the exits that we can take along the way. These exits provide information in various forms of media. So how does *HyperStudio* fit into all of this? *HyperStudio* is a means through which our travels along the information highway can be communicated to others. As mentioned in Lesson 2, *HyperStudio* is the ultimate creative environment in which media can be used and combined in all of its many forms.

HyperHardware:

- An active TCP Internet connection

- Web browser software, such as *Netscape, MacWeb,* or *Internet Explorer*

HyperPrerequisites:

- A good understanding of *HyperStudio* and some experience using the Internet

HyperClinic:

This lesson is but a very brief overview of ways to use *HyperStudio* to access and utilize information and media available on the Internet.

One method is to access FTP (File Transfer Protocol) servers for files to use in your stacks. There are numerous FTP servers on the Internet, many of which are *anonymous* sites, which means they are designed for the very purpose of locating and downloading files free of charge. Usually the only password required when logging onto such sites is your e-mail address.

Included with HSMac 3.0 is a folder called "HS Internet." Within this folder is a program called *MediaLinker.* MediaLinker allows you to create "medialinks" to files on  FTP servers. These files can be text, sound, art, photos, and the list goes on. The idea of establishing a medialink to an Internet file is that you don't need to store the actual file on your computer. With *MediaLinker,* you create virtual libraries of clip art, sounds, etc. The actual files are stored at the FTP sites. The Internet becomes your storage facility.

If you are not that familiar with accessing FTP sites, that is okay. What is nice is that you don't need to work with MediaLinker in order to use medialinks in your stacks. The HS Internet folder includes a "MediaLinks Folder" full of links already created for you. Want to add a medialink art file to your stack? Simply choose one of the medialink files for your art source rather than an image from the HS Art folder, Resource CD, etc. This example uses the "Marco Polo" medialink from the History folder within the MediaLinks Folder. The file itself is 239K, but its medialink is only 8K. *HyperStudio*

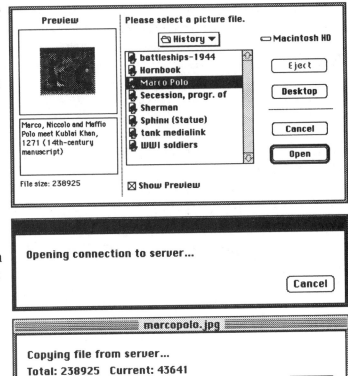

then accessed the Internet and implemented the link to the actual file. Once the file was downloaded, it was selected in the Clip Art window and placed it in the stack.

HyperHint→As mentioned in the "MediaLinker Read Me First!" text file, "Each time a MediaLink is generated, the actual image is downloaded. You can delete these or use them in HyperStudio as you wish." All this means is that when you create a medialink, the actual file from the FTP site is downloaded and saved on your computer. Likewise, if you access a medialink file for use in your stack, the actual file is also saved on your computer. In either case, it is a simple matter to delete the file. Once a medialink is created to the file's location on the Internet, there is no reason to also save the actual file on your hard drive. And once a file is added to your stack, then you don't need it as a separate file on your hard drive. So, if you create a medialink, trash the downloaded FTP file and just keep the medialink. If you use a medialink and the FTP file becomes part of your stack, then save the stack and trash the FTP file that was also stored on your computer.

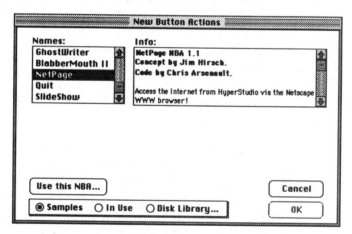

Another method is to use either the NetPage NBA (with Netscape) or the MacWebPage NBA (with MacWeb) to display web pages while using *HyperStudio*. Just like other NBAs, either of these can be assigned to objects, cards, or hypertext links. You simply enter the URL (Universal Resource Locator).

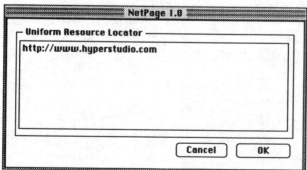

address into the dialog box for the web page you wish to access. Then, whenever the button, etc. is clicked, the URL address is located by the particular Internet application, and the web page is displayed. This is a powerful combination. Imagine showing a stack with links to *HyperStudio*-related sites on the web for a presentation to your administrators or board of education. Imagine sharing information about where you teach with a stack that has links to your school or district home page. Imagine creating a stack for a friend or colleague with links to your favorite sites on the web. Imagine having your students design stacks that access information on the web. As the web pages are changed and updated, so too is the information in the students' stacks. This opens up the possibility of creating stacks that are dynamic—that change from day to day as the pages and information they are linked to change.

There are a number of excellent *HyperStudio*-related web sites. Four that you will find especially useful and informative are the Roger Wagner Publishing home page (http://www.*hyperstudio*.com), the *HyperStudio* Journal home page (http://www.hsj.com/hsj.html), the *HyperStudio* Network home page (http://www.hsnetwork.com), and the HyperInternet home page (http://www.anoka.k12.mn.us/*HyperStudio*/HyperInternet.html). It is recommended that you take the opportunity to visit each site as you travel the information highway.

If you would like to learn more about using *HyperStudio* and the Internet, then the HyperInternet site is a must. It was created by Jim Hirsch, Director of Technology for the Plano Independent School District. Jim is a highly recognized and respected *HyperStudio* and Internet expert, and perhaps the greatest advocate in the *HyperStudio* community for the integration of *HyperStudio* and the Internet—a process he calls *HyperInternet*. He has authored numerous "Skiing the Internet" stacks, which are "Hypermedia productions that give a K–12, education-based overview of the Internet and the services it offers to staff and students." The HyperInternet site is just the starting point for the wealth of information Jim shares. Links include:

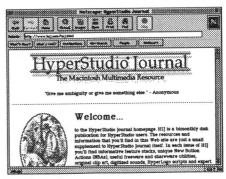

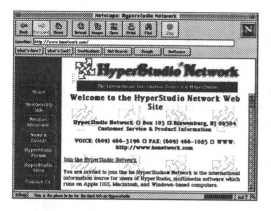 

- Multimedia Writing: yesterday and today
- Using data files found on the Internet
- Creating MediaLinks for use with *HyperStudio*
- Creating buttons that connect to Universal Resource Locators
- "Realtime" *HyperStudio* Stacks via Netscape.

HyperStudio Plug-in

In his section on "Realtime" *HyperStudio* Stacks, Jim describes how to configure Netscape to launch stacks directly as part of web pages. This includes taking advantage of the new *HyperStudio* plug-in for Netscape. As Jim mentions, "With this plug-in and the ability to use 'frames' on web pages, you can now combine all of the features of *HyperStudio* stacks along with standard HTML coding—all on the same page without launching *HyperStudio* separately."

Be sure to check out Jim's "Skiing the Internet" web site as well (http://www.anoka.k12.mn.us/Skiing/Skiing.home).

We have gone down the highway as far as we can. The Internet highway stretches infinitely before you, and *HyperStudio* will play an ever-increasing role in helping you and your students make the most of your journeys.

Tutorial Notes

Tutorial Notes

Tutorial Notes

Project Lesson Plan Index

Project Lesson Plans

Hyper-Book Report

HyperTutorial Mastery Level Required:

Beginner

HyperOverview:

A Hyper-Book Report would be appropriate for students in grade four or higher.

Book reports are a common assignment. Creating an electronic book report takes some of the drudgery out of a mundane assignment, for both the teacher and the student.

This is an excellent opportunity to advertise a book (a student recommendation can be more powerful than one from an adult). Completed projects could be placed on a computer in the Media Center for other students to view. Similarly, all projects could be placed on a computer in the classroom.

HyperObjectives:

Students will write brief character sketches for each of the main characters of the book.

Students will practice organizing information logically when they are formulating the summary portion of the book report.

They will then present this information in descriptive paragraphs.

HyperMedia Sources:

Scanned image of the book cover (optional)

HyperHardware and Other HyperMaterials:

Data Sheet

Planning sheet page (See Appendix page 322.)

HyperPrerequisites:

Prior to assigning this project, students should have had several opportunities to write descriptive paragraphs.

Students will complete a book report data sheet once the reading of the book has been completed.

A sample data sheet is on page 187. The data sheet can be customized if a particular genre of book has been read by all students. (If all students read biographies, specific information, such as birth date, birthplace, facts about why this person is famous, etc., may be included on the student data sheet.)

HyperInstruction and HyperTimeline:

The Hyper-Book Report project would take two to three class periods to complete. (More time may be needed if the data sheet is customized and it requires more information about the book.)

HyperExtensions:

Students may add another card (not a grouped card), on which he or she makes an illustration of the book.

An invisible button could be placed on the first card. The action of that button would be to **Play a Sound,** which is a recording of the student stating the title of the book and the author's name. Students should select **Automatic Timer** and click on **Do these actions as soon as card is shown.**

Hyper-Book Report Data Sheet

Student Name: _____

Date: _____

Card 1

Left Side

Title: _____

Author: _____

Right Side

Your Name: _____

Teacher Name: _____

Date: _____

Card 2

Left Side

Main Characters: _____

Right Side

Setting: _____

Card 3

Left Side

Summary of book: _____

_____

_____

_____

Right Side

Opinion of book: _____

_____

_____

_____

Hyper-Book Report Quick Guide

1. Open *HyperStudio*. Go to **File** and select **New Stack**.

2. When the following message appears, click **Yes**.

3. Go to **File** and select **Save Stack As...** to save the stack.

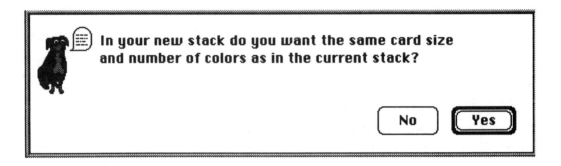

In your new stack do you want the same card size and number of colors as in the current stack?

No   Yes

4. Go to **Edit** and **Import Background**. The following screen appears:

Where do you want to get your picture?

◉ Disk file
○ Video
○ QuickTake camera

Cancel   OK

You want a background from the **Disk file**. Click **OK**. The following screen appears:

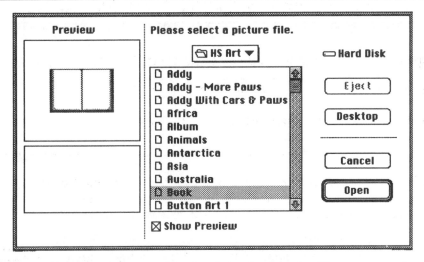

Click on **Book** and **Open**. The book background will appear on the first card. You will be using the same background on all cards of the book report.

By grouping cards, you will reduce the size (memory requirements) of the stack. Go to **Edit**, drag to **Ready Made Cards**, and **Group card**. This will create a new card with the same background. Repeat this process until you have the number of cards needed for the book report.

When you think you have made the required number of cards for the project, go to **Extras** and **StoryBoard**. This will show you the number of cards you have made.

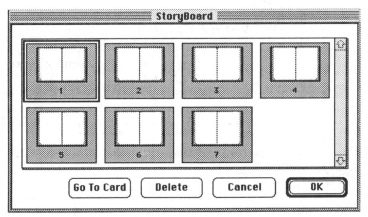

If you have too many, you can easily delete cards now. Click on the card you wish to delete and click **Delete**. You will be asked to verify that you want to delete the card:

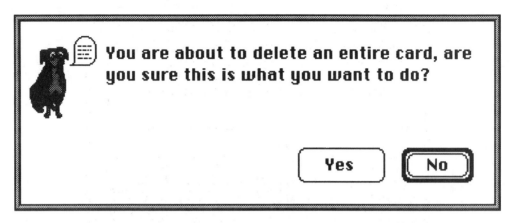

Click **Yes**. The "StoryBoard" screen will reappear. Delete all unnecessary cards. When you are satisfied you have the desired number of cards, click **OK**. Go to **File** and **Save Stack**.

5. Go to the **Objects** menu and select **Add a Text Object**. Move the text box to the left of the screen and resize it so that it fits inside the "page." Click outside the text box.

   The **Text Appearance** dialog box appears. Select the color of text and background for the text box. A good idea would be to leave the text black and the background white, so that this stack has the appearance of text on a printed page.

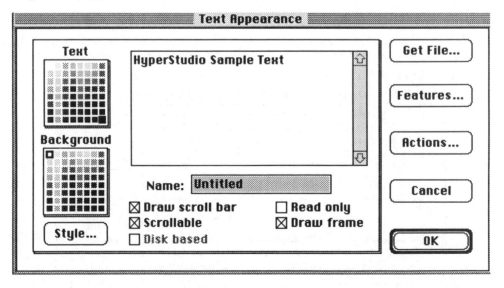

Click on **Style**. The "Text Style" dialog box appears.

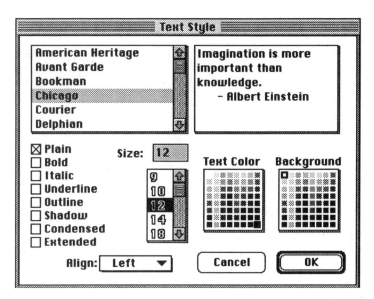

Select a font and size. (Keep in mind that only the title and author will be in this text box, so a large size is desirable.) Select **Align: Center**. Click **OK**.

This returns to the "Text Appearance" dialog box. You have one more opportunity at this point to make changes in text or background colors. Click **OK**.

Enter the title of the book and the author.

Pull the **Tools menu** down so that it is visible on the screen. Click the **Edit tool**. Double-click inside the text box. The "Text Appearance" dialog box reappears:

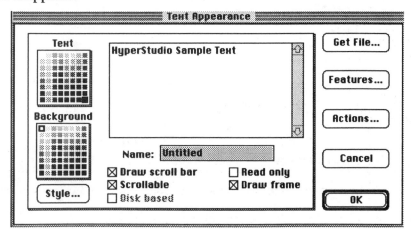

Select **Read only**. Select the **browse tool** again.

6. Go to the **Objects** menu and select **Add a Text Object**. Move the text box to the right side of the card and resize as necessary. Click outside the text box.

   From the "Text Appearance" box, select the color of text and background of the text box.

   Click **Style**. Select a font and a size no larger than 24. Select **Align: Center**. Click **OK**.

   This returns to the "Text Appearance" dialog box. You have one more opportunity at this point to make changes in text or background colors. Click **OK**.

   Type your name, teacher name, and the date in this text box.

7. The card should be edited for spelling errors. Once all corrections have been made, select the **edit tool** from the **Tools** menu. Double-click on the text box on the left side of the card. The "Text Appearance" dialog box appears:

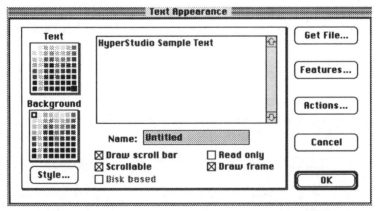

Select **Read only**. If the text box does not need to have a scroll bar or be scrollable, click off of **Draw scroll bar** and **Scrollable**. Click **OK**. Select the **browse tool** again. Repeat this process for the text box on the right side of the card.

8. Go to the **Objects** menu and select **Add a Button**.

   The **Button Appearance** dialog box appears.

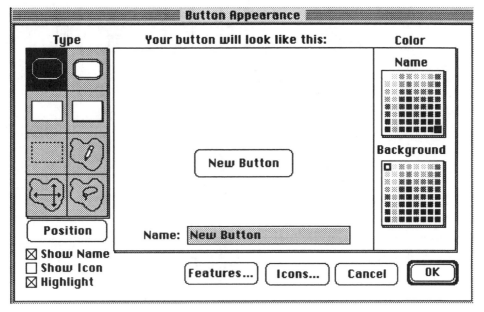

Select the dotted rectangle (the background of the button will be invisible). Click **Icons**. Select the icon and click **OK**. The "Button Appearance" dialog box reappears with the selected icon in the center of the screen. Click **OK**.

The button will appear as a dotted rectangle in the center of the card. Click, hold, and drag inside the button to place it on the card. Click outside the button.

The **Actions** dialog box appears. After choosing your actions, click **Done**.

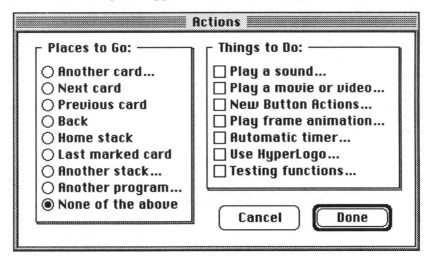

The **Transitions** dialog box appears.

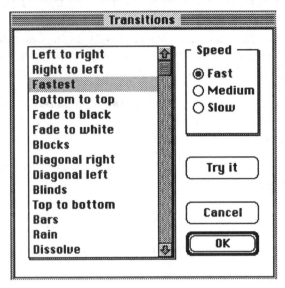

Select the transition and speed of the transition. Click on **OK**.

The "Actions" dialog box reappears. Under "Things to Do", students may choose to play a sound.

The **Tape Deck** window appears.

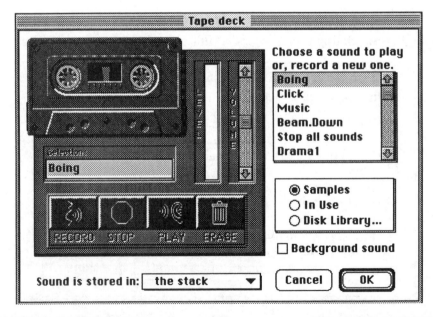

Students may select one of the sounds from the samples listed or choose disk library to select from more sounds. (Sounds may be tested by double-clicking on one or by highlighting a sound and clicking on **Play**.) Once a sound has been selected, students click **OK**. The "Actions" dialog box reappears. Students should check to be sure they have made a selection from "Places to Go" and have selected a sound. Students click on **Done**.

9. Click on the button to test it. If it works as intended, repeat the steps for making text boxes and buttons on all cards. You will select **Align: Left** on all other text boxes.

10. When you are finished, go to **File** and **Save Stack**. Go to **File** and **Quit** *HyperStudio*.

The Human Body

HyperTutorial Mastery Level Required:

Beginner

HyperOverview:

This project would be good for students in grade six or higher.

This project could be a culminating activity for a study of the human body.

Students will take advantage of content learned in the classroom, as well as independent research. Students (or the teacher) may choose to research a body system or a particular organ of the body, such as the heart, for this project.

Each student will create a *HyperStudio* stack which provides factual information about each part of the body system or an organ.

A graphic of a body system, such as the digestive system or a particular organ, will be on the first card of the *HyperStudio* stack. This graphic will include the name of each organ and a line pointing to the organ. If the graphic is a single organ, parts of the organ will be labeled with the identifying line drawn to the specific part.

Invisible buttons will be placed on the name of each organ (or part of the organ) which link to cards which provide factual information about that organ, such as position, size, function, etc.

HyperObjectives:

Students will learn about body systems or particular organs of the human body. Each, student will take notes on his or her body system or organ. Students will find information about their systems or organs from textbooks, encyclopedias, or other books available from the media center, the public library, or the Internet.

Once notes about the body systems or organs have been taken and a drawing of the system or organ (including identifying labels) has been made, students will build a *HyperStudio* stack which includes the graphic, as well as facts about the body system or organ.

HyperMedia Sources:

Pictures of organs can be brought into *HyperStudio* from a CD-ROM like a multimedia encyclopedia. (See Capturing Pictures pages 318 and 319.)

HyperHardware and Other HyperMaterials:

Scanner (optional)

Human body data sheet, page 199 (students will need to complete several of these, one for each part which has been labeled).

HyperPrerequisites:

Students make a drawing of a system of the human body or a particular organ, using any draw program.

If students are drawing a body system, a scanned outline or other digital picture of the human body could be placed in the draw program you are using and a copy saved on each student's disk prior to beginning this project. (Students may have a difficult time making a reasonably accurate drawing of an outline of the human body, where accuracy is somewhat important. Students do not need to feel frustration early in the project). Precise drawings of the organs are not crucial to the success of this project.

This would be a good opportunity to teach one or two students how to use the scanner, if time allows. These students can complete the scanning portion of the project and save each scanned image on student disks. (See Capturing Pictures pages 318 and 319.)

There are a variety of ways of presenting the factual information on each card. You need to consider the level of your students and their writing skills. If your students have not yet mastered formal paragraph writing, that should not necessarily deter you from assigning this project to your students.

Certainly, a paragraph presenting the required facts about each organ is an option. Another idea would be to have a bulleted list of facts about each organ.

Consider your ultimate goal: Is it to have students learn and present information about a particular system or organ of the human body, or is it to be able to develop a well-written paragraph? The point is that no teacher should dismiss this project as being too challenging for his or her class because the class does not have strong writing skills.

HyperInstruction and HyperTimeline:

This project will take three or four class periods, depending upon the amount of factual information the teacher would like included in the stack. (More time will be needed if this is the first *HyperStudio* endeavor for the class. Experience has shown that students perform tasks much more quickly on second or third *HyperStudio* projects. The comfort level for students increases dramatically with each project.) You will need to include an additional class period for the drawing of the body system or organ in the draw program you of your choice.

HyperExtensions:

1. Students can add an additional card to the stack entitled is "About the Artist." Each student would provide information about himself or herself on this card. An option of making a new card is to have a button on the first card whose label is the name of the student. The action of the button is **Play a sound**, in which the student records information "About the Artist". This is just for fun, yet provides an additional opportunity for the students to experience the joys of *HyperStudio.*

2. If an Internet connection is available, students can add a button ("More Facts About") on the final card which links to a URL relating to the project.

Human Body Data Sheet

Student Name _____ Date _____

Please complete this sheet in order to be ready to begin our *HyperStudio* project on the human body.

Name of body system or organ: _____

Facts

Location

Size

Function

Related Diseases

Interesting Information

Human Body Quick Guide

1. Open *HyperStudio*. Go to **File** and select **New Stack**.

2. When the following message appears, click **No**. (You need the cards to be as large as possible for your human body graphic and labels, whether it is the entire body, or just one of the organs).

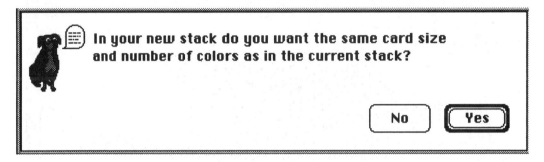

In your new stack do you want the same card size and number of colors as in the current stack?

No   Yes

Select **Change # of Colors of Size**. The following screen appears:

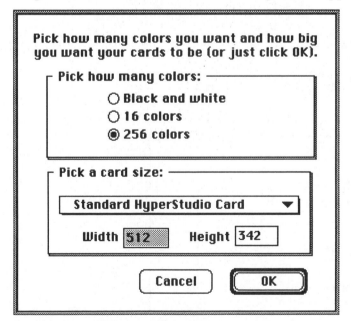

Pick how many colors you want and how big you want your cards to be (or just click OK).

Pick how many colors:
○ Black and white
○ 16 colors
◉ 256 colors

Pick a card size:
Standard HyperStudio Card ▼
Width 512   Height 342

Cancel   OK

Under Pick a card size, select **Current Screen Size**. Click **OK**.

3. Go to **File** and select **Save Stack As...** to save the stack.

4. Go to **Edit** and **Erase Background**. Select a background color. Click on **OK**.

5. Go the the **Objects** menu and select **Add a Graphic Object**. Select **Disk File**. Locate the disk on which the human body has been saved. Select the file.

The following screen appears:

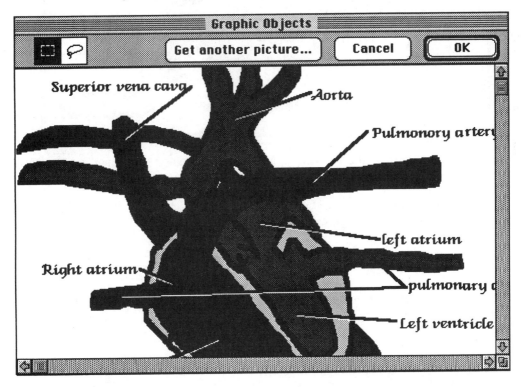

Using the **rectangular selector tool**, make a rectangle around as much of the image as you want to be included on your card, being sure to include the entire image as well as the labels of all body parts. Click **OK**.

The "Graphic Appearance" dialog box appears. A preview of the image is in the center of the window. On the left you may select a "Frame color" and "Frame width". To select the "Frame width," click on the up arrow key until you reach the desired width of the frame. (**Note:** The frame goes around the image. If your frame is too large, you lose part of the image.) Click **OK** when you have the desired frame color and width *or* if do not want a frame around the image.

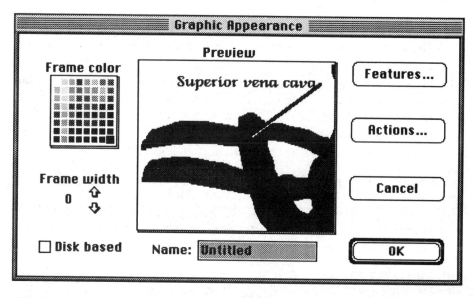

Place the cursor inside the image and drag it to place the image on the card. Click outside the image.

This card will have a series of buttons which will link to other cards, providing information about the human body.

6. Go to the **Objects** menu and select **Add a Button**. The "Button Appearance" dialog box appears.

Select the **retangle dotted** (the button will be invisible). Click on **OK**.

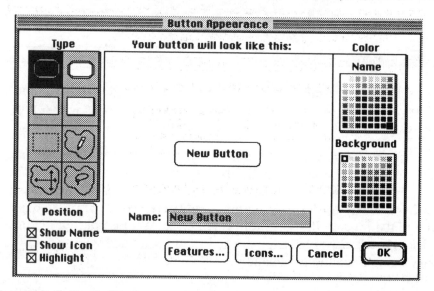

The button will appear as a dotted rectangle in the center of the card. Click, hold, and drag inside the button to place it on one of the body part labels. Since the buttons will be invisible, it is easier to keep track of which buttons you have made if you begin with the first button at the top of the screen and work your way down. If there are labels on both sides of the graphic, begin at the top of the left side of the screen and work your way to the bottom. Then begin with the label at the top of the right side of the screen and work your way to the bottom. Click outside the button.

The *Actions* dialog box appears.

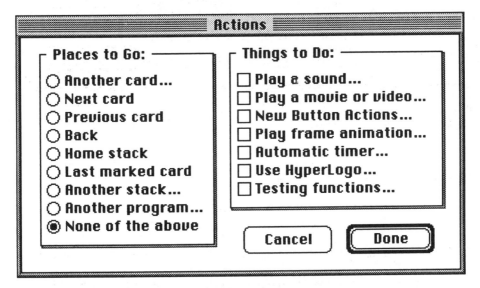

Under "Places to Go:", select **Another card.**

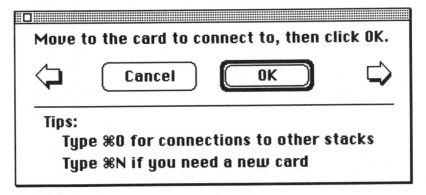

You need a new card, so follow the screen directions: **"Type ⌘ - N if you need a new card."** Click on **OK.**

The "Transitions" dialog box appears.

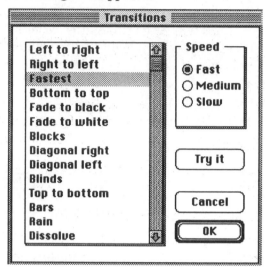

Select the transition and speed of the transition. Click on **OK**.

The "Actions" dialog box reappears. Under **Things to Do**, you may select to play a sound.

The **Tape deck** window appears.

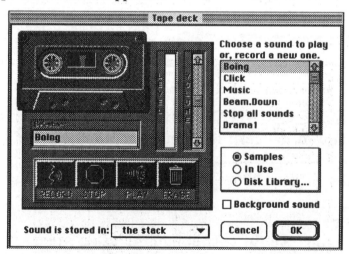

You may select one of the sounds from the samples listed or choose **Disk Library** to select from more sounds. (Sounds may be tested by double-clicking on one, or by highlighting a sound and clicking on "Play".) Once a sound has been selected, click **OK**. The "Actions" dialog box reappears.

Check to be sure you have made a selection from **Places To Go** and have selected a sound. Click **Done**.

Click on the button to test it. If it works as intended, you are ready to make a text box to enter information about that body part.

7. Go to the **Objects** menu and select **Add a Text Object**. Move the text box to place it on the screen and resize it so that it is large enough to view all of the information. (This may not be possible if you have a lot of information about a particular body part.) Click outside the text box.

The "Text Appearance" dialog box appears. Select the color of text and background for the text box.

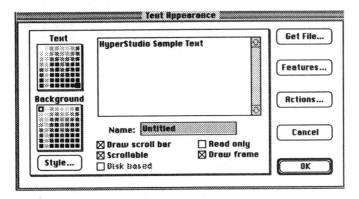

Click **Style**. The "Text Style" dialog box appears.

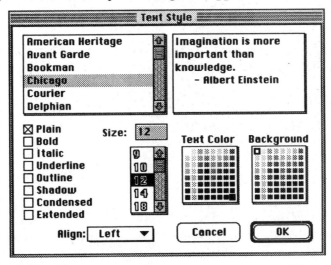

Select a font and size. Click **OK**.

This returns to the "Text Appearance" dialog box. You have one more opportunity at this point to make changes in text or background colors. Click on **OK**.

Enter the information about the body part here.

Pull the **Tools menu** down so that it is visible on the screen. Click on the **browse tool**. Double-click inside the text box. The "Text Appearance" dialog box reappears:

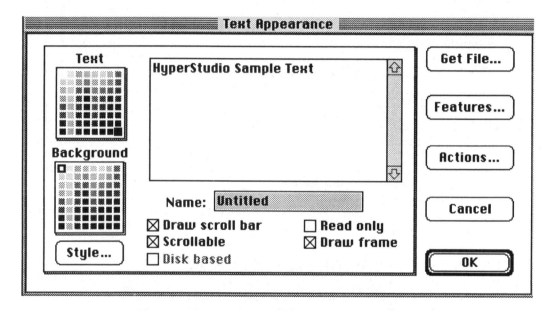

Select **Read only**. Click off of **Draw scroll bar** and **Scrollable** if they are not needed. Select the **browse tool** again.

You need to add a button which links back to the first card.

8. Go to the **Objects** menu and select **Add a Button**. The "Button Appearance" dialog box appears.

Select the dotted rectangle (the background of the button will be invisible). Click **Icons**. Select the icon and click **OK**. The **Button Appearance** dialog box reappears with the selected icon in the center of the screen. Click **OK**.

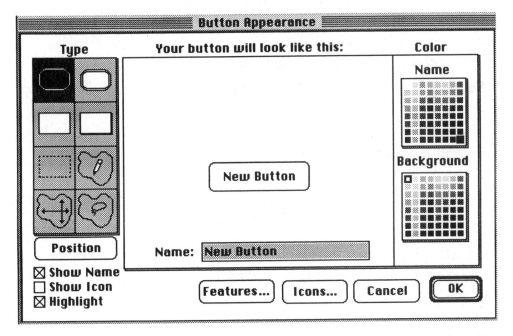

The "Actions" dialog box appears. Under "Places to Go", select **Another card**. Use the arrow key until you are back to the first card. Click **OK**.

The "Transitions" dialog box appears. Select the transition and speed of the transition. Click **OK**.

The "Actions" dialog box reappears. Under **Things to Do**, you may select to play a sound. The "Tape deck" window appears. You may select one of the sounds from the samples listed or choose **Disk Library** to select from more sounds. (Sounds may be tested by double-clicking on one, or by highlighting a sound and clicking on "Play.") Once a sound has been selected, click **OK**. The "Actions" dialog box reappears. Check to be sure you have made a selection from **Places to Go** and have selected a sound. Click **Done**.

At this point you are ready to repeat the process of making buttons and new cards until all buttons and cards are made.

9. When you are finished, go to **File** and **Save Stack**. Go to **File** and **Quit** *HyperStudio*.

Hyper-Yearbook

HyperTutorial Mastery Level Required:

Intermediate

HyperOverview:

Students will each create a one-card autobiographical stack which includes his/her digital image. All student stacks will be linked with buttons to create a class electronic yearbook.

HyperObjectives:

Students will gather autobiographical information to create one-card stacks. The autobiographical information as well as a digital image of the student is placed on the card. Buttons are made on each stack which link to another student's stack. The end result is an electronic yearbook.

HyperHardware and Other HyperMaterials:

Autobiographical data sheet (page 210)

Digital images (See Capturing Pictures pages 318 and 319.)

HyperPrerequisites:

Students have completed the autobiographical data sheet. A digital image has been taken of each student and placed on each student's disk.

HyperInstruction and HyperTimeline:

Students will be given the autobiographical data sheet to complete. The teacher can determine the specific data requested, according to age and grade level of students. An example data sheet has been included on page 210.

An option would be to have students brainstorm to generate the class data sheet. The students need to be aware of the audience for this project as they brainstorm.

This would be a good opportunity to discuss relevance of suggested topics and whether suggestions would be of interest to the intended audience. (Parents may be interested in seeing someone's favorite subject in school, but this may not be of interest to other classmates).

A digital image should be taken of each student and placed on each student disk. (See Capturing Pictures pages 318 and 319.)

Once all information has been recorded on data sheets and the digital image has been taken and transferred to student disks, students are ready to begin work on the computer.

Students can complete this project in the computer lab or in a one-computer classroom. (Obviously, the project will require more than the estimated amount of time if this project is being developed in a one-computer classroom. If developing the project in a one-computer classroom, try to schedule several students working on the project each day. The goal would be to have students complete the project during two school weeks).

Students working on the project in the computer lab should complete the one-card stack in one class period. (More time may be needed, depending on the amount of autobiographical information requested on the student data sheet.)

At least one class period would be required to put all students' stacks together and make buttons linking the stacks.

HyperExtensions:

Each student may add a button to his/her stack, which plays a sound that students record as a personalized greeting. Students do enjoy the sounds of their own voices.

Students can ask others to edit their autobiographical information.

Students may add additional autobiographical information that was not included on the autobiographical data sheet.

Hyper-Yearbook Data Sheet

Student Name_____ Date _____

Please provide the following information in order to be ready to begin our Hyper-Yearbook.

Birthdate:_____

Birthplace:_____

Names and ages of brothers & sisters: _____

Pets (what kind and name): _____

Hobbies: _____

Sports you play or like to watch: _____

Favorite food: _____

Favorite local restaurant:_____

Favorite TV show: _____

Favorite movie:_____

Favorite movie star: _____

Favorite book:_____

Pet peeve (What really bothers you?): _____

Hyper-Yearbook Quick Guide

1. Open *HyperStudio*. Go to **File** and select **New Stack**.

2. When the following message appears, click **Yes**.

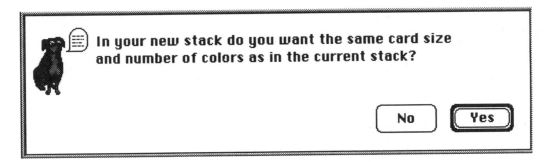

3. Go to **File** and select **Save Stack As...** to save the stack.

4. Go to **File** and select **Import Background**. When the following dialog box appears, select **Disk File**.

Select "Album" from the following selection and click **OK**.

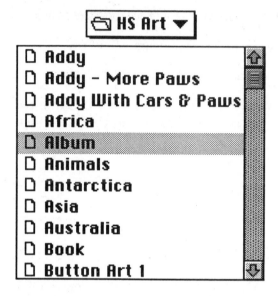

5. Go to the **Objects** menu and select **Add a Text Object**. Move the text box to the left side of the screen and resize it so that it fits in the space under "Photographs." Click outside the text box.

The "Text Appearance" dialog box appears. Select the color of text and background for the text box. White text on black background looks nice here, but this is a personal preference.

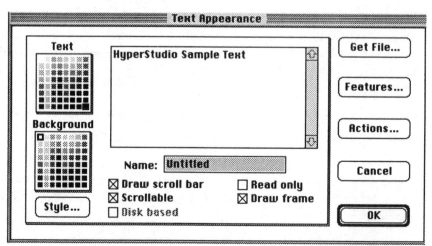

Click **Style**. The "Text Style" dialog box appears.

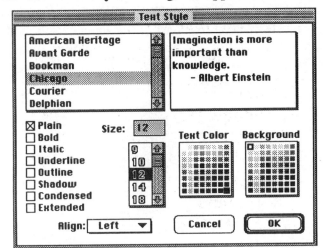

Select a font and size. The size of the text may be dictated by the amount of autobiographical information required on student data sheets. Another consideration may be whether you want all of the information visible at one time or to have a scrolling text box. Click **OK**. This returns to the "Text Appearance" dialog box. (You are given one more opportunity at this point to make changes in text or background colors.) Click **OK**.

Enter information from autobiographical data sheet.

6. After text has been entered, select the **Objects** menu and select **Add a Graphic Object**. Select **Disk File**. Locate the disk on which the student image has been saved. You may have to click on Desktop, open the student's disk, then select the student's image.

Using the **rectangular selector tool**, make a rectangle around as much of the image as you want to be included on your card, keeping the size of the card in mind, as well as the fact that you only have space on the right side of the card in which to place the image. Click on **OK**.

Place the cursor inside the image and drag it to place the image. (Remember to leave space under the image to add a text box for the student's name.) Click outside the image.

The "Graphic Appearance" dialog box appears. A preview of the image is in the center of the window. On the left you may select a **Frame color** and **Frame width**.

To select the **Frame width**, click on the **up arrow** key until you reach the desired width of the frame. (**Note:** The frame goes around the image. If your frame is too large, you lose part of the image.) Click **OK** when you have the desired frame color and width or if you do not want a frame around the image.

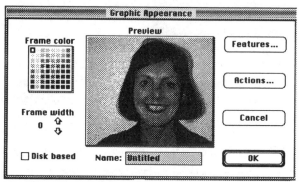

7. Go to the **Objects** menu and select **Add a Text Object** . Move the text box under the student's image and resize it so that it fits in the space under the image. Click outside the text box.

From the "Text Appearance" box, students select the color of text and background of the text box. A good idea might be to be consistent with colors selected in the autobiographical information text box.

Click **Style**. Students may select a font and size. Again, font and size that is consistent with the autobiographical information text box should be a consideration.

8. The card should be edited for spelling errors. Once all corrections have been made, select the **edit tool** from the **Tools** menu. Double-click on the text box. The "Text Appearance" dialog box appears:

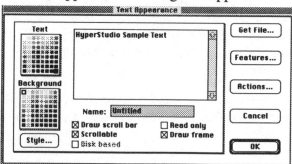

Select **Read only**. (Changes cannot accidentally be made to the student's card.) If the text box does not need to have a scroll bar or be scrollable, click off of **Draw scroll bar** and **Scrollable**. Click **OK**. Select the **browse tool** again. Repeat this process for the text box under the student's image.

9. When all the cards have been completed (including a title card for the yearbook, they should be saved in one place (either on one disk or in a designated folder on the hard drive).

10. Buttons can be added now to link all of the cards. The teacher may choose to add all of the buttons or to designate one student for this. (It is a one-person job from now on.) Go to the **Object** menu and select **Add a Button**.

The **Button Appearance** dialog box appears.

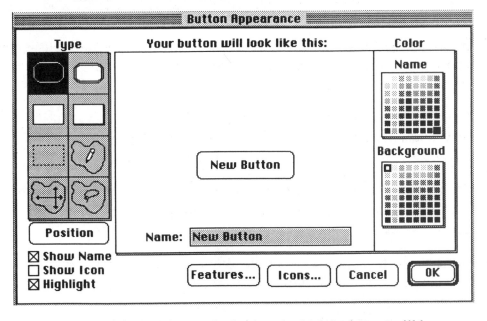

Select the rectangle selector (the background of the button will be invisible). Click on **Icons**. Select the icon and click **OK**. The "Button Appearance" dialog box reappears with the selected icon in the center of the screen. Click **OK**.

11. The button will appear as a dotted rectangle in the center of the card. Click, hold, and drag inside the button to place it on the card. Click outside the button.

12. The "Actions" dialog box appears.

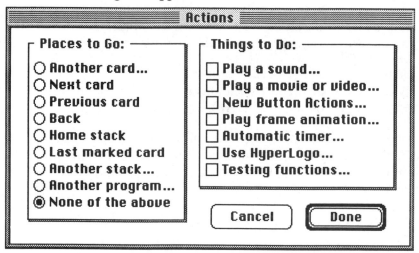

Under **Places to Go:**, select **Another Stack**. Select the stack you wish to be next in the sequence (alphabetical order, perhaps).

The "Transitions" dialog box appears.

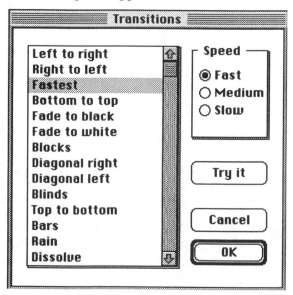

Select the transition and speed of the transition. Click **OK**.

The "Actions" dialog box reappears. Under **Things to Do**, students may select to play a sound.

The "Tape deck" window appears.

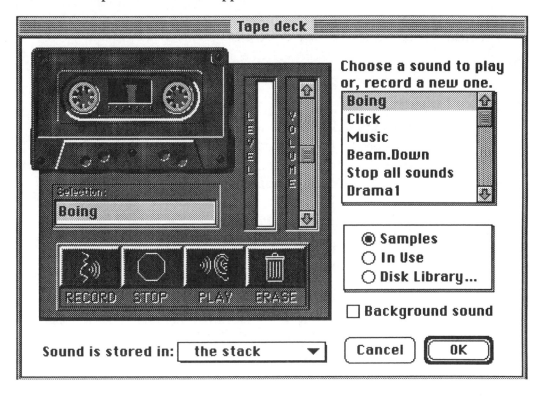

Students may select one of the sounds from the samples listed or choose
disk library to select from more sounds. (Sounds may be tested by
double-clicking on one, or by highlighting a sound and clicking on "Play.")
Once a sound has been selected, students click **OK**. The "Actions" dialog
box reappears. Students should check to be sure they have made a selection
from **Places to Go** and have selected a sound. Students click **Done**.

Click on the button to test it. If it works as intended, repeat the steps for
making a button on all student stacks.

If you want all student stacks to have the same button icon, transition, and
sound, the button can be copied from the first stack and pasted on all
other stacks.

Our Presidents

HyperTutorial Mastery Level Required:

Beginner

HyperOverview:

This project would be appropriate for students in grade five or above. Each student will take notes on one of the presidents of the United States. The information gathered about each president will be placed on a *HyperStudio* stack about the president. The president's data sheet is on page 221.

HyperObjectives:

Students will gain skills in note-taking, organizing, and presenting factual material, as well as gain knowledge about a president of the United States.

Once the president's data sheet is complete, the teacher will need to determine if the class is at the point of being able to present the information in paragraph form. An alternative to formal paragraph writing is to have students present facts as a list on the *HyperStudio* cards.

When all student projects have been completed, students can view others' projects in a variety of ways:

A. Stacks can be opened on all computers in the computer lab. Students rotate from one computer to another, going through several projects and taking notes on other presidents. Once back in the classroom, the teacher could lead a discussion comparing and contrasting the presidents.

B. Student stacks can be presented on a computer attached to a large-screen monitor or a LCD panel. Each project would be presented by the "author." This method of presentation has the virtue of all student projects being "formally" presented. The drawback of this approach is that students are sitting for a very long time, and students' attention spans may not allow for this to be productive.

C. Another approach would be to have all student stacks placed on one computer, perhaps in the school media center. The teacher or one of the students could create a one-card title stack, which contains a series of buttons. The buttons have the name of each president for which there is a *HyperStudio* stack. Once a student clicks on the button, it opens the stack about that president. (If this approach is taken, be sure to put a button on the last card of each president stack which links back to the title stack.) This is a good way to share information with all students in the school about our presidents. Students may be more inclined to look at these stacks because a sibling or friend has done the work, and there is the added benefit that they may learn something in the process.

HyperMedia Sources:

CD-ROMs with pictures of the presidents or scanned pictures (optional)

HyperHardware and Other HyperMaterials:

President's data sheet

Digital images (see Capturing Pictures pages 318 and 319) of the president or an image that has been copied from a URL on that president (you will need an Internet connection for this).

HyperPrerequisites:

Each student has completed the president's data sheet.

Each student has a digital image of his or her president and placed it on a disk.

HyperInstruction and HyperTimeline:

The construction of the actual *HyperStudio* stack will take three or four class periods, depending on the number of cards that the teacher requires in the stack. (Prior to beginning the *HyperStudio* project, a considerable amount of time will need to be devoted to gathering information.)

HyperExtensions:

A. Students can add a card on which he or she includes information that was learned during research about the president, but was not information required to be included in the stack.

B. If an Internet connection is available, students can add a button ("More Facts About...") on the final card which links to a URL on the president.

Our Presidents

Student Name_____ Date _____

Data Sheet

Please complete this data sheet about your president.

Name of President: _____

Date of Birth: _____ Date of Death:_____

Birthplace:_____

Early Life:_____

Education: _____

Political Party:_____ Years in Office: _____

Important events during his presidency:_____

_____

_____

_____

_____

_____

_____

_____

_____

_____

_____

_____

Our Presidents' Quick Guide

1. Open *HyperStudio*. Go to **File** and select **New Stack**.

2. When the following message appears, click **Yes**.

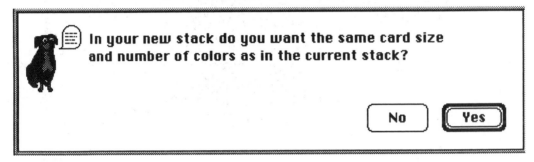

> In your new stack do you want the same card size and number of colors as in the current stack?
>
> No   Yes

3. Go to **File** and select **Save Stack As...** to save the stack.

4. Go to **Edit** and **Erase Background**. Select a background color. Click **OK**.

5. If you have a scanned image of the president, go to the **Objects** menu and select **Add a Graphic Object**. Select **Disk File**. Locate the disk on which the scanned image of the president has been saved. Select the image of the president.

   Using the **rectangular selector tool**, make a rectangle around as much of the image as you want to be included on your card, keeping the size of the card in mind. Click **OK**.

   Place the cursor inside the image and drag it to place the image. (Remember you need space for a text box in which you will type the name of the president and your name.) Click outside the image.

   The "Graphic Appearance" dialog box appears. A preview of the image is in the center of the window. On the left you may select a **Frame color** and **Frame width**. To select the **Frame width**, click on the up arrow key until you reach the desired width of the frame. (**Note:** The frame goes around the image. If your frame is too large, you lose part of the image.) Click **OK** when you have the desired frame color and width or if you do not want a frame around the image.

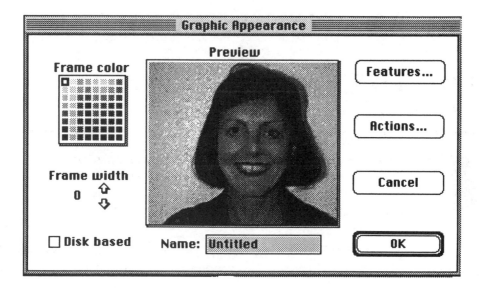

6. Go to the **Objects** menu and select **Add a Text Object**. Place the text box on the screen and resize it so that it is large enough for the name of the president and your name. Click outside the text box.

The "Text Appearance" dialog box appears. Select the color of text and background for the text box.

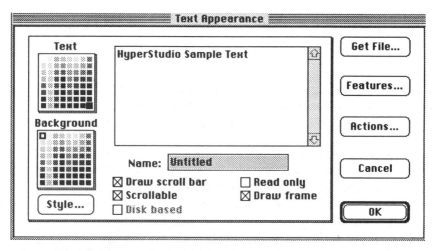

Click **Style**. The "Text Style" dialog box appears.

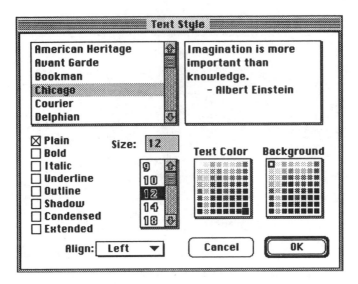

Select a font and size. (Keep in mind that this is only the title card, so a large size is desirable). Click **OK**.

This returns to the "Text Appearance" dialog box. You have one more opportunity at this point to make changes in text or background colors. Click **OK**.

Enter the name of the president and your name.

Pull the **Tools menu** down so that it is visible on the screen. Click on the **edit tool**. Double-click inside the text box. The "Text Appearance" dialog box reappears:

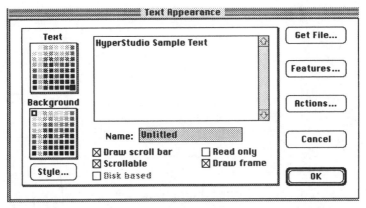

Select **Read only**. Click off. **Draw scroll bar** and **Scrollable**. Select the **browse tool** again.

7. Go to **Edit** and **New Card**. Caution: If you hold down "N" for too long, you make multiple new cards.

   Optional: Go to **Edit** and **Erase Background**. Select a background color. Click **OK**.

8. Go to the **Objects** menu and select **Add a Text Object**. Move the text box to the desired location on the card and resize as necessary. Click outside the text box.

   From the "Text Appearance" box, select the color of text and background of the text box.

   Click on **Style**. Select a font and a size no larger than 16 since you have several sentences to enter in this text box. Click **OK**. This returns to the "Text Appearance" dialog box. You have one more opportunity at this point to make changes in text or background colors. Click **OK**.

   Type biographical information about the president in this text box.

9. The card should be edited for spelling errors. Once all corrections have been made, select the **edit tool** from the **Tools** menu. Double-click on the text box. The "Text Appearance" dialog box appears. Select **Read only**. If the text box does not need to have a scroll bar or be scrollable, click off **Draw scroll bar** and **Scrollable**. Click **OK**. Select the **Browse** tool again.

10. Continue to add new cards, digital images (if there are more), and biographical information to each card by repeating steps 7–9.

11. When all cards have been made and completed, buttons must be added to link all of the cards. Go to the **Objects** menu and select **Add a Button**. The "Button Appearance" dialog box appears.

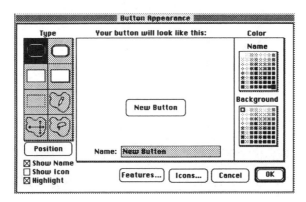

Select the dotted rectangle (the background of the button will be invisible). Click on **Icons**. Select the icon and click **OK**. The "Button Appearance" dialog box reappears with the selected icon in the center of the screen. Click **OK**.

12. The button will appear as a dotted rectangle in the center of the card. Click, hold, and drag inside the button to place it on the card. Click outside the button.

13. The "Actions" dialog box appears.

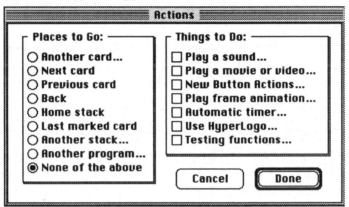

Under **Places to Go:**, select **Next card**. The "Transitions" dialog box appears.

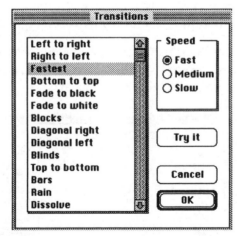

Select the transition and speed of the transition. Click **OK**.

The "Actions" dialog box reappears. Under **Things to Do**, you may choose to play a sound.

The "Tape deck" window appears.

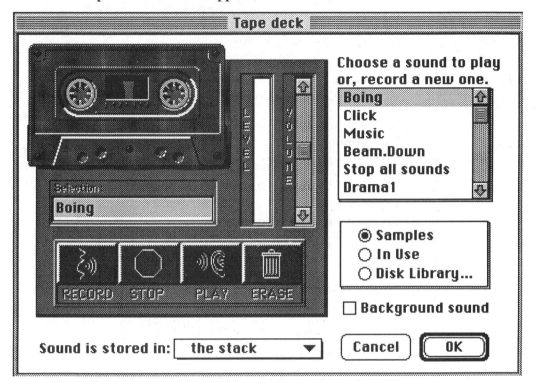

Select one of the sounds from the samples listed or choose **Disk Library** to select from more sounds. (Sounds may be tested by double-clicking on one, or by highlighting a sound and clicking on **Play**.) Once a sound has been selected, click **OK**. The "Actions" dialog box reappears. Be sure you have made a selection from **Places To Go** and have selected a sound. Click **Done**.

Click on the button to test it. If it works as intended, repeat the steps for making a button on all cards.

14. Go to **File** and **Save Stack**. Go to **File** and **Quit** *HyperStudio*.

The United States

HyperTutorial Mastery Level Required:

Intermediate

HyperOverview:

This project would be appropriate for students in grade five or above. Each student will take notes on one of the states of the United States. The information gathered about each state will be placed on a *HyperStudio* stack about the state. This project will bring to life a mundane assignment about the fifty states. This project would be a good opportunity for two classes on the same grade level to work together. By having both classes work on this project, perhaps all fifty states could be assigned! An example of a state data sheet is on page 231.

HyperObjectives:

Students will gain skills in note-taking, organizing, and presenting factual material, as well as gain knowledge about a state other than the one he or she presently resides.

Once the state data sheet is complete, the teacher will need to determine if the class is at the point of being able to present the information in paragraph form. An alternative to formal paragraph writing is to have students present facts in bulleted form on the *HyperStudio* cards.

When all student projects have been completed, students can view others' projects in a variety of ways:

A. Stacks can be opened on all computers in the computer lab. Students rotate from one computer to another, going through several projects and taking notes on other states. Once back in the classroom, the teacher could lead a discussion comparing and contrasting the states.

B. Student stacks can be presented on a computer attached to a large-screen monitor or a LCD panel. Each project would be presented by the "author." This method of presentation has the virtue of all student projects being "formally" presented. The drawback of this approach is that students are sitting for a very long time, and students' attention spans may not allow for this to be productive.

C. Another approach would be to have all student stacks placed on one computer, perhaps in the school media center. The teacher or one of the students could create a one-card title stack, which contains a series of buttons. The buttons have the name of each state for which there is a *HyperStudio* stack. Once a student clicks on the button, it opens the stack about that state. (If this approach is taken, be sure to put a button on the last card of the state stack which links back to the title stack.) This is a good way to share information with students in the school about other states.

HyperMedia Sources:

Electronic atlas or CD-ROM encyclopedia (optional)

HyperHardware and Other HyperMaterials:

State data sheet

Scanned images from books or from photographs students may have in a personal collection that was compiled while on a trip to that state. (See Capturing Pictures pages 318 and 319.)

Clip art from a graphics software package, such as SuperPrint

HyperPrerequisites:

Each student has completed the state data sheet.

Each student has scanned an image of his or her state and placed the scanned image on a disk or has planned to add clip art from a graphics package.

HyperInstruction and HyperTimeline:

The construction of the actual *HyperStudio* stack will take three or four class periods, depending on the number of cards that the teacher requires in the stack. (Prior to beginning the *HyperStudio* project, a considerable amount of time will need to be devoted to gathering the state information.)

HyperExtensions:

A. Students may add a card on which he/she makes illustrations of "Things (*Name of State*) is Famous For".

B. Students who complete this project quickly may be interested in researching a second state. This second *HyperStudio* stack may need to be completed independently by the student on a computer in the classroom if there is not adequate time for the completion of the second project in the computer lab.

C. If an Internet connection is available, students can add a button ("More Facts About ...") on the final card which links to a URL relating to the state.

D. Use an electronic atlas or other program that includes maps of the United States to show different views of the state (ie: physical, roads, etc.)

The United States Data Sheet

Student Name_____ Date _____

Please complete this sheet in order to be ready to begin your *HyperStudio* stack about your state.

Name of State: _____ Capital: _____

Location: (Surrounding states or geographic location within the United States)

_____

Major Cities: _____

_____

Climate:_____

_____

Natural Resources: _____

_____

_____

 Famous Landmarks:_____

_____

Major Industries and Crops: _____

_____

Important Events in This State's History: _____

_____

_____

_____

_____

The United States Quick Guide

1. Open *HyperStudio*. Go to **File** and select **New Stack.**

2. When the following message appears, click **Yes**.

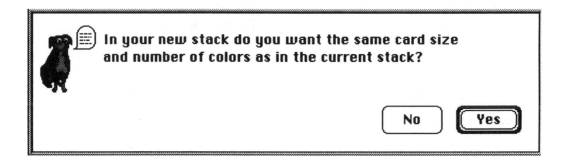

In your new stack do you want the same card size and number of colors as in the current stack?

No   Yes

3. Go to **File** and select **Save Stack As...** to save the stack.

4. Go to **Edit** and **Import Background**. The following screen appears:

Where do you want to get your picture?

◉ Disk file
○ Video
○ QuickTake camera

Cancel   OK

You want a background from the **Disk file**. Click **OK**. The following screen appears:

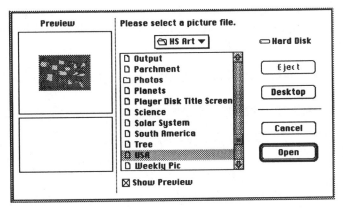

Click **USA** and **Open**. A map of the United States will appear on the first card.

5. Go to the **Objects** menu and select **Add a Text Object**. Move the text box to the top of the screen and resize it so that it fits above the map of the United States. Click outside the text box.

The "Text Appearance" dialog box appears. Click **Features**. The "Item Features" screen appears:

Note: If "Features" does not appear, you will need to set yourself up as an experienced user. To do this select **Preferences** from the **Edit** menu, then click **I'm an Experienced User**.

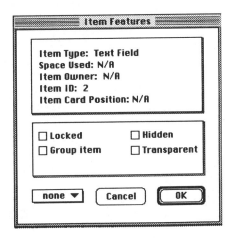

Click **Transparent**. The following screen appears:

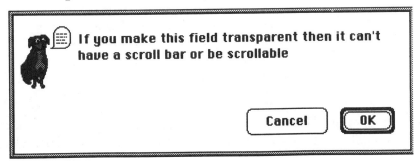

(This text box does not need to be scrollable or have a scroll bar since it will only contain the name of the state.) Click **OK**. The "Item Features" screen reappears. Click **OK**.

Select the color of text for the text box. A good idea would be to leave the text black.

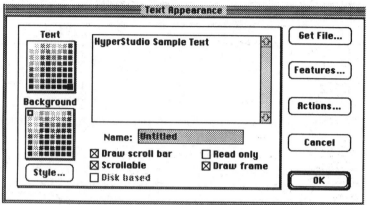

Click **Style**. The **Text Style** dialog box appears.

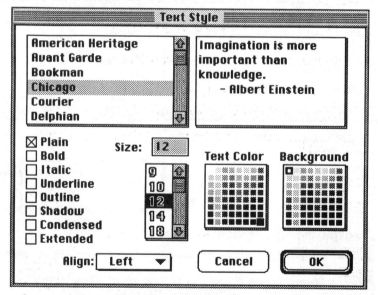

Select a font and size. (Keep in mind that only the name of the state will be in this text box, so a large size is desirable.) Select **Align: Center**. Click **OK**.

This returns to the "Text Appearance" dialog box. You have one more opportunity at this point to make changes in the text color. Click **OK**.

Enter the name of the state.

Pull the **tools menu** down so that it is visible on the screen. Click on the **edit tool**. Double-click inside the text box. The "Text Appearance" dialog box reappears:

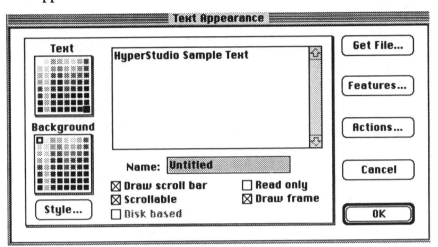

Select **Read only**. Select the **browse tool** again.

6. Go to the **Objects** menu and select **Add a Button**.

The "Button Appearance" dialog box appears.

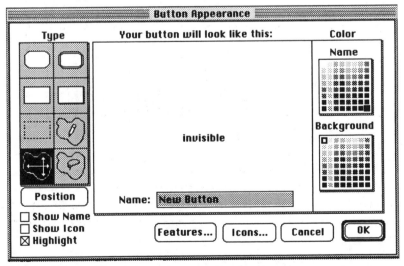

Select the expanding area button. Click **OK**. The following screen will appear:

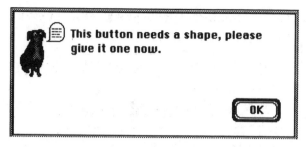

Click **OK**. Place the four-headed arrow cursor inside your state and click. The following screen appears:

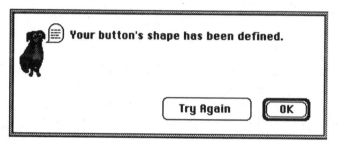

If you need to start over, click **Try Again**. If you correctly clicked inside your state, click **OK**.

The "Actions" dialog box appears.

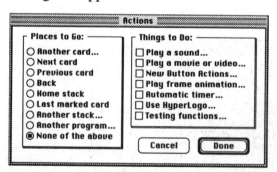

Under **Places to Go:**, select **Another card**. The following screen appears:

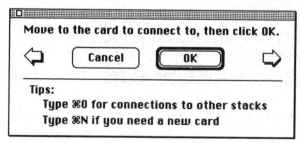

Make a new card. When the blank card appears, click **OK**. The
"Transitions" dialog box appears:

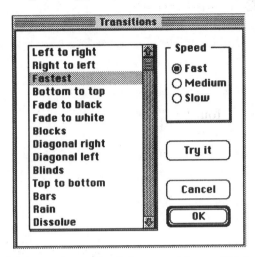

Select the transition and speed of the transition. Click **OK**.

The "Actions" dialog box reappears. Under **Things to Do**, students may
select to play a sound.

The "Tape deck" window appears.

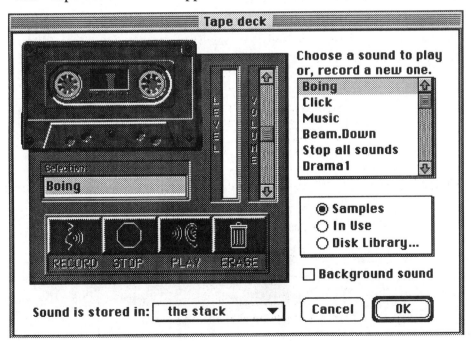

You may select one of the sounds from the samples listed or choose **disk library** to select from more sounds. (Sounds may be tested by double-clicking on one, or by highlighting a sound and clicking on **Play**.) Once a sound has been selected, students click **OK**. The "Actions" dialog box reappears. Check to be sure you have made a selection from **Places To Go** and have selected a sound. Click **Done**.

7. Click on the button to try it. If it works as intended, you should be on the second card of the stack. Go to **Edit** and **Erase Background**. Select a background color and click **OK**.

8. Go to the **Objects** menu and select **Add a Text Object**. Move the text box to place it and resize as necessary. Click outside the text box.

   From the "Text Appearance" box, select the color of text and background of the text box.

   Click **Style**. Select a font and a size no larger than 24. Click **OK**.

   This returns to the "Text Appearance" dialog box. You have one more opportunity at this point to make changes in text or background colors. Click **OK**.

   Enter information about your state from your data sheet.

9. The card should be edited for spelling errors. Once all corrections have been made, select the **edit tool** from the **Tools** menu. Double-click on the text box. The "Text Appearance" dialog box appears:

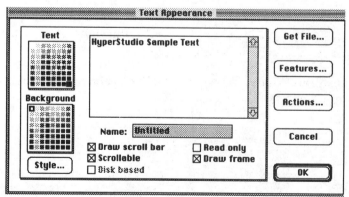

Select **Read only**. If the text box does not need to have a scroll bar or be scrollable, click off of **Draw scroll bar** and **Scrollable**. Click **OK**. Select the **browse tool** again.

10. Go to Objects and **Add a Button**.

The "Button Appearance" dialog box appears.

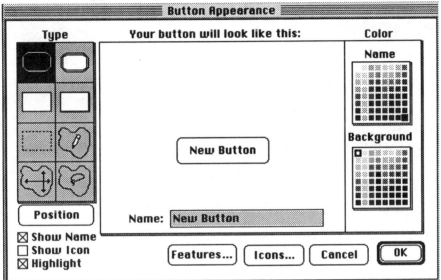

Select the dotted rectangle (the background of the button will be invisible). Click on **Icons**. Select the icon and click **OK**. The "Button Appearance" dialog box reappears with the selected icon in the center of the screen. Click **OK**.

The button will appear as a dotted rectangle in the center of the card. Click, hold, and drag inside the button to place it on the card. Click outside the button.

The "Actions" dialog box appears. Under **Places to Go:** , select "Another card". Create a new card. Click **OK**.

The "Transitions" dialog box appears. Select the transition and speed of the transition. Click **OK**.

The "Actions" dialog box reappears. Under **Things To Do**, you may choose to play a sound. The **Tape Deck** window appears.

You may select one of the sounds from the samples listed or choose **Disk Library** to select from more sounds. (Sounds may be tested by double-clicking on one, or by highlighting a sound and clicking on **Play**.) Once a sound has been selected, click **OK**. The "Actions" dialog box reappears. Check to be sure you have made a selection from **Places To Go** and have selected a sound. Click **Done**.

Click on the button to test it. If it moves to the next blank card, repeat steps 7–10 until all cards and all buttons have been made.

11. When you are finished, go to **File** and **Save Stack**. Go to **File** and **Quit** *HyperStudio*.

Extras!

Adding A Digital Picture:

If you have a scanned image of your state to include in your stack, move to the card on which you wish to place the image. Go to **Objects** and **Add a Graphic Object**. The following screen appears:

The image is on a disk, so click **OK**. You may need to click on desktop to locate the disk on which the image has been saved. Click on the name of the image and click **Open**. Using the **rectangular selector tool**, make a rectangle around as much of the image as you want to be included on your card. Click on **OK**. The image with "marching ants" will appear in the center of the card. You may move the image to place it on the card. Click outside the image.

The Graphic Appearance dialog box appears. A preview of the image is in the center of the window. On the left you may select a **Frame color** and **Frame width**. To select the **Frame width**, click on the up arrow key until you reach the desired width of the frame. (**Note:** The frame goes around the image. If your frame is too large, you lose part of the image.) Click **OK** when you have the desired frame color and width or if do not want a frame around the image. (The example shown is not a scanned image, but it serves to illustrate the procedure to follow.)

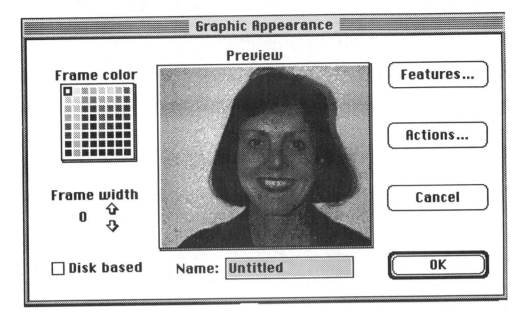

If you have placed the scanned image on the card after adding a text box, you may need to move the text box. Click on the **edit tool** from the **Tools menu**. Click once inside the text box to move and resize the text box, if necessary. Once it is in the desired location, click back on the **browse tool**.

Remember to go to **File** and **Save Stack** when you have finished this step.

Adding Clip Art:

If you are adding clip art from a graphics package such as *SuperPrint*, select the clip art. Copy the clip art. Open the *HyperStudio* state stack, move to the card on which you wish to place the clip art. Go to **Edit** and **Paste**. Place the cursor inside the clip art and drag to the desired location on the card. You can color the clip art by selecting the color from the **Colors menu** and the paint bucket in the **Tools menu**. Click inside the clip art to add color.

If you have placed the clip art on the card after adding a text box, you may need to move the text box. Click on the **edit tool** from the **Tools menu**. Click once inside the text box to move and resize the text box, if necessary. Once it is in the desired location, click back on the **browse tool**.

Remember to go to **File** and **Save Stack** when you have finished this step.

Go to **File** and **Quit** *HyperStudio* when you are finished.

Rolling Credits and Bibliographies for Projects

HyperTutorial Mastery Level Required:

Intermediate

HyperOverview

Students will use rolling credits for HyperProjects, video portfolios, live presentations, or transfer to video tape for a school news program. This project should be used in conjunction with other projects. One of the goals of this project is to help students think about giving credit to others they borrow materials from in order to create their own project. This project will also show students that most projects are a collaborative effort and more than one person almost always helps to create a project.

HyperObjectives:

Students will gather information needed for rolling credits and/or a bibliography as they create a project.

Students will design a card and stylize the text in a worksheet which includes size, font, color, and look of the rolling credits.

Students will demonstrate using the Roll Credits feature in *HyperStudio*.

Students will demonstrate understanding of giving credit to resources they borrow.

HyperMedia Sources:

This lesson should be done in conjunction with another project. All the information needed for this lesson will be obtained from the resources material used in a typical project. Examples: Students use music from a sound clips library as background for their slide show. Credit should be given to the sound clips library. Students use photographic images and clip art from the World Wide Web. Credit should be given to the source listing the web page address, title of each work used, and artist.

The *HyperStudio* Ready Made Card Bibliography Template is helpful but not necessary to complete this project.

HyperHardware and Other HyperMaterials:

Data Gathering for Project Credits Worksheet pgs 250

If the project requires transfer to video tape you will need an AV computer, a video recorder, RCA or S-VHS cables, depending on your equipment set up.

HyperPrerequisites:

Students should have a working knowledge of copyright issues and why they should give credit to others work when they use it in a project.

HyperInstruction and HyperTimeline:

When students are beginning a project other than this one, they should be given the *Data Gathering for Project Credits Worksheet (Page 250)*. The teacher should explain that this worksheet will help them to keep track of resources that they borrow from different places. This would be a good time to introduce information concerning the proper use of copyrighted materials in student projects. Another area to consider giving students information on, is how to create a proper bibliography. Bibliographies should be introduced for electronic projects just as they are for paper projects.

As the students make decisions about their projects they should begin adding the necessary information to the *Data Gathering for Projects Credits Worksheet.* Once all the elements have been added to their project, they will be ready to design the Roll Credits card.

Students should design the card on the paper template so when they go to the computer, the majority of their decision making is done. This technique also helps in classrooms where there is limited computer access. When all the decisions on what the Roll Credits card will look like have been completed, the students begin design of the card on the computer.

The Roll Credits card can be a completely separate stack or part of an existing stack. This is a decision that you and your students should make together.

If the project includes transferring the Roll Credits information to video tape, you will need to use the information that came with your audio/video card explaining how to hook your audio/video model computer to the VCR. Cue up your video tape, begin recording, and start your credits rolling!

HyperExtensions:

Students can add additional items to the Roll Credits cards.

Students can ask each other to check the information on the Roll Credits cards and try out the cards to make sure the credits scroll at a rate that others can read them.

Students can ask others to check spelling and grammar on their Roll Credits cards.

HyperStudio Roll Credits Quick Guide

This Quick Guide will explain how to create scrolling text in *HyperStudio* that can be used in video production.

1. The color red does not transfer well to video tape or live presentations. Also avoid variations of red. A dark color background with light color text shows up best. A dark blue background with yellow text is a good combination. Make the text large enough to read.

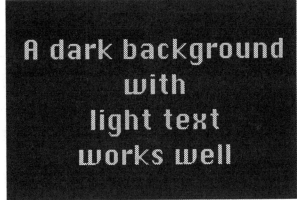

2. After opening *HyperStudio* go to the **File** menu and select **New Stack**.

3. After you create a new stack go back to the **File** menu and **Save Stack**.

4. In the **Objects** menu choose **About this Stack..** In About Stack click on **Change # of colors or size.**

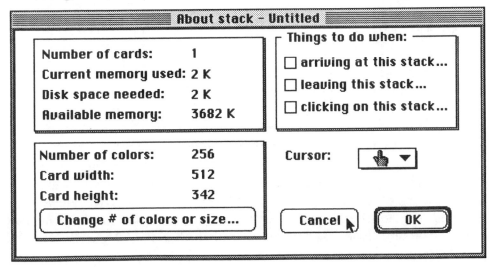

In 'Pick how many colors," click **256**. In the "Pick a card size" choose 640 x 480. This is a standard television screen size.

Click **OK**. Click **OK** again.

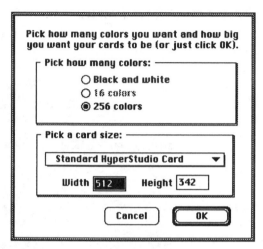

5. In the **Objects** menu choose add a **Text Object**. Size the text object to the size that you wish it to be and then click the mouse with the cursor outside of the text object.

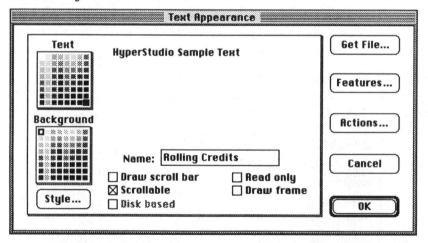

In the "Text Appearance" window turn off **Draw scroll bar** and **Draw frame**. Name your text object a name that you will remember. You will need this name again later. Click on **Style**. In the "Text Style" menu click the box next to **Align**, choose **Center**. Also select a text size large enough to read on the screen. (Nothing smaller than 18-point.) Make other choices as necessary.

6. If you need to resize the text object, change to the arrow tool and double-click inside the text object. Move the mouse over a corner intersection until you have one line with two arrows pointing in a diagonal direction. Resize to fill screen. Change back to the **browse tool**.

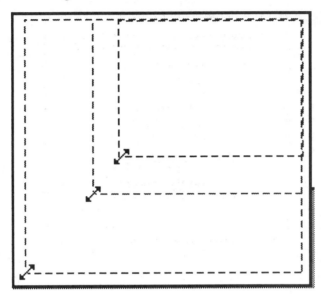

7. Now type the text you want to scroll into the **text object**. If the text doesn't look the way you want, select the **edit tool** and double-click on the **text object**. This allows you to change your selections.

8. In the **Objects** Menu choose **Add a Button**. In the "Button Appearance" window select the invisible button and make sure the **Highlight** is NOT selected. Click **OK**. The button outline appears on the screen.

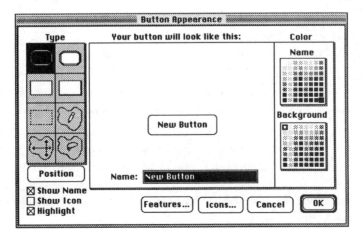

To move the button to a new location, place the cursor on the button, click down, and drag it to the new location. Place invisible buttons in the same place on each card so they are easy to locate. Click one time outside the button.

9. Choose **New Button Actions**.

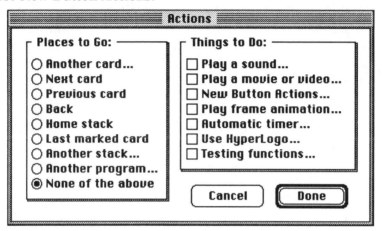

10. In the **New Button** "Actions" window click on **Roll Credits** and click on **Use this NBA.**

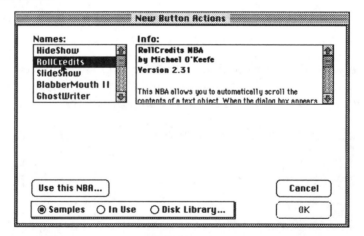

Type in the name of the **text object** that you want the button to activate. This is the name you chose earlier for the **text object** you made. Then click **OK** to close the "RollCredits" window.

Click **OK** to close the "New Button Actions" screen. Click **Done** to close the "Button Actions" window. Try out your button.

Hyperhints:

If you want the text to roll all the way off the screen you can add extra lines at the end of the text. You can even create a design with dots or other characters.

*To make the blinking cursor disappear from your **text object** you will need to lock the **text object**. Once you lock it you will not be able to make changes in your text until you unlock it again. To do this click on the **edit tool** in the tools palette. Double-click on the **text object** you want to remove the cursor from. Place an "X" in the **Read Only** box. Click **OK**.*

*If you want to make changes in either your Button or **text object** you must click on the **edit tool** and then double-click the object you want to change. When done make sure **browse tool** is selected. Click your invisible button and watch your text scroll.*

Data Gathering for Project Credits Worksheet

Anytime you create a Hyperproject, video production, or other project you should give credit to all the resources you have used. Another good thing to do is thank special people who have helped make your project a success. Review the information below. When you are ready to create your Rolling Credits or Bibliography page you will have all the information you need to complete the project.

As you work on your project, add information to the list below as you borrow it from different resources.

Written resources—List all books, pamphlets, web sites, and other printed written materials you used to create your project. If you wrote an original story make sure to give yourself credit! Make sure you include copyright dates, page numbers, company names, and authors.

Sample:

Cards 1,3,5 & 7 of stack 1 "Laura the Digital Pot Belly Pig," by Chris Carey, Educational Design Studio, Inc. P.O. Box 608013, Orlando, FL 32860-8013 ©1996

Card #	Stack	Description
all	Pig 1	"Pig noises." Steve Hall, Ms. Smith's Class, Edgewater School, Orlando, FL

Sound resources—List sound clip library parts used, narrator, and original sounds created for the project.

Card #	Stack	Description
all	Pig 1	"Pig noises." Steve Hall, Ms. Smith's Class, Edgewater School, Orlando, FL

Graphics resources—List all the clip art graphics and their sources including those you create yourself.

Card #	Stack	Description
6	Pig 2	"The Pig." ftp://ftp.eds.np.org/pub/images/gif/potbelly.gif
6	Pig 3	HyperStudio clip art "Animals" HyperStudio, Roger Wagner Publishing,
		El Cajon, CA 1995
7	Pig 3	"Pig nose." drawn by Laura Carey, Edgewater School, Orlando, FL

Video resources—List any moving video you have added to your project.

Card #	Stack	Description
4	Pig 1	"Laura lying on her side," photographed by Angel Hall with
		QuickTake camera, Edgewater School, Orlando, FL
6	Pig 3	"Laura Rooting," Educational Design Studio, Inc. P.O. Box 608013,
		Orlando, FL 32860-8013 ©1996

Still photographic resources—List all photographic pictures used in your project and where you found them. If you got a picture from the Internet it is a good idea to include the web address where you found the picture. If you took the pictures yourself, make sure to add your name.

Card #	Stack	Description
3	Pig 1	"Laura with Muddy Nose," by Chris Carey, Educational Design Studio,
		Inc. P.O. Box 608013, Orlando, FL 32860-8013 ©1996

Animation—List any animations in your project. Again, if you created them, give yourself credit.

Card #	Stack	Description
1	Pig 1	"Laura's Walk," by Chris Carey, Educational Design Studio, Inc.
		P.O. Box 608013, Orlando, FL 32860-8013 ©1996

Special Thanks—Make sure you give credit to those who were helpful in making your project a success.

Card #	Stack	Description
all	Pig 1	"Pig noises." Steve Hall, Ms. Smith's Class, Edgewater School, Orlando, FL

Shadows and Reflections

HyperTutorial Mastery Level Required:
Advanced

HyperOverview:
This lesson covers the principles of making drop shadows both rectangular and free-form, and as an extension, making shaded blocks and block letters. It then includes techniques for making shaped, foreshortened shadows for standing objects. Finally, it extends the tricks for shadows to making reflections. Only a minimum of freehand drawing is required.

HyperObjectives:
Learn the basic principles for making drop shadows, including the idea of the direction of the light source.

Extend this to drop shadows for free-form shapes, including text.

Use the same principles to form shaded blocks and text. This introduces some simple perspective.

Understand the principle of foreshortening, and use this to create shaped shadows on the ground.

Extend the same techniques to making simple reflections.

HyperMedia Sources:
Students will use clip art from the Media Library on the *HyperStudio* CD, and will create some original artwork.

HyperHardware and Other HyperMaterials:
None

HyperPrerequisites:
Students should be comfortable with the lasso and rectangular selectors, and know what each can do. In particular, they should know that the rectangular selector is needed to flip and stretch or squash a selection, either selector can be

used with Replace Colors, Gradients, and the cookie cutter command, and the lasso should be used whenever an exact shape is desired. They should know how to get to the Gradients option and choose the type and set up the colors. They should be able to use the line tool with the shift key and have at least some experience doodling with the brush. They should be able to use the Magnify option. And they should be able to start a new stack, make a new blank card, and add clip art from the Media Library.

HyperInstruction and HyperTimeline:

This is a fairly open-ended lesson. In each part, students will gain some general principles and techniques, which hopefully will suggest many experiments. If possible, do each of the three topics as a separate lesson, and then have some time for students to work at the keyboard applying what they have learned. It is hoped that after this practice, these tricks will be used in making stacks throughout the year.

The first topic could take an hour or more, the second about half an hour to an hour, and the third less than half an hour to work through. In a classroom with few computers, all three could be given initially as demonstrations, but students will need to work through at the keyboard at some later time. These tricks should be fun, especially those in the second two topics. Fairly extensive instructions for the basic exercises are included on the Quick Guides so that students will be able to remember how they were done. The drop shadows and standing shadows sheets have some further ideas described briefly, which some more advanced students may wish to try.

The first set of tricks goes through the creation of block text; all these are based on the drop shadow. The second topic relies on making a lassoed shadow, then squashing it to foreshorten it, to make shadows at 90° to the casting shape. The third topic is simple reflections.

Start by making a new stack, which can be named "Shadows". To get students to thinking about shadows, have them make a new button with a shadowed rectangle style. Explain that once they understand the idea, they will be able to make their own drop shadows, but they will not be limited to just one size and one direction as they are with the button. They can make their own shadowed clip art, turn it into graphics with actions, and use those as buttons specially designed for their stacks.

Topic 1: Basic Drop Shadows

Point out that the shadowed button style looks three-dimensional, and stands out more than the plain rectangular button. All that is required to produce that effect is a dark line on two sides of the rectangle. Ask the students to guess where the light would be coming from, to make the shadow on the right and lower sides. Then delete the button, and let the students start making their own shadowed art.

Make a rectangle about the size of a button, and fill it with a fairly bright color. Type a label in the rectangle. Alternatively, fill the rectangle with a pattern. Lasso the filled rectangle, option-drag a copy, and go to **Gradients** (**Edit:Effects**). Set the color in both palettes to black and click **OK**. This is a tricky way to fill a patterned shape. (The other method would be to drag the shape over a black area and use the cookie cutter, but this seems quicker.) Point out that this method of producing a shadow of the exact size and shape of the original would work just as well with free-forms, like lassoed clip art or text.

Be sure students put these two elements in a safe part of the card and work with copies from here on. This same rectangle and its shadow will be used many times, and then all the examples can be compared.

For the first example, hold down on the option key and drag a copy of the filled rectangle and magnify it 200%. Point out that this quick way of making a copy will be used throughout the lesson. Use the **pencil** or **line tool** with the shift key to make a black line along the left side and the bottom. Erase one pixel at each end so that the lines don't quite reach the upper left and lower right corners. If you had lined up a copy of the rectangle on a copy of the shadow and then moved the rectangle over one pixel in each direction, you would get the same result. The line not quite reaching the corner, and being on only two sides, is what creates the illusion of a shadow.

This is the thinnest possible shadow, and it makes the rectangle look like it has perhaps the thickness of an index card. For this minimum shadow, drawing the line is easier than actually working with a copy of the shadow. Lasso a copy of the shadow, paste it down, and then lasso another copy of the rectangle. Drag it to line up exactly on the shadow, then use the **arrow** keys to move the rectangle up and to the right, creating an offset. Deselect. For this wider shadow, it's easier to actually work with the two shapes. Lasso another copy of the shadow, paste it, and then fill it with a light gray. Get another copy of the rectangle, line it up, and this time offset it six pixels up and right. Now the rectangle really appears to float in front of the surface. Shadows thrown from a distance usually are not as dark as shadows up close, so the paler color looks more natural. Point out that shadows aren't just restricted to gray. If the shadow falls on a pale colored background, make the shadow a slightly darker and perhaps duller tone close to that color.

At this point, ask the students which way the light would come to make these shadows. We've carefully made all these shadows on the lower left, so they agree with each other, as if the light was coming in from the upper right. Just as easily, they could all be on the lower right, like the button. Or they could be all in the upper left or right, if lighted from below. The important thing is to have them all the same on one card. This is often neglected, even in professional web sites. Students may spot some unlikely collections of shadows, once they know this trick.

This is a good point to go to the **File** menu and save the stack.

Extension: Shaded Blocks

Have the students select both the rectangle and shadow shapes, put the selection on the clip board with the copy command, make a new blank card, and then paste the shapes. Point out that the first very narrow shadow actually looked more like the edge of a piece of thick paper than a separate shadow. Starting with the same basic shapes, we can create a thicker block to really make the rectangle look solid and stand out. We will start as if to make a shadow, but with a few additional steps, it will become a block.

Start by lassoing the shadow and dragging off a copy. Fill it with some color besides black, perhaps a medium gray. Option drag a copy of the rectangle, line it up on the gray shadow, and use the arrow keys to move it four up and four right. At this point, it will just look like a rectangle with a gray drop shadow. Magnify the upper left corners. Because the rectangle was offset the same number of pixels up and right, a line connecting the two corners will be the diagonal of a square. Use the eyedropper to make sure the color is set to the gray of the shadow. Use the pencil to connect the corners with three pixels, and then fill in the gap. Magnify the lower right corners, draw the three pixels of the diagonal, and fill that gap. The rectangle already looks like a block, but it will look even better if we custom shade the left side and bottom. Decide what color the shadowed bottom of the block would be. For example, if the rectangle is filled with a bright red, perhaps the shaded bottom would be a dull dark red.

Magnify the lower left corner. Draw that diagonal in the color you have chosen for the bottom, and then use the paint bucket to fill the area on the bottom. Fill the side of the shadow with a lighter shade of the bottom color. Of course, you can make a light gray copy of the original shadow and float this block on it, and suspend it in space. Before continuing, be sure to save the stack.

Extension: Block Text

Tell students the same technique helps in drawing three dimensional text. Make a new blank card. Get the paint text tool, and set the font to Chicago 36-point, bold. Have students choose a bright, clear color, type their first names, and then lasso it and drag off a copy. Go to **Replace Colors** and change it to a very pale tone of that color. Lasso and drag off another copy of the name, go to **Replace Colors**, and change it to a dark tone of the color. The three copies of the name will be the face, the highlight, and the shadow of the block text. Point out that the shadow and highlight are always on opposite sides, diagonally across from each other. Discuss the fact that the shadowed side should be wide since we are trying to create the illusion of depth, but we can't really see the brightly lighted side, only a highlight or glare off the very edge of the block. If the highlight is too wide, the effect will be an optical illusion. Of course, you could reverse the entire thing, and have a wide lighted side and very narrow shadowed edge across from it. Select and duplicate all three copies, leaving an extra unchanged set in case of problems.

Lasso the medium colored copy, line it up exactly on top of the pale copy, and use the **arrow** keys to move it one down and one left to expose a one-pixel wide highlight. It may be hard to see on a white card. Lasso this highlighted copy, line it up on the dark copy along the left and bottom edges, and use the arrow keys to move it up four and right four. You must use the left and bottom edges to get lined up, since the highlighted copy is bigger than the dark one at this point. Magnify each set of left side corners where there is a pair of right angles. Don't worry about curves or various slanted edges, just the straight angles such as the tops of E's and T's, for example. At each right angle gap, fill in the diagonal and the triangle it creates with the shadow color, just as was done for the corner of the rectangular block. Make a rectangle of the face color large enough for the entire name. This may work best on a new card, if the current one is fairly full. Paste the name on the rectangle for an embossed effect. Save the stack. This is a good stopping point for the day. Give students a chance to experiment with these tricks before tackling the next topic.

Topic 2: Standing Shadows

In all the examples so far, the shadows have been in the same plane as the casting shape. Floating upright letters have a shadow cast behind as if on a wall. Now we will learn to make shadows that lie down flat. Start by getting across art concept foreshortening. A good example is something circular, like a CD or the top of a can. As it tilts over flat, it no longer looks circular but oval, as if it has been squashed. Students may want to play around with the "Box Maker Extra," noticing the squashed shape of a rectangle when it is tilted down away from upright.

We can squash or stretch any shape selected with the **rectangular selector** by putting the cursor on top, so the double-headed arrow appears, changing just the height. So to make a shadow that lies down, we just make an upright shadow and then squash it flat.

Have the students make a new blank card, go to the **File** menu, and choose **Add Clip Art**. Look on the CD for the Media Library, and open the **Black Bear** screen in the **Mammals** folder under **Animal Kingdom**, select the bear, and click **OK**. Position the bear in the upper left quarter of the card, and make a rectangle in the upper right big enough to cut out a bear shadow. For variety, use the palest brown or a gray-blue instead of gray or black. Lasso the bear, option-drag a copy onto the rectangle, and cut out the shape with option–⌘–C. Without deselecting, drag the silhouette of the bear down to the lower part of the card. Deselect, and then capture the bear shadow again with the rectangular selector. Put the cursor on the top edge of the selection, so that the double-headed arrow appears, and squash down the height to about one-third. Lasso the bear picture, and paste it in position so the feet meet the shadow's feet. This trick will only work on some animal positions; a side view seems to work many times. It is okay to stretch part of the shadow or erase a part protruding below a foot.

The fill patterns make good shaped shadows, too. Try the gray and blue-pebbly ones. The green grassy pattern squashes down to look duller, so you can use it to make the squashed shadow in a background filled with that pattern. Try some foreshortened shadows with text, too. It works better with tall, skinny text, so that the shadow shows.

Have the students save the stack, and make a new card. We'll actually do a little bit of original art here. But it might surprise you and the students to see how easy original art can be, so give it a try. Get the smallest slant brush and sweep a brown curve for a trunk.

You may want to even off the base. You can add detail with the pencil, if you wish. Get the smallest dot brush and scribble the top of the palm tree with the black and green leaf fill pattern. Just sweep fronds out all around from a center point. Choose the lighter green grassy pattern, and streak over some of the fronds. Finish with a few streaks of the lightest green fill pattern. Lasso the top of the tree and put it on the trunk. By working in two subunits, it's easy to get them just right and then connect them.

Lasso the tree, option-drag a copy, and this time go to **Gradients** and apply a vertical gradient from the palest gray to black. Deselect the shadow, capture with the rectangular selector, and squash the shadow. Lasso and paste the tree in position. The gradient gives the shadow a more realistic look, darker next to the trunk and gradually fading out farther away.

The slant and back lighting examples are available to students who want an extra challenge. This is a good place to save the stack, and give students some time to absorb the lesson so far.

Topic 3: Reflections

Start by making a new card. Get the text tool and choose Chicago, bold, 18, or 24-point, in a bright color other than green. Type the student's name or some other word. Important: If there are any letters with tails below the surface line, upper case MUST be used. Prepare a pane of glass for the letters to sit on. Use a light green to make the slanting sides using the **line tool** and **shift**. They should be wider apart than the typed word, and long enough so that the space thus created is four or five times the height of the letters. Use the palest green and a thin line for the back edge, and a deeper green and thick line for the front edge. Fill the trapezoid with the palest green. Use the magnifying glass, and clean up protruding lines.

Select the word with the **rectangle selector** and option-drag a copy. While it is selected, go to **Edit Effects** menu and choose **Flip Upside Down**. Still selected, put the cursor on the bottom edge so the double-headed arrow appears, and stretch the selection about twice its height. Deselect. Lasso the stretched, flipped copy, go to **Gradients** under **Edit Effects**, and apply a vertical gradient.

The top color should be a duller tone similar to the color of the typed word, and the bottom should be the pale green of the glass. Click **OK**. **Line** up the reflection with the bottom of the word, but leave about a two pixel gap. Lasso both word and reflection, and paste on the glass. Be sure the entire reflection is in the glass. The upright letters can stick up above the top edge. The duller color is typical of reflections, and the gradient makes the reflection fade out smoothly into the glass.

HyperExtensions:

Lasso simple clip art shapes, create gray shadow copies, and paste the art offset on the shadow. These are useful with invisible shaped buttons. There are good arrows in the Clip Art folder, Media Library.

Try lassoed script with a pale shadow for titles. Try different offsets to see a floating effect. This works better with larger text.

Try working with color shadows. For example, the pale gray green fourth from the right in row seven of the standard 256 palette is a good shadow color on pale yellow backgrounds.

Make block text in various colors. Turn it into a graphic object, so that it is easy to position, and give it a name. Type the same word in the face color. Position the graphic object so that the shadowed edges line up with the edges of the painted text. Put an invisible button over it. Choose **New Button** "Actions", **Hide/Show**, **Graphic**, and enter the name. Be sure the button is created last, or you may have to use the **Bring Closer** command under **Objects** to get it on top. Try the button.

Turn some block text into a graphic object and position it on a gradient background for a dramatic title page. For variety, do a block lighted from below. Switch the position of the dark and highlight copies, and fill the corners with the light copy color.

Experiment making a slanted shadow for some text. Follow the directions on the Standing Shadows reference sheet. This technique, involves successive captures with the **rectangular selector** and moves with the arrow keys.

This reflection example is for glass, so there are no ripples. Try making a watery reflection. Make a copy of the reflection, and capture all but a small slice. Use the arrow keys to move right one. Capture within a small slice of the jog, and move right two. Capture again within a small slice of the jog, and move left two. Continue capturing progressively smaller rectangles and alternately shifting right and left. This is similar to creating a slant, except in this case you alternate the direction of the shifts. This should create ripples.

Shadows and Reflections Quick Guide

New Button   **New Button**

If you have been using *HyperStudio*, you have surely made many buttons. Have you noticed the button style that looks like it has a shadow? It really looks like it's standing out from the card. This three-dimensional effect is a very easy trick. The only difference between the shadowed button and a plain rectangle is a line around the bottom and right side that does not quite reach the corners. You can create shadows easily, in different widths and on any side of the artwork. This Quick Guide will make you a wizard with all kinds of shadows and reflections, too. Use your reference sheets to help you follow the instructions.

Basic Drop Shadows

Start by going to the **File** menu and choosing **New Stack.** Save the stack under the name **Shadows**. Make a rectangle about the size of a typical button, and fill it with a fairly light bright color. Type a label in the rectangle or fill it with a pattern. Lasso the filled rectangle, hold down the **Option** key, drag off a copy, and go to **Gradients**

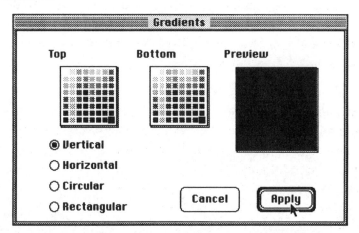

Set the color in both palettes to black and click **OK**. This is a tricky way to fill a patterned shape. Now you have a piece of clip art and a shadow just the right size for it. Of course, you would use this method to get a shadow just the right size for art of any shape, not just for rectangles. Put these two in a safe part of the card and work with copies. We will use this rectangle and its shadow many times and then compare all the effects.

For the first example, option-drag a copy of the filled rectangle and **Magnify** it 200%. Use the pencil or line tool with the **Shift** key to make a black line along the left side and the bottom. Erase one pixel at each end, so that the lines don't quite reach the upper left and lower right corners. If you lined up a copy of the rectangle on a copy of the shadow, and moved the rectangle over one pixel in each direction, you would get the same result. The line on only two sides, not quite reaching the corner, is what creates the illusion of a shadow.

This is the thinnest possible shadow. It makes the rectangle look like it has the thickness of an index card. For this thin shadow, drawing the line is easier than using a copy of the shadow. Notice that you have made a shadow on the opposite side from the shadow on the button. Try a wider shadow. Lasso and option-drag a copy of the shadow and paste it. Then lasso and option-drag another copy of the rectangle. Drag it to line up exactly on top of the shadow, then use the arrow keys to move the rectangle up four and right four, creating an offset. Deselect. For this wider shadow, it's easier to actually work with the two shapes.

Lasso and option-drag another copy of the shadow, paste it, and then fill it with a light gray. Get another copy of the rectangle, line it up, and this time offset it six pixels up and six right. Now the rectangle really appears to float in front of the surface. Shadows at a distance usually are not as dark as shadows up close, so the paler color looks more natural. Shadows are not just restricted to gray. For a shadow on a pale colored card, try making it a slightly darker, duller shade of that color.

Which way would the light come from to make these shadows? We have carefully made all of them on the lower left, as if light was coming in from the upper right. Just as easily, they could all be on the lower right, like the button. Or they could all be in the upper left or right, if lighted from below. The important thing is to have them all the same on one card since a real light would create all shadows on the same side. This is often neglected, even in professional web sites. You may spot some unlikely groups of shadows, now that you know to check for the light source. This is a good point to go to the **File** menu and save the stack.

Extension: Shaded Blocks

Select both the rectangle and shadow shapes, put the selection on the clip board with the copy command, make a new blank card, and use the paste command to paste the shapes. That first very narrow shadow looked more like the edge of a piece of thick paper than a separate shadow. Starting with our two basic shapes, we can create a thicker block to really make the rectangle look solid and stand out. Starting as if to make a shadow, with a few additional steps we will have a block. Refer to the **Drop Shadows** Quick Guide for help with the next steps.

Start by lassoing the shadow and dragging off a copy. Fill it with some color besides black, maybe a medium gray. Option-drag a copy of the rectangle, line it up on the gray shadow, and use the arrow keys to move it four up and four right. At this point it still looks like a rectangle with a gray shadow. **Magnify** the upper left corners. Because we offset the rectangle the same number of pixels up and right, a line connecting the two corners will be the diagonal of a square. Use the eyedropper to make sure the color is set to the shadow gray. Use the pencil to connect the corners with three pixels then fill in the gap. **Magnify** the lower right corners, draw the three pixels of the diagonal, and fill that gap, too. Now the corner looks like the slanted top edge of a block.

The rectangle already looks like a block, but will look even better if we custom shade the left side and bottom. Decide what dark dull color the shadowed bottom of the block should be. For example, if the rectangle is filled with a bright red, perhaps the shaded bottom would be a dull dark red. **Magnify** the lower left corner. Draw that diagonal in the dark color you have chosen, and then use the paint bucket to fill the area on the bottom. Fill the shadow on the side with a lighter shade of the bottom color. You can make a light gray shadow and float the block on it to suspend it in space. Before continuing, be sure to save the stack.

Extension: Block Text

The same technique helps in drawing three dimensional text. Make a new blank card. Get the **text tool** and set the font to **Chicago, 36, Bold**. Choose a bright clear color, type your first name, and then lasso it and option-drag off a copy. Go to **Replace Colors** and change it to a very pale tone of that color. Lasso and drag off another copy of the name, go to **Replace Colors**, and change it to a dark tone of the color. We will use the three copies of the name for the face, the highlight, and the shadowed side of the block text. Remember that he shadow and highlight are always on opposite sides, diagonally across from each other.

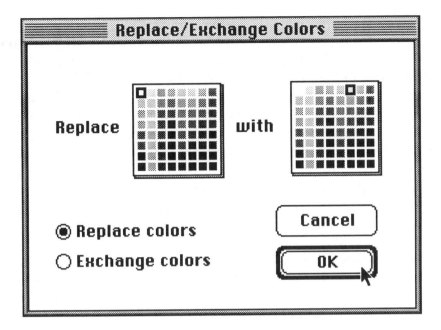

The shadowed side will be wide, since we are trying to create the illusion of depth, but we will not really see the brightly lighted side, only a highlight or glare off the very edge of the block. If the highlight is too wide, the effect would be an optical illusion. Of course, you could reverse the entire thing, and have a wide lighted side and very narrow shadowed edge across from it. Select and duplicate all three copies, so you will have an extra set for emergencies.

Lasso the medium-toned copy, line it up exactly on top of the pale copy, and use the **arrow** keys to move it one down and left one, exposing a one-pixel wide highlight. It may be hard to see on a white card. Lasso this highlighted copy, line it up on top of the dark copy along the left and bottom edges, and use the arrow keys to move it up four and right four. You must use the left and bottom edges to get lined up, since the highlighted copy is bigger than the dark one at this point. **Magnify** each set of left side corners where there is a pair of right angles. Don't worry about curves or various slanted edges, just the straight angles such as the tops of E's and T's, for example. At each right angle gap, fill in the diagonal and the triangle it creates with the shadow color, just as was done for the corner of the rectangular block. Make a rectangle of the medium color large enough for the entire name. This may work best on a new card, if the current one is fairly full. Paste the name on the rectangle for an embossed effect. Save the stack.

Topic 2: Standing Shadows

In the examples so far, shadows have been in the same plane—floating upright letters cast a shadow as if onto a wall behind them. Now we will learn to make shadows that lie down flat. Look at something circular, like a CD or the top of a can. As it tilts over, it no longer looks circular but oval, as if it had been squashed. Play with the **Box Maker Extra**, noticing the squashed shape of a rectangular box top when it is tilted down away from upright. This foreshortening has been used for hundreds of years to create the illusion of depth. To make a shadow that lies down, we simply make an upright shadow and then squash it flat. Anything selected with the **rectangular selector** can be squashed or stretched by putting the cursor on the top edge of the selection, so the **double-headed arrow** appears, changing just the height.

Make a new blank card, go to the **File** menu, and choose **Add Clip Art**. Look on the *HyperStudio* CD for the "Media Library," and open the "Black Bear" screen in the Mammals folder under "Animal Kingdom," select the **bear**, and click **OK**. Refer to the Standing Shadows sheet for details of the next steps. Position the bear in the upper left quarter of the card, and make a rectangle in the upper right big enough to cut out a bear shadow. For variety, use the palest brown or a gray-blue instead of gray or black. **Lasso** the bear, option-drag a copy onto the rectangle, and cut out the shape with **option-⌘-c**, the cookie cutter copy. Without deselecting, drag the silhouette of the bear down to the lower part of the card. Deselect, and then capture the bear shadow again with the **rectangular selector**. Put the cursor on the top edge of the selection, so that the **double-headed arrow** appears, and squash down the height to about one-third. Lasso the bear picture, and paste it in position so the feet meet the shadow's feet. This trick will only work on some animal positions; a side view seems to work many times. It is okay to cheat and stretch a part of the shadow or erase a part protruding below a foot.

The fill patterns make good shaped shadows, too. Try the gray and blue-pebbly ones. The green grassy pattern squashes down to look duller, so you can use it to make the squashed shadow in a background filled with that pattern. Try some foreshortened shadows with text, too. It works better with tall, skinny text, so that the shadow shows.

Save the stack and make a new card. We will actually do a little bit of original art here, and then give it a fancy shadow shaded with a gradient.

Get the smallest slant brush and sweep a brown curve for a trunk. You may want to even off the base. You can add detail with the pencil, if you wish. Get the smallest dot brush and scribble the top of the palm tree with the black and green leaf fill pattern. Just sweep fronds out all around from a center point. Choose the lighter green grassy pattern, and streak over some of the fronds. Finish with a few streaks of the lightest green fill pattern. Lasso the top of the tree and put it on the trunk. By working in two subunits, it's easy to get them just right before you connect them.

Lasso the tree, option drag a copy, and this time go to **Gradients (Edit:Effects)** and apply a vertical gradient from the palest gray to black. Deselect the shadow, capture with the rectangular selector, and squash the shadow. Lasso and paste the tree in position. The gradient gives the shadow a more realistic look, darker next to the trunk and gradually fading out farther away. Save the stack.

If you have time, experiment with the backlit and slanted shadows.

Topic 3: Reflections

Start by making a new card. Get the text tool and choose **Chicago, bold, 18 or 24**-point in a bright color other than green. Type your name or some other word. Important: If there are any letters with tails below the surface line, upper case MUST be used. Prepare a pane of glass for the letters to sit on. Use a light green to make the slanting sides using the line tool and **shift** key. They should be wider apart than the typed word, and long enough so that the space thus created is four or five times the height of the letters. Use the palest green and a thin line for the back edge and a deeper green and thick line for the front edge. Fill this trapezoid with the palest green. Use **Magnify** to check the corners, and clean up protruding lines.

Select the word with the **rectangle selector**, and option-drag a copy. While it is selected, go to **Edit:Effects** menu and choose **Flip Upside Down**. Still selected, put the cursor on the bottom edge so the **double-headed arrow** appears, and stretch the selection about twice its height. Deselect. Lasso the stretched, flipped copy, go to **Gradients** under **Edit:Effects**, and apply a vertical gradient.

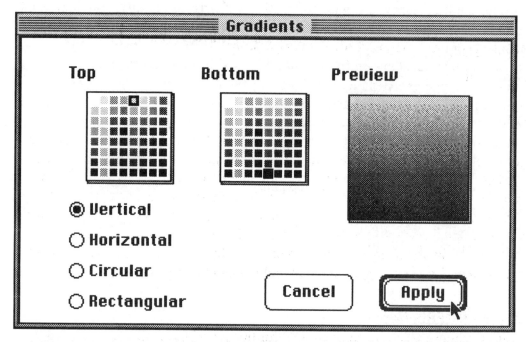

The top color should be a duller tone similar to the color of the typed word, and the bottom should be the pale green of the glass. Click **OK**. Line up the reflection with the bottom of the word, but leave about a two pixel gap. Lasso both word and reflection, and paste on the glass. Be sure the entire reflection is in the glass. The upright letters can stick up above the top edge. The duller color is typical of reflections, and the gradient makes the reflection fade out smoothly into the glass.

Understanding Color

HyperTutorial Mastery Level Required:
Advanced

HyperOverview:
The lesson begins with an introduction to the way the computer handles the 256 color palette, and explains why **Replace Colors** sometimes seems to miss areas. Students will explore the two-color editing modes available in *HyperStudio* to gain an understanding of the attributes of color including hue, saturation and lightness, and how they affect what actually appears on the display screen. They will also find out why the primary colors on the computer are red, blue, and green, and how to use these to mix colors. Finally, they will experiment with the use of color for mood (warm and cool colors) and the principles of contrast.

HyperObjectives:
Learn to choose colors to set the mood for titles, backgrounds, etc.

Learn to choose contrasting colors where things need to stand out, such as text on a background, and how to use low contrast for things that should be unobtrusive, such as neutral backgrounds or buttons on a photo or drawing.

Introduce students to the color editing modes.

Introduce elementary color theory, as it applies to computer displays, including the rather different form of primary colors and color mixing.

HyperMedia Sources:
Students will work primarily within *HyperStudio*. Have a text file that can be loaded into a text object. The subject is not important since it will be used only to experiment with the effect of colors on text appearance. It may be useful to have some stacks available to look at, to find examples of contrast, warm and cool colors, etc.

HyperHardware and Other HyperMaterials:

None

HyperPrerequisites:

Important: Be sure to go to **Preferences** and check **Experienced User** for this lesson. Otherwise, you will not be able to get to the 256-color palette by double clicking a color on the 64-color palette. This is especially necessary in this lesson, in order to be able to access the color editing dialogs.

Students should be comfortable with *HyperStudio*, able to make simple shapes with the paint tools, understand how to change the font in paint text, and how to tear off the color menu. They should be able to make a button, a text object, a new card, and a graphic object from the screen.

HyperInstruction and HyperTimeline:

This is a very open-ended exercise. It will not take long to introduce each idea, but students could spend quite a bit of time experimenting.

It is hoped that they will be able to apply these ideas to projects throughout the year. Much of the lesson could be given as a demonstration, so it is readily adaptable to a one-computer classroom. Going through the entire discussion with the class as a whole could be done in less than an hour.

Palette Positions Versus "Colors"

Start by making a new stack. Tear off the 64-color palette, and have students double click on it to bring up the 256-color palette. If your students aren't used to working with this extended palette, you should mention that they can also get to it from the any 64-color palette, including the buttons, text color, set eraser color, **Replace Colors** and **Gradients** dialogs, by double clicking on a color. Click on the black at the end of the top row, and click **OK**. Go to the **tools** menu, choose filled rectangle, and make a black rectangle. Double click the palette again, choose the black at the end of the bottom row, click **OK**, and then make a filled circle. Then go to **Replace Colors (Edit:Effects)** and set it to replace the current black with red. Only the circle will become red. Discuss the reason for this. To the computer, the palette is a table of number codes which it uses to set the color of pixels on the screen. It does not really know what they look like. If two palette boxes happen to have the same number stored, they are still different to the computer, since they have a different address.

So when you set the palette to replace a color, other areas in the picture that look the same color will not change, if their color instruction is found in a different mailbox.

HSL Editing

Next, go back to the 256-color palette, have the students set the current color to red, and double click it. This brings up the first color editing dialog. Mention that they can also get to this dialog by double clicking a color in the 256-color palette. The first editing dialog uses the hue, saturation, and lightness system. We will get an overview of what these three color attributes are, and how they affect the color we see on the screen as they change.

Hue

Hue is the easiest concept. It is what we normally think of as color names. The hues are located around the color circle, which you can think of as a prism with a white beam coming in to the center. The spectrum spreads around in a complete circle so that the purple colors join up with red. Have the students examine this circle, to get a rough idea where hues are located. Notice that red is taken as 0°, green is a third of the way around counter-clockwise at 120°, and blue is two thirds of the way around at 240°. The hue angle is recorded in the entry box to the right of the word **Hue** as you move the crosshair, or you may type in the position in degrees. Start at red (0°) and have the students carefully move the cross hair in toward the center, checking to keep it on 0°. Watch what happens to the color in the **New** box.

Saturation

The color becomes duller and grayer, as the crosshair gets to the center. Yet all these colors are the same hue; that is, it is light of the same wavelength. What is actually changing? The clue is that the numbers are changing in the **Saturation** box. So what exactly is saturation? It can be thought of as the amount of color present. Think about the color adjustment on a television. Sometimes if reception is poor, there is no color, and the picture is just shades of gray. If you turn up the appropriate control, you can pour more and more color into the picture, until there is so much that it looks unnaturally intense. This is what happens as you move the crosshair to the rim of the color circle, and the saturation gets close to 100%. Have the students do this, and notice the color in the **New** box become more intense.

In this editing dialog, you can do this with one color at a time, instead of all the colors in the picture. Remember that changes you make here only affect the color you double-clicked. When you go back to the stack, all paint areas using that single color position on the palette will change on that card.

Lightness

The third attribute you can change in this dialog is **lightness,** which is a function of the amount of light present. Think about what happens as the sun goes down. The colors do not actually change hue or saturation. For example, your red shirt is still red, and it doesn't fade out. But it certainly looks different. Lightness can exist separately from color, as a gray scale. The lowest lightness is black, and the highest is white. In between are different levels of visibility. If the color is completely unsaturated, lightness can vary from black through all the gray scale to white. This is the center of the wheel. If the color is low saturation, lightness can vary from black through slightly tinted grays to white. If color is 50% saturated, lightness can vary from black through medium intense colors through pastels to white. If the color is very high saturation, lightness can vary from black through dark tones, Day-Glo type colors, clear pastels, and then to white. Have the students pick a hue, and then try moving the lightness slider up and down using 0, 30, 50, 80, and 100% saturation, and observe the changes to the color in the **New** box. Then choose another hue, and try to design a dull, dark version of it, an intense version, and a clear pastel. Discuss what saturation and lightness settings should give these effects. Don't get too involved with exact numbers, but think of low, medium, and high saturations. If the equipment permits, go back to the stack and make a circle of each color. Label it with the hue (either the name or the angle), general saturation level, and lightness.

RGB Editing

In the upper right of the dialog box, click **Apple RGB** to bring up the second type of color editing. This is the color mixing dialog, and it uses sliders for the three primary colors red, blue, and green to mix any hue. Many students have been taught that the primary colors are red, blue, and yellow, so this may be very confusing to them. They also have been taught that if all the colors are mixed together, the result is white. Yet they also know that if you try this with paint on paper, the result is not white but black or a dark muddy brown.

Mixing Paint vs. Mixing Light:

Why Two Sets of Primary Colors?

The explanation is that the familiar primary colors are for paint or other pigments, which are mixed by **subtractive mixing.** For example, red paint has a mixture of ingredients that absorb all the wavelengths but the ones in the red part of the spectrum, which they reflect. So when white sunlight falls on it, only the red part is reflected, and that's what we see. Similarly, blue paint reflects only the blue part of the spectrum, and yellow reflects the yellow part. If you mix these, there are then materials present that absorb most of all the parts of the spectrum, so very little light of any color is reflected and it looks black or dark brown.

The computer colors are mixed as if you were mixing beams of light, or **additive mixing.** Here the primary colors are the ends and middle of the spectrum, red, green, and blue (hence RGB). It is easy to see that if mixing light beams adds them up, then mixing equal amounts of all three colors would give back the whole spectrum—white. The secondary colors in this system are also different. A mix with just red and green makes yellow, blue and green make cyan (turquoise or aqua), and red and blue make magenta.

Put one slider at 100 and the other two at 0 for each of the three colors to see the three primary colors. Have the students prove to themselves that mixing all three colors makes white by sliding all three sliders all the way up. Next, move the sliders to the middle, but keep them all lined up so the amounts are equal. What effect do you get with the same proportion but less total light? The result is a medium gray. Move each pair of sliders to 100%, while putting the third slider at 0. This will generate the three secondary colors. Other colors can only be mixed by using all three primaries, and then adjusting the saturation and lightness. For example, browns are low saturation, low lightness reds, with a touch of green. Push the red slider to about 40% and put the blue at 0 and the green at something low, about 3%, and you will have a brown.

Using Colors to Set the Mood

Go back to the stack and make a new blank card. Go to the **Edit** menu and choose **Gradients** under **Effects.** Make a vertical gradient from light to dark blue. Click **OK**, then get the **circular** selector. Select an oval in the left half of the card, and make a circular gradient from green to a blue. On the left, select another circle and make a gradient from red to golden yellow. Do the blues and greens look cool, calm, and relaxing, and the reds and yellows warm? Ask the students why they think these colors affect us this way. What do they think would be the effect of putting text in hot colors on a cool background? What about the reverse?

Intense vs. Neutral colors

Make a new card, and add a text item. Load in a text file, just so there is some text to look at. Set the font to **Chicago 12**. Have the students pick an intense color for both the text and the background, perhaps a bright clear red and blue. Intense colors are pretty, but are they always the best choice? Get the **text tool,** double-click the text object to edit it, and choose a dark, unsaturated color for the text, such as a brown or dark gray, and a light color for the background. Which arrangement is easier to read? Which would tire the eyes more if there was a long string of text? Edit the text object again, and pick a light text color and a dark color for the background. This also is easy to read, but which do the students like better and why? Which background color would be best for a serious history stack? Which would be most dramatic? Edit the item again, and pick two pale colors. Would this be a good choice? The idea is to think about how the colors make them feel, which ones are happy, sad, ugly, exciting, depressing, etc. At the same time, some combinations are hard to read, so in those cases being practical would be better than choosing your favorite color. Notice that opinions vary, but some combinations give most viewers the same feelings. Some of these are especially worth noting, for stacks that will be exchanged with others.

Contrast

Edit the text item again. Choose a dull dark red for the background, and the lightest pink for the text. Then go back and change the text to a light pink to a light blue. Which is easier to read? This last choice is easiest because it has the most contrast. *Contrast* refers to opposites, and here is a light on a dark color, a cool on a warm color, and a saturated on an unsaturated color. The greatest contrast of all is black on white, but that can be boring or harsh. You can show rather dramatically how contrast works. Make a new card, get the paint text tool, set the text color to bright red, and set the text style to **Chicago 48 (Options:** "Text Style"). Type the word "Contrast" and center it on the card. Change the text setting to a bright blue, and **Chicago 36**. Under the first word, type "makes things visible." and center that. Lasso both words together, use the copy command to put it on the clipboard, and then make it into a graphic object. Select it with the graphic tool, and use copy command again.

Make a new card and paste twice. Be certain it's the graphic object being pasted here. Move back to the first card of the three. The two words are both intense, bright colors. Is this why they show up so well?

Move to the next card. Add a button, position it in the lower left, name it **Next**, choose light blue for the name, choose invisible type button, show name, and make it go to the next card with a dissolve. Go to the next card, add a button, position it in the lower left, choose light pink for the name, choose invisible type button, show name, and make it go to the previous card with a dissolve. Fill the card with the previous button with the same red as the word "Contrast." (If you don't remember, go back two cards and set the color with the **eyedropper**. That card still has the words as paint.) Click the button. Fill that card with the same blue as the words "makes things visible." Now click back and forth between these two cards. What creates the effect? Not just intense colors, but contrast. Notice that the button colors use low contrast to be unobtrusive. Sometimes it is good to have elements that don't stand out on a card. If all the items are equally attention-getting, it's confusing. So use different color types to help prioritize card elements.

HyperExtensions:

Students may want to experiment further with the editing dialogs. Open **RGB editing**, slide two sliders to 100%, and see what happens to the color as the third color is added to the mix. Pick a color mix, switch to **HS editing**, and type in a much higher or lower saturation. Then return to **RGB editing**, and see how this effects the color.

Experiment with trying to produce a particular color. Load in a background such as the Tree screen (HS Art folder), and try the effect of editing just the sky color. Choose one of the greens and edit it.

Try making cards in the following styles:

Paint a background using all one hue. The easiest way is to just use one column of the 64-color palette. It can be an original free-form drawing or a composition of shapes with the shape tools. The student must use contrast here since variety can only be obtained with various lightnesses and saturations.

Do similar cards using just primary colors, just secondary colors, or a primary and its complement—the color opposite it on the wheel.

Do cards with all cool, all warm, and a mixture of colors. Use some gradients, as well as geometric shapes. Try a gradient from a cool to a warm color or from a neutral to an intense color.

Make two rectangles in different colors, but about the same saturation and lightness. Put a smaller rectangle in one of them, in the same hue but a different saturation and lightness. Lasso the little rectangle, copy, and paste it in the other larger rectangle. Compare the results. Do the small rectangles still look the same color?

Color Quick Guide

This quick guide will help you use colors on the computer. You will learn how the computer keeps track of which colors you choose, how to edit colors to get just the ones you want, and how to use them to get just the effect you are looking for in your stacks.

Palette Positions

Start by making a new stack. Check **Preferences** under **Edit** to make sure you have checked that you are an experienced *HyperStudio* user.

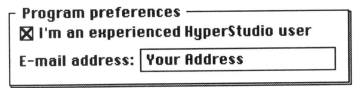

Tear off the 64-color palette, and double click on any color to bring up the 256 color palette. Click on the black at the end of the top row, and click **OK**. Go to the **tools** menu, choose **filled rectangle**, and make a black rectangle. Double click the palette again, choose the black at the end of the bottom row, click **OK**, and then make a filled circle.

Then go to **Replace Colors (Edit:Effects)** and set it to replace the current black with red. Why doesn't the rectangle turn red?

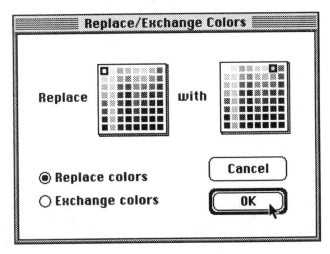

To the computer, the palette is a table of number codes, which it uses to set the color of pixels on the screen. It does not really know what they look like. If two palette boxes happen to have the same number stored, they are still different to the computer, since they have different addresses. So when you set the palette to replace a color, other areas in the picture that look the same color won't change if their color instruction is found in a different mailbox.

HSL Editing

Set the current color to red, and double click it. This brings up the color editing dialog. Make sure the top choice in the upper left, **Apple HSL**, is chosen. You can also get to this dialog by double-clicking a color in the 256-color palette.

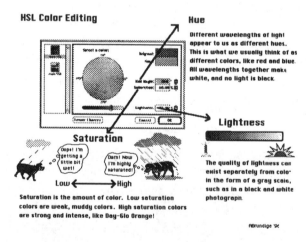

This editing dialog uses the hue, saturation, and lightness system. We will get an overview of what these three color attributes are, and how they affect the color we see on the screen as they change.

Hue

Hue is the easiest concept. It is what we normally think of as color names. The hues are located around the color circle, which you can think of as a prism with a white beam coming in to the center. The spectrum spreads around in a complete circle so that the purple colors join up with red. Notice that red is taken as 0°, green is a third of the way around counter-clockwise at 120°, and blue is two thirds of the way around at 240°. The hue angle is recorded in the entry box to the right of the word **Hue** as you move the crosshair, or you may type in the position in degrees. Start at red (0°) and carefully move the cross hair in toward the center, checking to keep it on 0°. Watch what happens to the color in the **New** box.

Saturation

The color becomes duller and grayer as the crosshair gets to the center. Yet all these colors are the same hue; that is, it is light of the same wavelength. What is actually changing? The clue is that the numbers are changing in the **Saturation** box. So what exactly is saturation? It can be thought of as the amount of color present. Think about the color adjustment on a television. Sometimes if reception is poor, there is no color, and the picture is just shades of gray. If you turn up the appropriate control, you can pour more and more color into the picture, until there is so much that it looks unnaturally intense. This is what happens as you move the crosshair to the rim of the color circle, and the saturation gets close to 100%. Do this, and notice the color in the **New** box become more intense. In this editing dialog, you can do this with one color at a time (the one you are editing), instead of all the colors in the picture at once like the television control. Remember that changes you make here only affect the color you double clicked. When you go back to the stack, all paint areas using that single color position on the palette will change on that card.

Lightness

The third attribute you can change in this dialog is **lightness**, which is a function of the amount of light present. Think about what happens as the sun goes down. The colors don't actually change hue or saturation. For example, your red shirt is still red, and it doesn't fade out. But it certainly looks different. Lightness can exist separately from color, as a gray scale. The lowest lightness is black, and the highest is white. In between are different levels of visibility. If the color is completely unsaturated, lightness can vary from black through all the gray scale to white. This is the center of the wheel. If the color is low saturation, lightness can vary from black through slightly tinted grays to white. If color is 50% saturated, lightness can vary from black through medium intense colors through pastels to white. If the color is very high saturation, lightness can vary from black through dark tones, Day-Glo type colors, clear pastels, and then to white. Pick a hue, and then try moving the lightness slider up and down using 0, 30, 50, 80, and 100% saturation, and observe the changes to the color in the **New** box. Then choose another hue, and try to design a dull, dark version of it, an intense version, and a clear pastel. Notice what saturation and lightness settings should give these effects. Don't get too involved with exact numbers, but think of low, medium, and high saturations. Go back to the stack and make a circle of each color. Label it with the hue (either the name or the angle), general saturation level, and lightness.

RGB Editing

RGB Color Editing

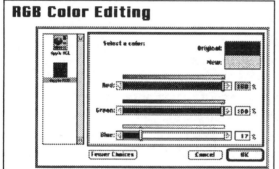

Additive Mixing (Beams of Light)
The primary colors are red, green, and blue, from the two ends and the middle of the visible spectrum. Mixing beams adds the

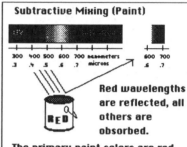

Subtractive Mixing (Paint)

Red wavelengths are reflected, all others are absorbed.

The primary paint colors are red, blue, and yellow. Mixing all three paints together absorbs most of the wavelengths, leaving black or a muddy brown.

wavelengths together to form new colors. In the RGB system, you are mixing colors as if you were mixing beams of light. Red and green make yellow, red and blue make magenta, and blue and green make cyan (tourquoise). Colors like brown are low saturation versions of some RGB colors. Choose a red-orange, go to the HSL dialog, and lower the saturation. Adding the third color to a mix lightens it. If all the sliders are at 100%, you have the entire spectrum--white!

ABrundige '96

In the upper right of the dialog box, click **Apple RGB** to bring up the second type of color editing. This is the color mixing dialog, and it uses sliders for the three primary colors (red, blue, and green) to mix any hue. You may have been taught that the primary colors are red, blue, and yellow, so this may seem confusing. You've been taught that if all the colors are mixed together, the result is white. Yet you know that if you try this with paint on paper, the result isn't white but black or a dark muddy brown.

Mixing Paint Vs. Mixing Light:

Why Two Sets of Primary Colors?

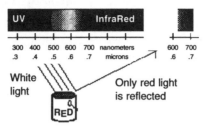

The explanation is that the familiar primary colors are for paint or other pigments, which are mixed by subtractive mixing. For example, red paint has a mixture of ingredients that absorb all the wavelengths but the ones in the red part of the spectrum, which they reflect. So when white sunlight falls on it, only the red part is reflected, and that's what we see. Similarly, blue paint reflects only the blue part of the spectrum, and yellow reflects the yellow part. If you mix these, there are then materials present that absorb most of all the parts of the spectrum, so very little light of any color is reflected and it looks black or dark brown.

White Light

Red, Green, and Blue Light Beams

The computer colors are mixed as if you were mixing beams of light—additive mixing. Here the primary colors are the ends and middle of the spectrum, red, green, and blue (hence RGB). It's easy to see that if mixing light beams adds them up, then mixing equal amounts of all three colors would give back the whole spectrum—white. The secondary colors in this system are also different. A mix with just red and green makes yellow, blue and green make cyan (turquoise or aqua), and red and blue make magenta.

Put one slider at 100% and the other two at 0% for each color, to see each of the three primary colors in the **New** box. Slide all three sliders all the way up. What color is in the **New** box? Next, move the sliders to the middle, but keep them all lined up so the amounts are equal. What effect do you get with the same proportion but less total light? The result is a medium gray. Move each pair of sliders to 100%, while putting the third slider at 0%. This generates the three secondary colors. Other colors can only be mixed by using all three primaries and then adjusting the saturation and lightness. For example, browns are low saturation, low lightness reds, with a touch of green. Push the red slider to about 40% and put the blue at 0 and the green at something low, about 3%, and you will have a brown.

Using Colors to Set the Mood

Go back to the stack and make a new blank card **(Edit:New Card)**. Go to the **Edit** menu and choose **Gradients** under **Effects**. Make a vertical gradient from light to dark blue.

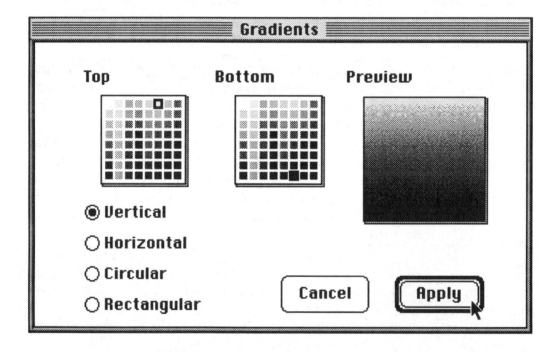

Click **OK**, then get the **circular selector**. Select an oval in the left half of the card, and make a circular gradient from green to a blue. On the left, select another circle and make a gradient from red to golden yellow. Do the blues and greens look cool, calm, and relaxing and the reds and yellows warm? Why do you think these colors affect us this way? What do you think would be the effect of putting text in hot colors on a cool background? What about the reverse?

Intense vs. Neutral colors

Make a new card, and add a text item (**Objects:Add a Text Object**).

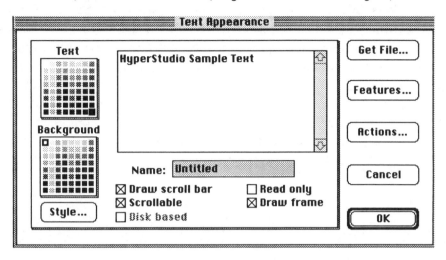

Load in a text file, just so there is some text to look at. Set the font to **Chicago, 12**. Pick an intense color for both the text and the background, perhaps a bright, clear red and blue. Intense colors are pretty, but are they always the best choice? Get the text tool, double-click the text object to edit it, and choose a dark, unsaturated color for the text, such as a brown or dark gray, and a light color for the background. Which arrangement is easier to read? Which would tire the eyes more if there was a long string of text? Edit the text object again, and pick a light text color and a dark color for the background. This also is easy to read. Which do you like better ? Why? Which background color would be best for a serious history stack? Which would be most dramatic? Edit the item again, and pick two pale colors. Would this be a good choice? Think about how the colors make you feel. Which ones are happy, sad, ugly, exciting, depressing, etc. Some combinations are hard to read, so in those cases being practical would be better than choosing your favorite color. Notice that opinions vary, but some combinations give most viewers the same feelings. Some of these are especially worth remembering for stacks that will be exchanged with others.

Contrast

Edit the text item again. Choose a dull, dark red for the background, and the lightest pink for the text. Then go back and change the text to a light pink to a light blue. Which is easier to read? This last choice is easiest because it has the most contrast. *Contrast* refers to opposites, and here is a light on a dark color, a cool on a warm color, and a saturated on an unsaturated color. The greatest contrast of all is black on white, but that can be boring or harsh. Make a new card, get the paint text tool, set the text color to bright red, and set the text style to **Chicago 48 (Options:** "Text Style"). Type the word "Contrast" and center it on the card. Change the text setting to a bright blue, and **Chicago 36**. Under the first word, type "makes things visible!" and center that. Lasso both words at once, use the copy command to put it on the clipboard, and make it into a graphic object. Select it with the graphic tool, and use the copy command again. Make a new card and paste twice. *Be certain it's the graphic object being pasted here.* Move back to the first card of the three. The two words are both intense, bright colors. Is this why they show up so well?

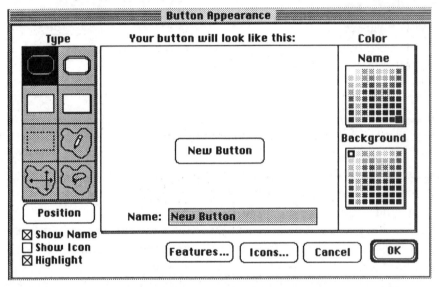

Move to the next card. Add a button, position it in the lower left, name it **Next**, choose light blue for the name, choose invisible type button, show name, and make it go to the next card with a dissolve. Go to the next card, add a button, position it in the lower left, name it "Previous", choose light pink for the name, invisible type button, show name, and make it go to the previous card with a dissolve. Fill the card with the "Previous" button with the same red as the word "Contrast." (If you don't remember, go back two cards and set the color with the **eyedropper**. That card still has the words as paint.) Click the button to move to the previous card. Fill that card with the same blue as the words "makes things visible!" Now click back and forth between these two cards. What creates the effect? Not just intense colors, but contrast. Notice that the button colors use low contrast to be unobtrusive. Sometimes it's good not to stand out.

Easy Custom Clip Art

HyperTutorial Mastery Level Required:

Advanced

HyperOverview:

Using capture, copy, paste, the cookie cutter, and replace colors, students will modify some of the familiar clip art samples in the HS Art folder. One goal is to encourage students to vary the art they paste into their stacks rather than always using the same few clips. Another is to empower students by showing them that with a little thought, anyone can design customized artwork to illustrate a specific stack rather than being limited to loading just what may be on the disk. The tricks in this lesson do not require freehand drawing ability.

HyperObjectives:

Learn the power of using multiple copies of an art clip to make changes, and introduce the option-drag copy shortcut.

Learn how to isolate elements of the art with Replace Colors, eraser, pencil, and paint bucket so that the parts can easily be modified.

Introduce the idea of masking the transparent color when combining clip art, and then restoring it with Replace Colors.

Introduce the cookie cutter command as a way of getting patterns into complex areas.

HyperMedia Sources:

This lesson shows how to extend the usefulness of resources already in the classroom. Therefore, students will work entirely with the clip art that came with *HyperStudio*, found in the HS Art folder. Step-by-step instructions are included for art from the Science and Computer 1 screens. Students should be encouraged to find other art clips that can be combined and modified using the ideas in this lesson.

HyperHardware and Other HyperMaterials:

None

HyperPrerequisites:

Important: Be sure to go to Preferences and check Experienced User for this lesson. Otherwise, you won't be able to get to the 256 color palette by double clicking a color on the 64 color palette. This is especially necessary in Replace Colors.

Creating a new stack and adding clip art should be routine for students doing this lesson. Make sure students are comfortable using the lasso, and understand how to deselect by clicking outside the selection outline, i.e. the "marching ants".

Have some practice with the cookie cutter command. This can be combined with using the **lasso**, by having students lasso art, drag it onto a patterned background, and make a cutout, and then paste it on a card. This works nicely with large text, so students could try typing their names in a large font and then adding a texture. There are some good texture backgrounds in the Media Library for this.

Students should also have some practice using the **Replace Colors** option found under **Edit:Effects**. Point out that the current painting color is the default color to replace, so it is a good idea to use the **eyedropper** to choose the color to replace before selecting the art. Also make sure they realize that if no specific area is selected, ALL parts of the screen with the chosen color will change. Depending on how experienced your students are, a preliminary session with **Replace Colors** might be in order. Load in clip art, and practice changing it up by using **Replace Colors**. Do some simple original art such as frames with fill patterns, and change them using **Replace Colors**. If you have one computer, put this up on the screen in front of the class and make it a group exercise, or let small groups take turns working with **Replace Colors** before doing the lesson. Besides getting students used to this option, this will also introduce them to the idea of using the clip art they already have to produce new art.

HyperInstruction and HyperTimeline:

This fairly short lesson could be completed in as little as an hour if your classroom has the resources to have every student work "hands on." It breaks down into two shorter lessons, the first on masking and the second on combining parts of copies to form new art. You may want to do these on two different days to give the lessons time to "soak in." If computers are limited, the best strategy would be for you to work through the exercises as a demonstration and then let students do the same work on their own using the Quick Guide. It is very important that students actually work on the computer screen, rather than just watching this being done.

Start by creating a new working stack. Reinforce the idea of using rough sketch stacks for creating and assembling artwork, which can later be pasted into a finished stack. This gives plenty of working area, and encourages the use of copies of the work at various stages, a strong defense against disaster. In the following exercise, it is especially important to use the specified selection tool for each step.

Masking

The first half of the lesson covers masking transparent areas in an art clip so that it can be pasted onto a patterned background. Begin by bringing in the boy at the keyboard from the Computer 1 screen, HS Art folder, and preparing a simple desktop and brick backdrop on which it will be pasted. Detailed instructions for this are in the Quick Guide. As soon as the desktop is finished, save the stack.

Point out that the stack should be saved whenever enough work has been done, so you will not have to do it over.

Make a rectangle filled with the brick pattern large enough to serve as a background to the art, and paste a copy of the desktop at its lower right. Point out that by using a copy, the desk just sketched can be used again in a different piece of art, saving time later. When the backdrop is all ready, save the stack and export the screen. You will need to reload the stack or screen in a minute, so this is important.

To mask the art clip, the first step is to make a copy to change up using the lasso and the **option-drag** method. Point out that this is a good shortcut when you need a copy on the same card. It does not, however, put a copy on the clipboard. At this point, have the students drag the art over to the backdrop and paste it. Point out that the background shows through. This demonstrates the challenge of this lesson—how to protect those transparent areas.

Discuss the problem of transparent parts in clip art. Whatever color is in the background where the tail of the **lasso** starts is transparent, so areas within the captured art using that color will let background show through. This is a great help if you want transparent areas, such as when you lasso text, but here it's a problem. In this case, the transparent color is white, since the background is white. How can these areas be protected?

Reload the stack without saving to restore the background, or reimport the screen as a background. Point out that saving frequently is one way to back up from mistakes, and so is exporting screens. Exporting screens also stores art students have created.

If there was only one solid white area, you could fill it with the paint bucket in some contrasting color, lasso and paste the art, and then fill the area again with white. This would hide that area from the lasso, just as if it were wearing a mask. Then when it was safe, you could take off the mask. Use **magnify** mode to look at the art clip. Notice that there are many tiny white areas. It would take a very long time to fill all of them.

The answer is to use the **Replace Colors** option to fill all the white areas at once. Use the **rectangular selector** (not the lasso!) to capture the art, **option-drag** a copy to an empty spot, and go to **Replace Colors** under **Edit:Effects**. Mark the palettes to replace white with a color that is not used anywhere in the art clip, such as the lightest purple-pink. It's very important that this mask color be one unused in either the clip art or the background onto which you will paste it, since you will be getting rid of it later. Emphasize this point: no magic color is used for masking. It will be a different color for different clips. The key is that it be a color not used in the clip or its immediate background so that at the end the color can safely be restored to white.

To finish the mask, fill the excess masking color in the rectangle around the clip with white. This leaves the mask only on the parts you want to protect, with one possible exception. It's important at this point to check for totally enclosed areas which you do not want white in the final picture. For example, if the mouse cable had a loop in it, it would be masked at this point, yet you wouldn't want a white area to show inside the loop in the final art. So any such areas should also be filled with white at this point.

Then lasso, drag, and paste the masked art clip into position on the backdrop. *Very important: deselect the art at this point.* If you do the last color replace while it's still lassoed, the areas will become transparent again. After deselecting, go back to **Replace Colors**, and replace the masking color with white. The art should then be back to its original appearance, but be pasted onto the background. If a background has many colors, it may still be possible to use one of them as a mask, so long as that color is not near the pasted area. If you can select the area close to the pasted art and replace the mask with white, the rest of the background won't be affected.

Notice that if the art had started out on another color background, yellow for example, then that color would be transparent and yellow areas would need to be masked. You should make this point clear.

Multiple Copies

The second exercise demonstrates the use of copies to combine several bits of clip art. Making copies is something we take for granted, but it can be a powerful drawing tool. We'll use many copies of art clips and parts of art clips as we modify the art with **Replace Colors** and the cookie cutter command, and finally paste them all back together to form some new art.

Start by making a new card and bringing in some of the clip art from the Science screen, HS Art folder. They will need the graduated tube with the spout and cut-off screw, the stopper, the larger flask and ring stand, and the Bunsen burner (see the Combining Art sheet). This could be brought in ahead of time. The goal is to change both vessels so they look like they have some liquid and then assemble the entire bunch of glassware on the card. The secret is to work with copies, so that the layers can be reassembled. Always using a copy for the next step also leaves the previous version handy as insurance. Be sure students paste things in the right order, that is, with the correct thing on top.

Filling the flask is similar to masking. Point out that capturing with the circular selector is an easy way to work with the surface of a liquid in any round container. This art happens to have an open pattern of blue and white, so we can change just the white and get translucent effects. Much of the HS art has this pattern, since it was originally 16-color art.

Make the surface a pale color. Then use the rectangle selector to capture the rest of the flask bottom, and replace white with a darker shade of the same color. Fill the excess of the rectangle outside the flask with white. Point out that you'll always need to do this clean-up fill when using the rectangle selector.

Next, lasso the stopper and paste it onto the spout at the bottom of the tube. Point out that the stopper must be dragged to the tube, not the other way around, or the spout would come out in front. It's important to get this across in this first simple example, because the order of pasting is vital in the more complicated parts to come. Point out that simply pasting the two pieces together works for this example, as long as the correct item is dragged and pasted on top.

The next task is to fill the tube, and in this case with a pattern instead of just a color. "Color Replace" won't put in a pattern. A pattern could be added to an open outline, but here there are details inside the outline so filling won't work very well either. The way to get a pattern into this artwork is to use both multiple copies and the cookie cutter. First, you will need to make a masked copy of the tube to use with the cookie cutter. Use the rectangle selector to capture the tube down to the metal fitting, drag off a copy **(option-drag)**, and mask it with any unused color. Be sure to fill the spill-over area with white. This needs to be masked because the original tube has many white areas which will be transparent when it is lassoed.

Make a little rectangle of the pattern you want inside. It should be a little wider than the tube. Lasso the masked tube and drag it over the pattern so the top is above the pattern, use the copy command, and drag the cutout to an empty spot. You should have a little cutout shaped like the bottom half of the tube. Now lasso the original tube and stopper, and paste it on top of the cutout. We need the transparency in this second copy. The pattern will show through the areas that were transparent.

Have the students copy and mask the Bunsen burner as well. Capture the flame only, and mask it with pale yellow. Use a pale blue for the base, and be sure to fill the spillovers. In this case, we will leave the masking colors in place. Choosing colors that look good in the final art lets us both protect the transparent areas and customize the colors in a single step. This is another variation on the first masking trick.

To put the flask assembly into the ring stand, students will have to solve a trickier problem. If they paste the flask on top, the front of the ring is covered by the flask. But if the ring is pasted on top, the entire ring and back leg will show in front. Here is where multiple copies really helps in combining bits of art. The trick is to use two copies of the ring stand. Paste the flask and tube on top of one copy, with the flask bottom a little below the rim of the ring. Erase the back leg and back of the ring in the second copy of the ring stand. If it's easier, students can do this in magnify. They will probably just need the eraser, but point out that in some work they might need to use the pencil with white as a precise eraser, and sometimes if a big area needs to be removed they can use the paint bucket.

Lasso the front of the ring stand and paste it in place. Point out that they really used three layers—the ring stand, the flask, and the front of the ring stand. And in fact, the entire piece of art has many more layers—the stopper, the tube, etc. This would be very hard to draw from scratch, but pasting small units together is easy. Lasso the Bunsen burner and paste it in place for the final touch.

HyperExtensions:

Students should be encouraged make further changes to the art used in this lesson. Several hints for doing this are included in the Quick Guide. They can also find other art clips that can be combined and modified using the ideas in this lesson, and add their original bits to clip art they bring into the stack. The general idea is to get them in the habit of putting some thought into customizing art to fit their projects, and to give them techniques so that this will be easy and fun for them.

Masking and Multiple Copies Quick Guide

Masking

Have you ever had trouble pasting clip art because the background showed through? This Quick Guide will show you how to solve that problem so your clip art always looks good!

Open *HyperStudio*, go to the **File** menu and start a new stack. Go to the **File** menu again and choose **Add Clip Art...** Select the boy at the keyboard from the **Computer 1** screen in the **HS Art** folder, and place this in the left corner of the screen. We will customize the art by creating a backdrop with a desktop and then paste in the clip art.

To draw the desktop, make two horizontal brown lines (use the **shift** key and line tool) far enough apart that the entire computer and mouse in the clip art would fit between them. These will be the back and front edges of the desktop. Make slightly slanted sides, to form a trapezoid. Run a third horizontal line just below the front edge, and two vertical line from the corners to form the side of the desk.

Sketch a desktop.

Fill and tidy up.

Use the eraser and pencil in **Magnify** mode to clean up the sketch, and use the paint bucket to fill it with the mottled tan pattern. Go to the **File** menu and choose **Save as... ?** to save the stack at this point. You might call it something like "Mask Stack."

Make a rectangle filled with the brick pattern large enough for a background to the art. Paste a copy of the desktop at its lower right. *Save the stack at this point.* You should also export the screen. Lasso the clip of the boy and computer, hold down the **Option** key, and drag off a copy. Drag the still-selected art clip onto the backdrop, position it on the desk, and deselect. Notice that the background shows through in places. How can we prevent this?

We need something like the masking tape used to protect areas from paint. If there was only one solid white area, we could fill it with the **paint bucket**, and lasso and paste the art. This would hide that area from the **lasso**, just as if it were wearing a mask! Then when it was safe, we could take off the mask by filling the area again with white.

Let's go back and try that idea. Go to the **File** menu, choose **Open Stack...** and reopen your stack. Important: when Addy asks you if you want to save the stack, choose **Don't Save**. Then you'll get back to the step before you pasted the art. Or, if you exported the screen earlier, you could import it at this point and get back one step that way.

Using **Magnify** mode, notice that there are many tiny white areas. It would take a very long time to fill all of them. The answer is to use **Replace Colors** to fill all the white areas at once. Capture the art with the **Rectangular selector** (not the lasso!), **Option-drag** a copy, and go to **replace Colors** under **Edit:Effects**.

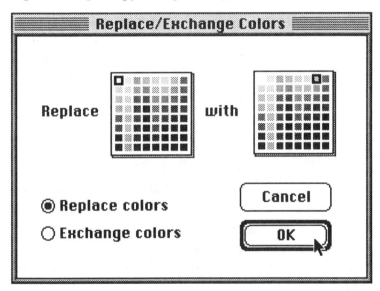

Mark the palettes to replace white with a color that is not used anywhere in the art clip, such as the lightest purple-pink. It's very important that this mask color be one unused in either the clip art or the background onto which you will paste it since you will be getting rid of it later.

Now all the white areas are protected, but there is still excess masking color around the art. Fill it with white, using the **paint bucket**. This leaves the mask only on parts you want to protect, with one possible exception. It's important to check for totally enclosed areas which you do not want white in the final picture. For example, if the mouse cable had a loop in it, it would be masked at this point, yet you don't want a white area, but a desk to show inside the loop in the final art. So any such areas should also be filled with white at this point. Save the stack.

Lasso the masked art, move it into position on the desk in front of the bricks, and deselect to paste it down. Be sure to deselect. If you do the next step without deselecting, you'll be back to having transparent art. Go back to **Replace Colors**, and this time replace the masking color with white. Now the art is on a background, with white areas intact.

A Few More Ideas:

Make some other changes to customize the art work. Use **Replace Colors** to change the color of the boy's shirt.

You could also change his hair color, but if you try to fill the hair or use **Replace Colors**, some of the black outline will change, too. You would have to make a copy of his head and erase everything but the hair first, fill just the hair, and then paste it in place.

Make a new card. Make a different pattern rectangle for a wall, add your desktop as clip art, and go back to the Computer 1 screen to get the clip of the girl at the keyboard. See if you can use masking to get the girl and her computer together with the desk.

Multiple Copies

If you've ever watched a magician do tricks, you know that the trick to many of the things you see is to have an extra coin or card hidden someplace. It's easy to make an extra copy on the computer, by selecting and using the the copy command keys or by holding down the **option** key and dragging off a copy. This guide will show you how to use those extra copies to do some tricks with clip art. You'll be able to change clip art to just the way you want it, and stack up bits of art to make something new.

Start by going to the **File** menu and choosing **New Card**. Then go to **File**, choose **Import Background**, and find the Science screen in the **HS Art** folder. You only need some of this art. Erase everything EXCEPT the black stopper, the large round-bottom flask, the large ring stand, the graduated tube with the spout at the bottom, and the Bunsen burner. As you work through this exercise, if the card gets crowded make a new one and do some of the work there. Always remember that you have an endless stack of scratch paper.

You will put all this lab equipment together on the card, as if you are illustrating a laboratory experiment. The tricks used here will work with any clip art you need to combine. The trick you will use most will be to make extra copies at each step. Sometimes you actually do something different to the copies, and then paste them back together. Sometimes working with a copy is just for safety, in case things go wrong. Just think of it as a hidden coin, or an ace up your sleeve!

You'll start by putting something into the flask. If you look at the flask in **Magnify** mode, you can see that the glass is mostly a pattern of blue and white. You will often find this open pattern in the art in the **HS Art** folder, which was originally 16-color art. If you change just the white, you will have a translucent effect. Use the **circular selector** to capture a narrow oval area stretching across the flask.

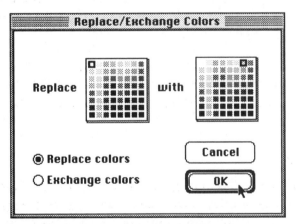

Go to **Replace Colors**, and replace white with pale green. Then use the **rectangular selector** to capture the bottom of the flask. Your selection will overlap the oval area you just changed, but it will not change again because there isn't any white there now. Go to **Replace Colors** and replace white with a darker green. Use the **paint bucket** to fill the spillover around the flask with white.

Lasso the stopper, and paste it on top of the spout at the bottom of the graduated tube. This is all that's needed to combine these pieces, but notice that it is important to drag the stopper to the tube, not the tube to the stopper. Now put something into the tube. Instead of just a solid color, put in a pattern. Because of the pattern already there, and the graduation marks, you can't just use the paint bucket to fill the tube. It's time to do one of those coin tricks. Use the **rectangular selector** to capture the tube down to the metal fitting, hold down the **option** key, and drag off a copy. While it's still selected, go to **Replace Colors** and choose a mask color. Fill the spilled area with white. You need to mask this

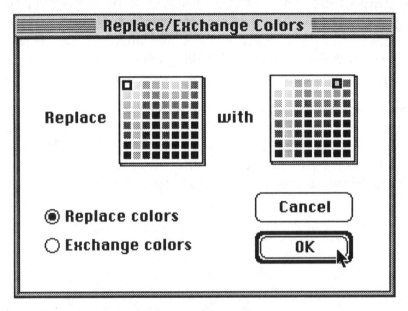

copy since it should be solid for the next step, but any mask color will do. Make a small rectangle of the pattern you want to use. Make it a little wider than the tube and not as tall.

Lasso the masked copy of the tube, drag it onto the pattern rectangle with the top sticking up past the edge of the rectangle, and hit the keys the cookie cutter copy. Drag the cutout off the rectangle and deselect. Lasso the tube and stopper, so the white areas will be transparent, and paste it in place on top of the cutout. By working with two copies, you have replaced all the white areas with a pattern. Give yourself a pat on the back, while you save the stack.

You will need to mask part of the Bunsen burner, so do that now. Use the **rectangular selector** to capture the flame, and replace white with pale yellow. Use the **rectangular selector** to capture the base and replace white with pale blue. Fill both spillover areas with white. This time you will leave the mask colors in place. By choosing colors that will look okay in the final art, you've customized the colors and masked transparent areas all in one step. You can use this shortcut whenever the mask colors will look okay.

Lasso the filled flask, option-drag a copy, and paste it so that the neck covers part of the stopper. The tip of the stopper should show inside. Now you need to get the flask and tube combination into the ring stand, but there is a problem. If you paste the flask on top, the front of the ring stand will get covered up. But if you paste the ring stand on top, the entire ring and back leg will show. As you can probably guess, it's another time when you need to use an extra copy. Lasso the ring stand, and option-drag a copy to an empty spot. Use the eraser to remove the back leg and the back of the ring. You should end up with just the front of the ring and the two outside legs.

Lasso the flask assembly and paste it on the other copy of the ring stand, so that the bottom of the flask is a little below the ring. Lasso the front of the ring stand and paste it on top. Add the Bunsen burner, and your lab setup is complete!

If you want to experiment more, bring in some more of the lab equipment and hook it together. Or look for other clips you can combine. You can also combine clips with bits you have drawn.

It is often the easiest way to do a complete piece of original art, too. For example, to do a bowl of apples, draw the bowl tilted so that you can see into it and one apple. Make a copy of the bowl. Lasso the apple, and option drag copies into the bowl to make a pile. Erase the back of the extra copy of the bowl, and paste on the front just like you did the front of the ring stand. It's easier than trying to guess what part of each apple will show!

Stories Where You Are the Main Character!

HyperTutorial Mastery Level:
Advanced

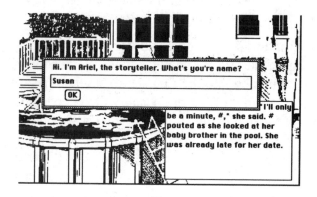

Figure 1: Story Stack

HyperOverview:

Imagine reading a story where you are the main character! That is exactly what this project lets you do.

You create a story, as simple or as complex as you like. When your story stack runs, it starts by asking for the reader's name. The story stack uses simple Logo scripts to pepper the reader's name throughout the story text at just the places you pick. The result is a story with the reader as the main character.

HyperObjectives:

You will learn how use scripting to manipulate text in a text field. The method used is list processing, where a long string of text is turned into a list of words, and you work on the list word by word. This technique of list processing is the opening door to the real power behind artificial intelligence languages like Logo. You will see these specific Logo features: Reading text from a text item, sending text to a text item, turning text into lists, and manipulating lists. In the process, we will use these HyperLogo commands:

;	Starts a comment line.
BUTFIRST	Returns all but the first word in a list.
CHAR	Takes a number and returns a character.
COUNT	Counts the number of words in a list or the number of characters in a word.
EMPTYP	Looks to see if a list is empty (has no more words).
END	Ends a procedure started with TO.
FIRST	Returns the first word from a list.
GETFIELDTEXT	Returns all of the text in a *HyperStudio* text object as a HyperLogo word.
IF	Checks to see if a condition is true, and executes one or more statements if it is.
LOCAL	Creates a HyperLogo variable. LPUT Places a word at the end of a list (Last PUT) and returns the new list.
MAKE	Assigns a value to a HyperLogo variable.
NOT	Reverses a true or false value.
OUTPUT	Returns a value from a Logo procedure.
READWORD	Reads a word by displaying a dialog, waiting for the reader to type something, then returning what the reader typed.
SETFIELDTEXT	Places a HyperLogo word into a *HyperStudio* text object.
SETRWPROMPT	Sets the prompt string for a HyperLogo input dialog. (See READWORD.)
SETRWRECT	Sets the position and size for a HyperLogo input dialog. (See READWORD.)
TO	Starts a procedure.
WHILE	Repeats one or more statements as long as a condition is true.
WORD	Combines two words into a longer word.

HyperMedia Sources:

This project does not require any outside art, but add it if you have it!

The background you see in the illustration is from a black and white clip art collection that came with a set of CD ROMs.

HyperPrerequisites:

Students should already know how to create buttons and text items, and how to add art to a card.

HyperInstructions and HyperTimeline:

The making of this project should be preceded by the writing of a short story in which there is one main character. This character's name will be that of the user and should be represented by the "#" symbol. The logo script will replace this symbol by any name that is entered. Once the story is finished, have students use one of the *HyperStudio* Planning sheets (pages 322–330) to storyboard the project.

Once the writing and storyboarding is done, the teaching of the script can be done on the blackboard. Introduce students to the logo scripting terms below. Have them try to guess how they would put the script together in a logical sequence so that the story would enter the user's name in the story.

Once the stories are done, figure that the creation of the stack and entering the logo scripts will take two to four class periods, depending on the keyboarding skills of the students.

HyperExtensions:

Add some background art. This step is optional, but really improves the stack.

The scripts used in this stack can easily be extended to handle longer, more complex stories that extend over multiple cards. Once you read the next section, you'll understand how the scripts do their job. Even if you don't feel up to writing a script from scratch, the explanation suggests ways you can modify the scripts you see to handle bigger stories.

Optional Section-HyperLogo Inside Out:

Learning to script in Hyperlogo is a great way to teach students logical thinking skills. The point of this section is to explain exactly how the scripts do their job. You can treat the scripts you see in this project as a black box, not worrying how they work. If so, you can skip this entire section.

If you decide to read this section, keep your HyperLogo reference manual handy! It's a great idea to read the descriptions of the commands you see as you study the scripts.

All of the action in this stack takes place automatically, as soon as the card is shown. When a script is organized this way, it's basically divided into two parts: the subroutines and the lines that call them.

In Logo, subroutines start with the word TO and continue until a line with just the word END. Everything in between these lines is part of a new command you are creating. The word TO, in fact, comes from the idea that you are teaching Logo TO do something. Looking at the script, you can see that everything but the last two lines is a collection of subroutines. Logo remembers them, but doesn't do anything with them right away.

At the bottom of the script you see the two lines that actually do something right away. The first is

```
Make "who GetName
```

This line calls a subroutine named GetName which asks the reader for her name and returns whatever the reader types. This is one of the subroutines in the script; we'll look at it in detail later.

The Make command is Logo's way of putting something in a safe place for later use. That safe place is called a variable, and in this statement, the name of the variable is who. The name returned by GetName is stuffed into the variable who.

```
ChangeStory [] "story :who
```

The next line calls our workhorse subroutine. ChangeStory reads a story from a text item, replaces all # characters with a name we supply, and replaces the text in the text item. As you'll see later, the commands we use to grab text from a text item and put text into a text item can work on the current card or a different card, and they can work on several text items on the same card. Because of this, we pass three parameters to our subroutine.

Parameters give us a way to pass a value that might change to a subroutine. If you think of the mathematical operation + as a subroutine, the numbers we write on either side of the + character are the parameters or values we want to change from time to time, since + isn't a very useful idea if we can only use it to add two fixed numbers!

In this case, the first parameter is []. In Logo terminology, this is an empty list. HyperLogo commands that take a card name as one of their parameters use the empty list to indicate the current card.

The next parameter is the name of the text item containing the story. Since we named the text item story when we created it, that's the name we use here. Since the word story is a series of constant characters, we use the " before the characters to tell Logo the characters are a name.

Last, we pass the name read by GetName.

Creating Longer Stories

Without going any further, you can use what you've just learned to create stacks with longer stories. Let's look at a specific example to see how.

Let's assume for a moment that you create a stack with several cards, and each of those cards has one or more text items containing parts of the story. You can add more calls to `ChangeStory` to change all of the various parts of the story.

The first step in making this work is to name your cards. This is something you might not normally do, but HyperLogo always needs a name so it knows what card or object to work on.

To give a card a name, move to the card and select **About This Card** from the **Objects** menu. You'll see a dialog like the one in the picture below. Type whatever name you want to use in the field labeled Card Name and press **OK**.

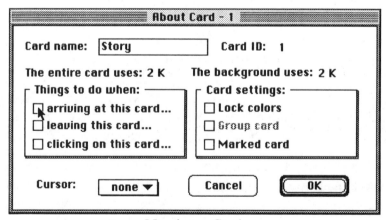

Naming a Card

Tip: You can put spaces in card names, but it is much easier if you don't. Names with spaced must be typed with a\character before each space in your Logo scripts, so the card name My Card would be typed "My\Card.

The text item you need to update also needs a name. The one we created in this sample stack has the name "Story."

Putting all of this together, to change a text item named "Story" on a card named Story43, we would use the line

```
ChangeStory "Story43 "story :who
```

You can put several calls to ChangeStory at the end of your script, changing all of the cards in the stack at once. The last few lines of the script might look like this:

```
ChangeStory [] "story :who
ChangeStory "Story43 "story :who
ChangeStory "Title "author :who
ChangeStory "Ending "credits :who
```

Colons and Quotes

If you have really been looking at these lines carefully, you may have noticed that who has a " character before it in one spot and a **:** in another. Why?

Like other list processing languages, Logo uses the one-letter commands **:** and **"** to tell what to do with a named variable. You put a quote before the variable when you are telling Logo to use the name of the variable, like the Make statement. You put a colon before the variable to tell Logo to use the current value of the variable.

If you have programming experience in numerically oriented languages like C or BASIC, this seems pretty weird, but Logo isn't a number crunching language— it's a word crunching language. The way it treats variables has some clever uses when you move on to artificial intelligence programming.

```
GetName
```

Digging through the script, we find the line

```
TO GetName
```

This is the start of the procedure that reads the reader's name. Logo uses TO to start a procedure because you are teaching Logo *to* do something new. All of the lines between that one and the line END are part of the procedure.

The next line is a comment. It doesn't do anything when the script runs, but it does remind us what the subroutine is for. How you comment depends a lot on your experience. At first, you might want to comment every line in a script, but eventually you'll get to the point where you just use a few comments to remind you about the overall flow in the script.

```
; Get the name of the person to put in the story.
```

This is followed by a blank line. Blank lines are a kind of comment, too. They don't do anything when the script runs, but they break a script up the same way paragraphs break up prose, making the major ideas in a subroutine easier to pick out.

The lines that really do the work are:

```
SetRWPrompt 'Hi.  I\'m Ariel, the storyteller.
What\'s you\'re name?'
SetRWRect [-180 30 180 -40]
```

Output ReadWord

It's easiest to understand these lines if we start with the last one. Output is Logo's way of taking a value and returning it. Looking back at the line that uses this procedure,

Make "who GetName

you see that the line stuffs a value into the variable who. It's this Output command that returns the value.

ReadWord is a Logo command that puts a dialog on the screen. The dialog has a prompt string, a text edit box that let's the reader type something, and a button labeled OK. When the reader clicks on OK, ReadWord returns whatever is in the text edit box.

There are two things you might want to change in this dialog, and that's what the other two lines do. SetRWPrompt is a HyperLogo command that remembers a string. This string is used as the prompt in the next ReadWord dialog. SetRWRect remembers a rectangle that changes the position and size of the next ReadWord dialog. These two lines, together, are responsible for the appearance of the dialog you see in Figure 1.

ChangeStory

This procedure is different in the two versions of the script. The script for newer versions of *HyperStudio* takes advantage of a feature that wasn't in the older version to create a faster script. This explanation starts by looking at the newer version. Later, it looks at the differences between the two versions.

The procedure that actually changes the story in a text item starts with these lines:

```
TO ChangeStory :card :item :name

; Put a name into a story.
```

As in GetName, the TO command starts the procedure and the next line is a comment. There is one new feature of Logo here, though, and that's the three variables you see after the name of the procedure. These are called *parameters*. They are three variables that come into being when ChangeStory is called and disappear when ChangeStory finishes. These variables start off with the values typed on the line that calls ChangeStory.   Looking at the line from our script,

```
ChangeStory [] "story :who
```

you can see that card has the value [], item has the value "story, and name has whatever value who contained.

ChangeStory needs two more variables to keep track of the words in the story. The next two lines create two variables called s1 and s2.

Local "s1

Local "s2

ChangeStory starts by getting the text from the text item, breaking it up into a list of words, and saving this list of words in the variable s1. It then works its way through the list of words, changing and # characters into the characters name, and saves the processed words in s2. Once all of the words are processed, ChangeStory places the modified words back into the text item.

The first step, then, is to get the list of words from the text item. The command GetFieldText :card :item from the line

Make "s1 Parse GetFieldText :card :item

reads all of the text from a text item and returns it as a single chunk of characters. It uses whatever card and item name we passed ChangeStory when it was called. That's a key concept-since this command uses the card and item names passed to ChangeStory, it can work on different text items each time it is called.

GetFieldText returns the text as a single Logo word. The Parse command takes a logo word and breaks it up into a list of words, pretty much the way you break strings of characters into words. Just like you, Logo separates the characters by looking for spaces. Unlike you, Logo doesn't care about standard punctuation marks. A period at the end of a word is just another character to Logo, so the period at the end of a sentence becomes part of the Logo word. Logo also treats certain special characters, such as the - sign, as word separators. For what we're doing, these minor technical details don't really matter, so we'll ignore them.

We save the list of words in the variable s1.

The next line initializes s2 to be an empty list. We'll put the finished words in this list as they are processed.

Make "s2 []

With all of the preparation out of the way, the real work is done by this line:

```
While not EmptyP :s1 [Make "s2 LPut Process First :s1
:name :s2 Make "s1 ButFirst :s1]
```

Like many Logo statements, this one is made up of several individual Logo commands. The best way to understand it is to build it up from the individual commands, just as it was written.

The idea behind this line is to take each word from the original list s1, one word at a time, replace and # characters with the reader's name, and place the processed word at the end of the finished list s2.

To do this, we use a while loop. Logo's While command. The While command has this basic form:

WHILE condition [statements]

The command evaluates the condition. If the condition is true, all of the Logo statements between the brackets are executed, and the process repeats. As soon as the condition is false, the While loop stops and Logo moves on to the next line.

In our program, the condition is not EmptyP :s1. This says to keep looping as long as the variable s1 has something left in the list. In terms of what our stack is doing, this loop keeps going as long as there are words in the list.

Naturally, that means we need to take words out of the list! Otherwise the loop will keep going "forever"—which, to the computer, means until the power is turned off or you press Command-. to stop the script.

The list contains several Logo statements. The one we're interested in right away is `Make "s1 ButFirst :s1`, which replaces the list in `s1` with a new list containing everything but the first thing in the list. For example, if the variable `s1` contains the list of words

Run Spot run.

then, after executing this statement, it will have the list

Spot run.

The other statement in the loop is

```
Make "s2 LPut Process First :s1 :name :s2
```

Like the loop itself, this is made up of smaller pieces. What we're trying to do is take the first word from the list contained in the variable s1, replace the # characters (if there are any) with the name of the reader, and put the result at the end of the output list.

The first step is to grab the first word from the list in `s1`. That's what `First :s1` does. The command

```
Process First :s1 :name
```

passes this word and the name of the reader to another procedure in our script. That procedure, which we'll look at in a moment, replaces the # character with the reader's name and returns the result.

Logo's `LPut` command places a word at the end of a list, making it the last thing in the list. The name is an abbreviation of Last PUT, and yes, there is a First PUT, too. It needs two inputs: the thing to put into the list and the list to put it into. LPut returns a new list.

To see how this works, let's assume that `s1` contains a list with just the word

`run`

The list in `s2` already has two words,

`Run Spot`

When the statement executes, the first thing that happens is First :s1 grabs the word run from s1. This is passed to the procedure Process, along with the name of the reader. Since there is no # character, Process returns the word to us. LPut takes this word, grabs the two words from the list in `s2`, and combines them together to form the new list

`Run Spot run`

The Make command places this into the variable `s2`, replacing the older, shorter list.

After looping through all of the words and changing them as needed, `ChangeStory` uses the `SetFieldText` command to place the processed list of words back into the text field. The `SetFieldText` command looks a lot like the `GetFieldText` command we looked at earlier. This time, though, we're stuffing text into the field, so the text is a new parameter instead of something the command returns to us.

`SetFieldText :card :item :s2`

If you remember, GFT returned a long sequence of characters which we broke up into words using the P command. In older versions of *HyperStudio*, HyperLogo would only take a long sequence of characters as the last parameter to SFT, too. What we just passed was a list of words, though. The newer version of *HyperStudio* automatically converts the list back into a long series of text characters by inserting spaces in the appropriate spots. If you're using the older version of *HyperStudio*, though, you have to do that step before passing the result back to SFT.

That explains the two differences between the scripts. In Listing 2, s2 is initialized with

```
Make "s2 "
```

rather than

```
Make "s2 []
```

This initializes the variable as an empty word, or a word with no characters, rather than an empty list. While in the loop, the script uses the Word command to combine words, returning a longer word, rather than LPut, which returns a list. The part of the command that changes is

```
(Word :s2 Char 32 Process First :s1 :name)
```

which replaces

```
LPut Process First :s1 :name :s2
```

This command actually combines three words to form a longer one, not two. The first of the three words is whatever is already in s2, and the last is the word returned by Process, as you would expect. The middle word is Char 32, which is a space character. That's how we force spaces to appear between the words.

The parenthesis around the command tell Logo where to stop. Without the parenthesis, the Word command expects exactly two words as inputs, and would never look for the third word. By using parenthesis, we can combine as many words together using a single command as we like. Most Logo commands don't work this way; you have to look carefully in the reference manual to find this sort of shortcut.

Process

The last procedure in our script has the job of taking a word and replacing # characters with the reader's name. It needs two inputs, the word and the readers name, which are called w and name. As always, we follow the TO statement with a comment telling what the procedure does.

```
TO Process :w :name
; Replace # characters with the reader's name.
```

There are several possible inputs, and we need a way to decide which is which and handle them differently. The first possibility is that the word doesn't start with a # character, so we don't need to do anything. That possibility is handled by the line

```
if not ("# = First :w) [Output :w]
```

This line uses a Logo if statement to see if the first character in the word is a # character. You've seen the `First` command before, when we used it to get the first thing from a loop-if we use it on a word, however, we get the first character in the word.

As with the `While` command, the `if` statement executes the statements between the brackets if the condition is true. In this case, if the word does not start with #, the procedure returns right away by using the `Output` command to return the original word.

If we get past that line, we know the word starts with the # character. There are two possibilities left to deal with. The first is an input word that contains only one letter, which we know is #. In that case, the procedure returns the reader's name. Logo's Count procedure tells us how many letters are in a word, and the line that carries out the test is

```
if (Count :w) = 1 [Output :name]
```

The last case is when # appears at the start of a longer word, like #'s. In this situation, we want to place the last two characters on the end of the reader's name and return the combination. That's done by the line

Output Word :name ButFirst :w

Stories Where You are the Main Character Quick Guide

1. Start *HyperStudio* and make a new Stack. Pull down the **File** menu and pick **New Stack**. You will be asked if you want your stack to have the same size and number of colors as the current stack. Click **Yes**.

2. This stack contains a story, and that story gets modified. We need is a place to put the story. Create a text item named "Story." Put it wherever you like on the card, and make it any size you like. Pull down the **Objects** menu and select **New Text Item...** You will see the familiar marching ants outline. Drag it to some convenient spot, resize it if you like, and click outside the marching ants box to accept the position.

   Next, you'll see a dialog for setting up a text box. The name of the text box is important, since you tell HyperLogo what objects to work with using the name of the object. Be sure you type "Story" for the object name, as shown in the sample dialog.

   The other options aren't critical, but the defaults you see in the sample dialog work well. Click **OK** once you select all of the options.

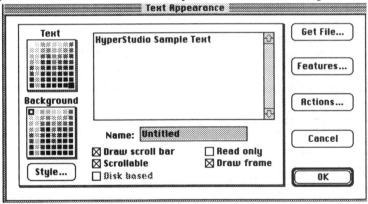

3. Type your story into the text item. Use "#" wherever the reader's name should be inserted. Click in the new text box to select it and type in any story you like.

   This script is fairly simple, so the story needs to be a single paragraph. You can, of course, stretch the story out across several cards, putting different paragraphs on each card. In the story, type the "#" character wherever the reader's name should appear. Later we'll add a script that will ask for the reader's name and replace all of the "#" characters.

You can use punctuation after the "#" character, but not before. For example, you can use "#'s" in a sentence, but the "#" character must appear either at the start of the paragraph or after a space or it will not be replaced.

Here's a short sample story you can enter if nothing better comes to mind:

#'s mom had promised. "I'll only be a minute, #," she said. # pouted as she looked at her baby brother in the pool. She was already late for her date.

4. If you are using *HyperStudio* 3.0.4 or later, add the script shown in Listing 1 to the card as something to do when arriving at the card. If you are using an earlier version of *HyperStudio*, create an invisible button that is executed as soon as you arrive at the card, and add the script to that button, and use the script from List 2.

   Spaces are important! Don't mess with the format unless you know enough Logo already to know what is important and what is not important.

   If You Have *HyperStudio* 3.0 or Greater Finish Here

5. Pull down the **Objects** menu and select **About this Card...** This brings up a dialog showing information about the current card.

   Click on the check box **arriving at this card...** This brings up a second dialog called "Actions". Click **Use HyperLogo...**

6. You will see the HyperLogo scripting environment with a blank window

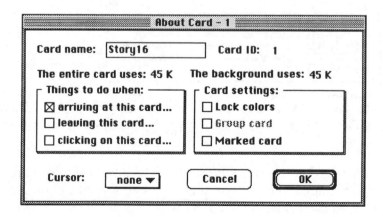

called HyperLogo Script. Type the script from Listing 1 into this window. Spacing is important. If you see a space in the listing, you should type a

space in your script, and if you do not see a space, you should not type one. People familiar with Logo know that there are places in the script where spaces can be removed or added without causing problems. If you're one

of those people, make whatever changes you like-but if you don't know Logo, assume everything is critical. It will save you a lot of time correcting problems later!

Two lines are too long to show in this book. The extra part of the line shows up left justified, like this:

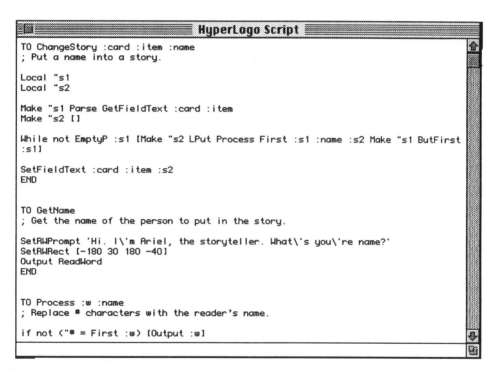

```
While not EmptyP :s1 [Make "s2 LPut Process First
:s1 :name :s2 Make "s1 ButFirst :s1]
```

When you type this line, do not press the return key to put `Make "s1 ButFirst :s1]` on a new line! If your Logo window is small, the editor may wrap the line for you-that's not a problem-but you should never press the Return key to break up a line from the listing.

```
TO ChangeStory :card :item :name
; Put a name into a story.
Local "s1
Local "s2Make "s1 Parse GetFieldText :card :item
Make "s2 []

While not EmptyP :s1 [Make "s2 LPut Process First
:s1 :name :s2 Make "s1 ButFirst :s1]

SetFieldText :card :item :s2
END

TO GetName
; Get the name of the person to put in the story.

SetRWPrompt 'Hi.  I\'m Ariel, the storyteller.
What\'s you\'re name?'
SetRWRect [-180 30 180 -40]
Output ReadWord
END

TO Process :w :name
; Replace # characters with the reader's name.

if not ("# = First :w) [Output :w]
if (Count :w) = 1 [Output :name]
Output Word :name ButFirst :w
END

Make "who GetName
ChangeStory [] "story :who
```

Listing 1

7. Once you finish typing the script, pull down the **File** menu and select **Quit HyperLogo.** This leaves the scripting environment, taking you back to *HyperStudio.*

8. Click **Done** in the actions dialog to indicate that you don't need to add any more actions.Click **OK** in the **About Card** dialog to indicate that you don't need to make more changes to the card.

If You Have *HyperStudio* 2.0 Finish Here

5. Pull down the **Objects** menu and select **Add a Button....** This brings up the button dialog. Click on the dashed outline icon to make the button invisible. This invisible button will hold the script, but the person using the stack shouldn't see it. Click **OK**. The button will appear on the card. Drag it to the top right of the card to get it out of the way, then click outside the button to accept the position.

Click **Use HyperLogo...** in the button actions dialog. This takes you to the HyperLogo scripting environment, where you will see a blank window called **HyperLogo Script**. Type the script from Listing 2 into this window.

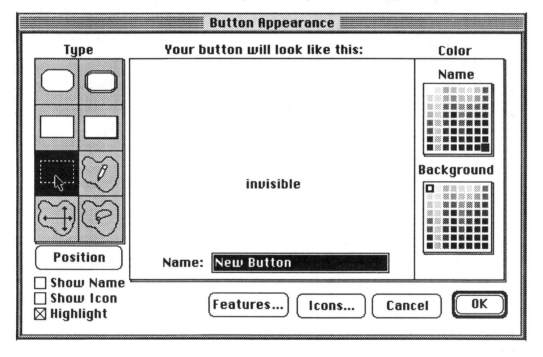

Spacing is important. If you see a space in the listing, you should type a space in your script, and if you do not see a space, you should not type one. People familiar with Logo know that there are places in the script where spaces can be removed or added without causing problems. If you're one of those people, make whatever changes you like-but if you don't know Logo, assume everything is critical. It will save you a lot of time correcting problems later.

```
┌─────────────────────── Actions ───────────────────────┐
│  ┌─ Places to Go: ──────┐  ┌─ Things to Do: ──────────┐ │
│  │  ○ Another card...    │  │  ☐ Play a sound...       │ │
│  │  ○ Next card          │  │  ☐ Play a movie or video...│
│  │  ○ Previous card      │  │  ☐ New Button Actions... │ │
│  │  ○ Back               │  │  ☐ Play frame animation...│ │
│  │  ○ Home stack         │  │  ☐ Automatic timer...    │ │
│  │  ○ Last marked card   │  │  ☐ Use HyperLogo...      │ │
│  │  ○ Another stack...   │  │  ☐ Testing functions...  │ │
│  │  ○ Another program... └──────────────────────────┘ │
│  │  ◉ None of the above     ┌─ Cancel ─┐  ┌═ Done ═┐   │
│  └──────────────────────┘                            │
└───────────────────────────────────────────────────────┘
```

Two lines are too long to show in this book. The extra part of the line shows up left justified, like this:

```
While not EmptyP :s1 [Make "s2 (Word :s2 Char 32
Process First :s1 :name) Make "s1 ButFirst :s1]
```

When you type this line, do not press the return key to put Make :s1 :name) Make "s1 ButFirst :s1] on a new line! If your Logo window is small, the editor may wrap the line for you-that's not a problem-but you should never press the Return key to break up a line from the listing.

```
TO ChangeStory :card :item :name
Local "s1
Local "s2

Make "s1 Parse GetFieldText :card :item
Make "s2 "

While not EmptyP :s1 [Make "s2 (Word :s2 Char 32
Process First :s1 :name) Make "s1 ButFirst :s1]

SetFieldText :card :item :s2
END

TO GetName
SetRWPrompt "Hi\.\ I'm\ Ariel\,\ the\ storyteller\.\
What's\ you're\ name\?
SetRWRect [-180 30 180 -40]
Output ReadWord
END

TO Process :w :name
if not ("# = First :w) [Output :w]
if (Count :w) = 1 [Output :name]
Output Word :name ButFirst :w
END

Make "who GetName

ChangeStory [] "story :who
```

Listing 2

Once you finish typing the script, pull down the **File** menu and select **Quit HyperLogo.** This leaves the scripting environment, taking you back to *HyperStudio.*

This button should execute automatically as soon as the card is shown. Click **Automatic Timer…** in the button actions dialog. Select the radio button **Do these actions as soon as the card is shown.** Click **OK** to leave the dialog.

Click **Done** in the actions dialog to indicate that you don't need to add any more actions.

Tips for Capturing Pictures

One of the strengths of new computers is their ability to capture and manipulate digital photography. Students and teachers use these pictures to bring more meaning to their writing. But how do you get digital photos that relate to your curriculum? Here are several ways.

Photo Collections

Several software manufacturers, like Adobe, market photo collections on CD-ROM. These royalty-free collections can be quite expensive and tend not to have exactly what you want.

Screen Capture Programs

There are several freeware (free to the public), shareware (full version given free with documentation that tells you where to send a fee if you like the program) and retail screen capture programs available for both IBM and Macintosh compatible computers. These programs allow the user to "capture" any picture that can be displayed on the screen and save it as a digital photo for use in any type of document. Freeware and shareware can be found through on-line services, on the Internet, or at some smaller software retailers.

Digital Cameras

Cameras like the Apple **Quicktake**, the Connectix **Quickcam**, and the Kodak **DC** are tools that can be used to take pictures just like regular cameras. The only difference is that they don't have film. The digital pictures are shown on the computer. The pictures can then be used in documents, presentations, or just printed. These cameras range from less than $100 for a tethered, black and white model to over $800 for an exceptional quality color portable.

Digital Developing

Several photo processors like Kodak and Seattle Film Works (mail order) provide digital developing of 35MM film. Pictures can be placed on disks or photo CD-ROM for a small additional fee. Classes will not require the professional quality images that developers charge a premium for.

Scanners

Scanners can be used to digitize photos and other images from nearly any source.

The Internet

The Internet has millions of photographic resources available for the taking. Internet users can search for media by subject, then download (copy a picture from a remote computer to yours) by a click of a mouse button.

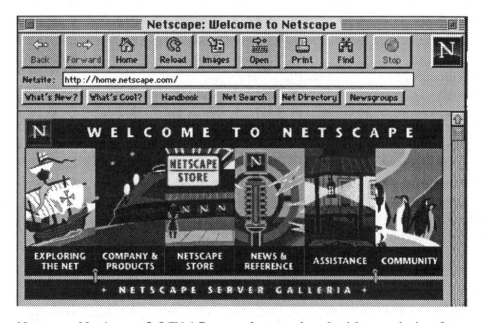

Netscape Navigator 2.0 ™ (Screen shot reprinted with permission from Netscape Communications)

Copy and Paste

Many educational programs, like encyclopedias, allow the user to copy non-copyrighted images from their programs. Consult your software documentation for instructions on how to do this.

Planning for Success

If you're like most teachers, you have far fewer computers in your classroom than you do students. If you have access to a computer lab, scheduling enough time for your class each week can be very difficult.

And that's what it takes to have students create projects with *HyperStudio*—computers and time. Therefore, it's essential that we help our students to make the most efficient use of computers and time as they work.

Task cards accompany many of the lessons in the tutorial. These cards are designed to help students practice the essential skills each lesson addresses. By providing specific directions for the students, these cards should help them acquire the basics of using *HyperStudio* in a realistic amount of time.

But the true goal of using *HyperStudio* in the classroom is not just to teach students how to use it. Rather, the goal is to provide students with opportunities to use *HyperStudio* to teach and learn from one another. *HyperStudio* must be given importance in the classroom. It should be as valued a tool for assessing student creativity and knowledge as handwritten reports, worksheets, and tests currently are. In fact, as we move toward the 21st Century, *HyperStudio* holds far greater potential than any of these assessment tools as a means of integrating and enhancing the curriculum.

HyperStudio should not be a once-in-a-while frill. It should not be a "toy" students play with when they finish their "work." Stacks should be treated as legitimate pieces of creativity and research. Computer time is far too precious a commodity to be wasted, and students should be held accountable for the time they spend at computers, just as they are in other pursuits at school.

HyperStudio for Terrified Teachers contains numerous examples of multimedia-based projects for you to use or modify for use in your classroom. The educators who developed these projects spent many hours outside of the classroom planning for ways to put *HyperStudio* to good use in the classroom. Like the saying goes, "Those who fail to plan, plan to fail." With proper planning, *HyperStudio* can be used successfully in the classroom to help students design projects that relate to the curriculum. But the responsibility for planning doesn't lie solely on the teacher's shoulders.

Students must take ownership and responsibility in the success or failure of their projects as well. It's the teacher's role to provide the opportunity for students to use *HyperStudio*, but the students must take advantage of this opportunity.

It's the teacher's task to develop meaningful goals, objectives, and requirements for multimedia projects. Students must take this framework and build upon it.

Students should be required to do their research and planning on paper first, before ever going to the computer. This helps ensure that they will develop projects of substance, not just cute special effects. It also helps ensure that they will maximize their time at the computer. Students should not spend computer time deciding what they're going to do and how they're going to make it. These decisions should be made beforehand. Just as builders start with blueprints, students should start with sufficient plans. That's where student stack planning sheets can come in handy.

A number of sample planning sheets have been included in this book. These sheets vary in scope and complexity. Some are better suited for use with younger students, or with students who are just beginning to make stacks with *HyperStudio*. Other sheets, can be used with experienced students who are capable of more sophisticated applications of the software.

As students complete their planning sheets, they should submit them to the teacher for evaluation. Planning sheets should be precise, detailed plans, not just sketches, of what students hope to achieve in their stacks. Sheets which show a lack of planning should be returned to the students for revision and resubmission. Details which should be addressed on the planning sheets include such things as colors, fonts, backgrounds, and buttons. In fact, each card should be "drawn" on paper before the students even sit down at the computer. The actual computer version of the card may not end up exactly as planned, and that's okay. The important thing is that a plan was made.

Try to meet with students as part of the process of evaluating their planning sheets. Have them explain choices they've made, and provide suggestions when necessary. Your role will be that of a facilitator, offering advice on such things as color choice, font selection, maintaining consistent card designs, using effective card transitions, button placement, etc. In the end, however, the final decisions need to be made by the students, provided they're putting forth effort and producing quality work.

Good stacks are the result of good planning. And good planning occurs when you set your expectations for your students high. Develop meaningful ways to incorporate *HyperStudio* into your curriculum. That way, projects will not only be worthwhile, but worth doing. Allow your students to assume ownership of their work, and hold them accountable for the time they spend at the computer. Before long, *HyperStudio* will transform the way you teach and your students learn — for the better.

HyperStudio Stack Student Card Planning Sheet

Name(s): _____ **Subject:** _____ **Project:** _____

Stack: _____ **Card #/Name:** _____ **Topic:** _____

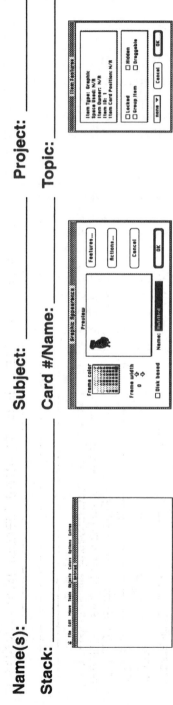

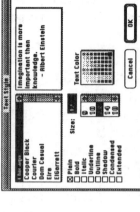

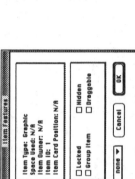

ART: Describe any backgrounds, clip art, or graphic objects used on this card. What sources will you be using (clip art library, paint tools, scanned)? Graphic objects "float" on top of the background, and can do things regular clip art can't! If you're using HS 3.0 on the Mac, describe any actions the graphic objects might carry out. Remember, artwork in your stack should relate to your topic and enhance its overall impact. Select art because it serves a purpose, not just because it "looks good!" **Be specific. Items must be indicated on the screen to the left.**

Backgrounds (Sources): _____

Clip Art (Sources): _____

Graphic Objects (Features/Actions/Sources): _____

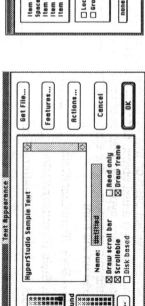

TEXT: Describe any text used on this card. Will the text be painted or in a text object? What fonts, sizes, and colors will you be using? If using a text object, describe the object itself (scrollable, transparent, hidden, etc.). If using HS 3.0 on the Mac, will you have any hypertext links or other actions connected to the text object? Remember, keep your number of different fonts to a minimum—your stack will look more consistent and professional! Be specific. Items must be indicated on the screen on the front.

Painted Text Style (Font/Size/Color): _____

Text Object Style (Font/Size/Color): _____

Text Object (Appearance/Features/Actions): _____

BUTTONS:
Describe the use of any buttons on this card. What types of buttons will you be using? Will the buttons include icons and names? What actions will the buttons carry out (another card, sound, animation, NBA, scripting, etc.)? Remember, try to maintain a consistent design and location for your buttons—you want your stack to be easy to use. Buttons should serve a purpose, not just add "special effects"! Be specific. Items must be indicated on the screen on the front of this planning sheet.

Appearance: _____

Actions: _____

Features: _____

WISH LIST: Describe something you would like to do with *HyperStudio* on this card but aren't sure if it's possible. If it's a possibility, I will meet with you to discuss how to go about doing it. Or, it might make a good topic to present to the entire class during a *HyperStudio* Clinic. Be specific, and use additional paper if necessary.

_____
_____

This sheet is (UNAPPROVED) (PARTIALLY APPROVED) (FULLY APPROVED) because _____
_____

HyperStudio Stack Student Card Planning Sheet

Name(s): _____

Subject: _____

Project: _____

Stack: _____

Card #/Name: _____

Topic: _____

Detailed Description of This Card

_____

_____

_____

_____

_____

This section is for teacher use only.

This planning sheet is (UNAPPROVED)   (PARTIALLY APPROVED)   (FULLY APPROVED) for the following reasons:

_____

_____

ART

Describe the use of any backgrounds, clip art, or graphic objects on this card. What sources will you be using (clip art library, paint tools, scanned)? Graphic objects "float" on top of the background, and can do things regular clip art can't! If you're using HS 3.0 on the Mac, describe any actions the graphic objects might carry out. Remember, artwork in your stack should relate to your topic and enhance its overall impact. Select art because it serves a purpose, not just because it "looks good"! **Be specific. Items must be indicated on the screen on the front of this planning sheet.**

Backgrounds (Sources): _____

Clip Art (Sources): _____

Graphic Objects (Features/Actions/Sources): _____

TEXT

Describe the use of any text on this card. Will the text be painted or in a text object? What fonts, sizes, and colors will you be using? If using a text field, describe the field itself (scrollable, transparent, hidden, etc.). If using HS 3.0 on the Mac, will you have any HyperText Links or other actions connected to the text object? Remember, keep your number of different fonts to a minimum—your stack will look more consistent and professional! Be specific. Items must be indicated on the screen on the front of this planning sheet.

Painted Text (Font/Size/Color): _____

Text Object (Font/Size/Color): _____

Text Object (Appearance/Features/Actions): _____

BUTTONS

Describe the use of any buttons on this card. What types of buttons will you be using? Will the buttons include icons and names? What actions will the buttons carry out (another card, sound, animation, NBA, scripting, etc.)? Remember, try to maintain a consistent design and location for your buttons—you want your stack to be easy to use. Buttons should serve a purpose, not just add "special effects"! Be specific. Items must be indicated on the screen on the front of this planning sheet.

Type: _____

Features: _____

Actions: _____

Buttons

Button Type:
O Rounded Rectangle
O Rounded Double
  Rectangle
O Rectangle
O Drop Shadow
O Invisible
O Freehand Area
O Expanding Area
O Lasso Area

Button Appearance:
O Show Name (give name)
O Show Icon (what icon?)
O Highlight

Color:
O Name (color of text)
O Background (color of
  button itself)

Places to Go:
O Another card…
O Next card
O Previous card
O Back
O Home stack
O Last marked card
O Another stack…
O Another program…
O None of the above

Things to Do:
O Play a sound…
O Play a movie or video…
O New Button Actions…
O Play frame animation
O Automatic timer…
O Use HyperLogo…
O Testing functions…

Features:
O Locked
O Group Item
O Drop Off only
O Hidden
O No Click
O Cursor (if using a
  special cursor)

Button #1:

Button #2:

Button #3:

Button #4:

Type:

Appearance:

Color:

Places to Go:

Things to Do:

Features:

Additional Information: (List sources for button icons, give specifics about any use of New Button Actions or HyperLogo, card transitions, etc.)

Text Objects

Style:
- O Font (give name)
- O Size (give number)
- O Plain
- O Bold
- O Italic
- O Underline
- O Outline
- O Shadow
- O Condensed
- O Extended
- O Align (left/center/right)

Appearance:
- O Draw scroll bar
- O Scrollable
- O Disk based
- O Read only
- O Draw frame

Color:
- O Text (identify font color)
- O Background (identify field color)

Actions:
(Same as "Places to Go" and "Things to Do" in the Buttons section)

Features:
- O Locked
- O Group Item
- O Hidden
- O Transparent
- O Cursor (if using a special cursor)

Text Capabilities:
- O HyperText Links
- O Roll Credits NBA
- O Hide Show NBA
- O GhostWriter NBA
- O HyperLogo

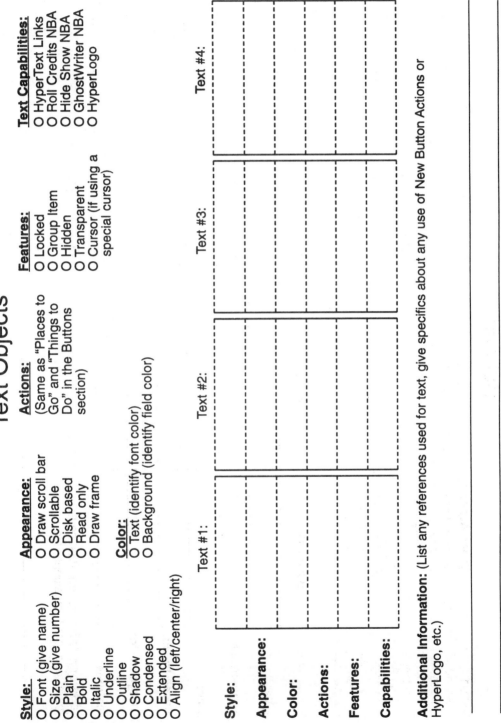

Text #1:

Text #2:

Text #3:

Text #4:

Style:

Appearance:

Color:

Actions:

Features:

Capabilities:

Additional Information: (List any references used for text, give specifics about any use of New Button Actions or HyperLogo, etc.)

Graphic Objects

Frame Color:
(color of border)

Frame Width:
(give number)

Actions:
(Same as "Places to Go" and "Things to Do" in the Buttons section)

Features:
O Locked
O Group Item
O Hidden
O Draggable
O Cursor (if using a special cursor)

Graphic #1:

Graphic #2:

Graphic #3:

Graphic #4:

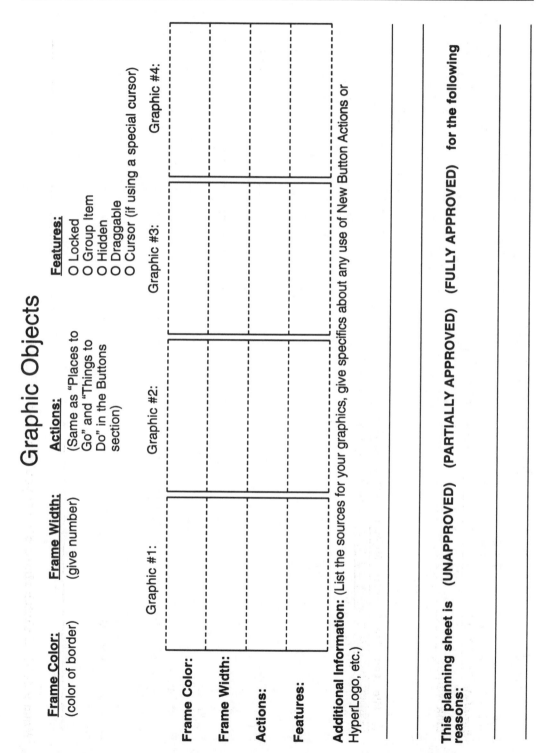

Frame Color:

Frame Width:

Actions:

Features:

Additional Information: (List the sources for your graphics, give specifics about any use of New Button Actions or HyperLogo, etc.)

This planning sheet is (UNAPPROVED) (PARTIALLY APPROVED) (FULLY APPROVED) **for the following reasons:**

Multimedia Menu

Name(s): _____

Project: _____

Subject: _____

Stack Name: _____

Card #/Name: _____

Topic: _____

Information on Clip Art, Backgrounds, and Painted Text
(Be sure to identify your sources, fonts, etc.)

_____

_____

_____

_____

_____

_____

_____

_____

File   Edit   Move   Tools   Objects   Colors   Options   Extras

Untitled

Make a detailed sketch above of what you think your card will look like.

HyperStudio Stack Student Card Planning Sheet

Name: _____   Project: _____

Stack: _____   Card # and Topic: _____

```
  File  Edit  Move  Tools  Objects  Colors  Options  Extras
████████████████████████ Untitled ████████████████████████
```

Notes

1. Describe the use of any backgrounds, clip art, or graphic items on this card. What source(s) will you be using (clip art library, paint tools, digital)? Indicate item(s) on the screen above.

2. Describe the use of any text on this card. Will the text be painted or in a text field? What font(s), size(s), and color(s) will you be using? If using a text field, describe the field itself (scrollable, transparent, hidden, etc.) Indicate item(s) on the screen above.

3. Describe the use of any buttons on this card. What type(s) of button(s) will you be using? Will the button(s) include icons and names? What action(s) will the button(s) carry out? Indicate item(s) on the screen above.

Glossary of HyperStudio Terms

Action—Something that a button or object carries out when activated (e.g., moving to another card, playing a sound, playing an animation, etc.)

Advanced User—A user that has learned the basics of *HyperStudio*. Also a preference that, when activated, allows the user to access additional features.

Automatic Timers—They are associated with buttons or other objects that activate an action automatically at a user specified amount of time.

Backgrounds—This is paint and/or clip art that is added to a card. Objects float above the background.

Browse Tool—This tool allows a user to interact with a stack.

Button—A spot that is added to a card, which is used for interacting with a stack (e.g., moving from card to card, activating multimedia, etc.)

Button Tool—This tool allows an author to edit buttons.

Card—This is an electronic screen with a presentation built on it. Similar to an index card.

Cell or Frame Based Animation—This is animation done by linking together several pictures into an electronic "flip book." For true animation see path based animation.

Fill Tool—This is the paint bucket tool. It is used to spill color within enclosed lines in a drawing.

Graphic Object—It is art that floats above a background. Once something become a graphic object, it cannot be painted over.

Graphic Tool—This tool is used to edit graphic objects.

Group Cards—These are cards that share backgrounds and/or are grouped in order to save memory requirements.

Glossary of HyperStudio Terms (cont.)

HyperStudio Player—This is a piece of software that comes with *HyperStudio*. It allows you to interact with a *HyperStudio* Stack even if you do not have *HyperStudio*.

Hypertext—It is text in a text object that carries out an action when clicked.

Invisible Button—It is a transparent button.

Line Tool—This tool is used to draw straight lines.

Magnifying Glass—This tool allows a card to be magnified (enlarged) for fine tuning.

Oval Tool—This tool creates ovals and circles.

Path Based Animation—This type of animation lets a user specify a path for a still object to follow on a card.

Pencil Tool—This tool is used for creating fine detail.

Presentation Mode—This setting blanks out the surrounding area around a card.

Ready Made Cards—These are pre-made cards that serve as a template for projects.

Rectangle Selector—This tool allows a user to select a rectangular portion of the screen to size, move, cut/copy, and paste, as well as a variety of other effects.

Rectangle Tool—This tool creates rectangles.

Rounded Rectangle Tool—This tool creates rectangles with rounded corners.

Sound Tool—This tool is for editing buttons that contain sounds.

Stack—This is a file of one or more cards, that along with buttons, graphics, sounds, and other multimedia elements make up an electronic presentation.

Storyboard—This is a graphic list of cards in a stack.

Text Object—This is a box that can be placed on top of a card, then similar to a word processor, allows a user to type in text.

Notes

Notes

Notes

Notes